RISING STAR

RISING STAR

DANDYISM,

GENDER, AND

PERFORMANCE

IN THE

FIN DE SIÈCLE

Rhonda K. Garelick

PRINCETON UNIVERSITY PRESS

PRINCETON, NEW JERSEY

Library of Congress Cataloging-in-Publication Data
Garelick, Rhonda K.
Rising Star : dandyism, gender, and performance in the
fin de siècle / Rhonda K. Garelick.
p. cm.
Includes bibliographical references and index.
ISBN 0-691-01205-9 (cl : alk. paper)
1. French Literature—19th century—History and criticism.
2. Dandies in literature. 3. Sex role in literature.
4. Decadence (Literary movement)—France. I. Title.
PQ295.D37G37   1998   840.9'008—dc21   97-21429   CIP

CONTENTS

ILLUSTRATIONS

ACKNOWLEDGMENTS

ALTHOUGH this book represents virtually a total rewriting of my dissertation, I very gratefully acknowledge the support I received during the time I was working on the original version, particularly from the Gilles Whiting Foundation, which granted me a year-long fellowship, and the Department of French at Yale University, which supported my studies and arranged for me to spend a year at the Ecole normale supérieure in Paris. More recently, I have benefited from the generosity of the Eugene M. Kayden Committee at the University of Colorado, Boulder.

For their advice, encouragement, and challenging questions, I would like to thank my friends and colleagues as well as the students in my graduate courses at the University of Colorado, Boulder. I am also grateful to April Alliston, Peter Brooks, Barbara Browning, Mary Ann Caws, Margaret Cohen, Margaret W. Ferguson, Julia Frey, Ellen Gainor, Thomas Greene, Wayne Koestenbaum, Jeffrey Nunokawa, Julie Stone Peters, and Richard Stamelman.

For their generous assistance, I thank Hélène Pinet-Cheula of the Musée Rodin, and the staffs of the Bibliothèque nationale, the Bibliothèque de l'Arsenal, and the Library for Performing Arts in New York City. I have also benefited from conversations with Daniel Garric, Giovanni Lista, Mickey Maroon, and Brygida Ochaim. Sadly, it is too late to thank Philippe Néagu, who kindly shared with me both his considerable art-historical knowledge and his photographic archives at the Musée d'Orsay.

For her intelligence and helpfulness, I thank Mary Murrell of Princeton University Press; I am also indebted to the careful work of Sara Bush, Beth Gianfagna, and Sherry Wert.

Finally, Richard Halpern has sustained and delighted me for over a decade with his subtlety of mind, unerring ear for language, generous spirit, and wit. This book is dedicated to him.

A word about translation: All translations here are my own unless otherwise noted. In order to keep this book a manageable length, I have, regretfully, eliminated many of the original French passages when they were not needed to make a point.

RISING STAR

INTRODUCTION

OVER ONE HUNDRED years ago, a crucial part of contemporary American culture was born—in France. The media cult personality is the mass-produced charismatic figure whose photograph graces supermarket check-out lines, whose likeness is rendered in doll form for children, and whose image appears and reappears on television and movie screens. This is a personality that encompasses its own mechanically reproduced versions, and eventually seems indistinguishable from them. Overcited but still relevant examples of this phenomenon include John F. Kennedy, Marilyn Monroe, Jackie Onassis (the connection among these three only intensifies their iconicity), Michael Jackson, Madonna, and Arnold Schwarzenegger.[1] But strangely, although such mass-produced icons are now considered pure Americana—creations of industrial Hollywood—the media cult personality finds its roots in French (and to a certain extent British) cultural and literary history.

Long before the pop-music star and the motion-picture idol, the dandy had made an art form of commodifying personality. Dandyism is itself a performance, the performance of a highly stylized, painstakingly constructed self, a solipsistic social icon. Both the early social dandyism of England and the later, more philosophical French incarnations of the movement announced and glorified a self-created, carefully controlled man whose goal was to create an effect, bring about an event, or provoke reaction in others through the suppression of the "natural." Artful manipulation of posture, social skill, manners, conversation, and dress were all accoutrements in the aestheticization of self central to dandyism. During decadent dandyism—the latest stage of the movement in the final twenty years of the nineteenth century—the socially detached hero turned his attention from the spectacle of the self to the spectacle of the other, to the woman onstage. My point of departure will be this encounter between the decadent dandy and the female performer, because when studied carefully, it narrates the creation of the media star, and particularly the related category of the camp icon. I choose this particular couple (the dandy and the female performer) because both members wear their sexuality with such drama. Both indulge in self-conscious, highly theatrical gender play—the dandy in his sexually ambiguous social polish, the woman in her explicitly staged and painted erotic charms. Placed side by side so often in fin-de-siècle culture, these two figures cast a curious light on each other's performances, then ultimately fuse their roles, forming something beyond androgyny, giving birth to the concept of the "star" as we know it today.

When the dandy confronted the female performer, in real life and in literary texts, he forged a creative response to an exterior performance, bringing about a new spectacle in conjunction with it. The critical relationship with the female performer, particularly with the dancer, shatters the dandy's hermetic shell of narcissism and questions his singularity. As a responsive audience member in a mass-cultural space, the decadent dandy exchanges his isolated corner for a place in the crowd. Once content simply to provide anecdotes to be related by others, the dandy now grapples with the difficulty of recounting experience himself, struggling to seize and represent the ephemeral event of performance in a world of crowd politics and mechanical reproduction. When the decadent dandy meets the woman of the popular stage, he looks into a distorted mirror, and from the confrontation of the two images—sharply divided by social class, gender, art form, and level of culture—the charged political, social, and cultural subtexts of the commodified personality emerge.

The dandy and the popular female performer come from the worlds known as "high" and "low" culture, and meet at the moment when such distinctions begin to blur. Mass entertainment did not simply supplant other cultural forms that had preceded it, nor did it spring to life ex nihilo, apart from those forms. On the contrary, despite its mechanistic nature, the commercial popular stage maintained visibly close connections with many other aspects of culture, including folklore, the medieval fair, and even (or especially) "high" literary culture.[2] This book will look at the last element in this series, studying the complex relationship between early mass culture and the contemporaneous Decadent literary movement.

I want to be careful about labels here, though. Almost all cultural criticism lays claim to "transitions," or shifts from one era to another, from one literary movement to another, from one century to another. We have adopted the habit of justifying our observations by invoking historical labels whose clear significance might be handily dismantled by us in any other context. "The apocalyptic types," writes Frank Kermode, "empire, decadence, and renovation, progress and catastrophe . . . underlie our ways of making sense of the world from where we stand, in the middest" (*Sense of an Ending* 29). It is for this reason that I wish to qualify my use of the label "decadent" here. Dating the Decadent movement is an imprecise task. Though the October 1886 publication of Anatole Baju's review *Le Décadent* may inaugurate the movement, Huysmans's novel of rare jewels and secret vices, *A Rebours*, came out in 1884 and is considered the breviary of decadence. And even as early as 1862, Flaubert, for his *Salammbô*, relied upon such staples of decadence as orientalism, densely ornate prose, and themes of disease, sex, and the femme fatale. For my purposes, I shall locate decadence mainly within the 1880s and

1890s—the fin de siècle—but I shall also include under this rubric texts by Mallarmé from the 1860s and 1870s.

I shall be using the term "fin de siècle" not because a magical transformation occurred when the century turned, but because the term provides a commonly accepted description of Europe in the 1880s and 1890s, conjuring certain accepted aspects of the period that will, in fact, be important to my study. These include the industrialization of culture in the form of music halls and eventually cinema; the fascination with the public, commercialized personality; the great rise of mass-produced goods and entertainment; and a concomitant concern for the decay of high culture.

The popular stage and the theatricality of the self fascinated the decadents. Yet at the same time, their work demonstrated extreme concern for preserving their own pristine distance from the rabble of mass culture. The self-conscious artificiality of decadence, and the elaborately posed persona of the decadent dandy, can be read as rebellion against an economy of ever-increasing "exchangeability" and the accumulation of mass-produced products. The dandy attempts to block this development by stepping outside of the system.[3] He turns his back completely on the outside world, sequestering himself, as Huysmans's Des Esseintes did, in a rarefied world of luxury and Oriental splendor. The decadent dandy aspires to the status of a nonreproducible, irreplaceable object, fixed in a perpetual "now" outside of time, in the manner of Wilde's Dorian Gray, who battles time by appropriating the characteristics of an ageless art object, his portrait. The dandy is never reducible to a sum of money, nor is he posed in counterbalance with a woman. In a world of universal equivalence, he is exchangeable with no one, remaining enclosed in a hermetic, autoseductive circle of narcissism.

As a movement founded against nature, decadent dandyism seems to leave no space for the woman. It prizes perpetual, artificial youth and a reified, immobilized self. By virtue of their association with the human life cycle and reproduction, women threaten the dandy's eternal present with temporality, and hence become objects of fear and disdain in decadent literature. Women also reveal the essential device behind dandyism, because their very existence gives the lie to the dandy's pose as a double-sex being.

A female character permitted into the decadent hero's world serves normally only as a tabula rasa upon which the dandy spectator projects his own creative musings, for to grant a woman consciousness or creativity would be to threaten the dandy's most important attribute: his self-containment. "Woman's place, for the artists and writers of the decadence," writes Jennifer Birkett, "was inside the work of art, as an image to fix the male imagination" (Birkett 159). Femaleness allies itself here primarily with a mute, hieratic power, which exists—as in Pater's *Mona Lisa* or Flaubert's *Salammbô*—only to be read and deciphered by a male interpreter. That the decadent dandy nonetheless exhibits great interest in the spectacle of the woman is not surprising, since dandyism attempts to incorporate into the male persona something of the highly social performance usually expected only of women.

But in order to discuss the figure of the dandy within decadent literature, I must first go still further back in time to the early dandyist movement. The dandy has a very long tradition in both France and England; indeed, he is a hybrid of both cultures. The first dandy celebrated specifically as such was the English George "Beau" Brummell (1778–1840) (Fig. 1), whose brilliant reign coincided with the Regency (1795–1820) of the future King George IV, who became, for a time, Brummell's closest friend. Born to commoners, Brummell effectively launched dandyism in both England and France, and in the worlds of both literature and society, with his meteoric social ascendancy and his theatrical originality. In his landmark essay of 1843, *On Dandyism and George Brummell* (*Du Dandysme et de George Brummell*), Barbey d'Aurevilly insisted that Brummell was unique and unreproducible, despite the countless dandies who would follow him to make up the movement; "Indeed, there was only one dandy," wrote Barbey,[4] while maintaining paradoxically that Brummell was responsible for generations of dandies. Brummell's life, then, was singular yet replicable, his influence (in England and France) both social and literary. This dandy's curious blend of contradictions creates the model for all further discussion of the subject.

The crucial and irresolvable complexity at the root of dandyism is that dandies are both real historical people and literary heroes. Beau Brummell's life influenced the English dandyist movement in that his world of gentlemen's sports clubs, sartorial elegance, and outré behavior inspired a whole generation of young men to emulate his social conduct. At the same time, Brummell's example inspired the literary dandyism found in the work of Lord Byron and in the so-called fashionable novels, such as *Vivian Grey*, written in 1826 by future British prime minister Benjamin Disraeli (Fig. 2), or Bulwer-Lytton's 1828 *Pelham*, the story of a young dandyist arriviste. *Pelham* quickly attained a kind of nonfictional status as "the hornbook of dandyism" (Moers 68), and was used as a manual for behavior by many young men aspiring to dandyism. Sometimes these young men became in their turn dandyist novelists, continuing the cyclical merging of life and literature. (Bulwer, for his part, had been much impressed by *Vivian Gray* and took up a correspondence with Disraeli that influenced the work of both.) In 1843, Captain William Jesse chose Beau Brummell as the subject for a biography; and when Barbey d'Aurevilly read this nonfictional work, it spurred him to write his famous essay, which then inaugurated the French dandyist movement.

1. George "Beau" Brummell, by Aubrey Hammond. Frontispiece from Lewis Melville (pseudonym of Lewis Benjamin), *Beau Brummell: His Life and Letters*.

2. Prime Minister Benjamin Disraeli as a young dandy.

Barbey's essay, while anecdotal and filled with many long scholarly footnotes, leans in its style more toward the art-movement manifesto than toward biography. Having come to Paris from his native Normandy in 1833—at the height of Parisian anglomania—Barbey was highly influenced by the literary dandyism of Lord Byron (all of whose work he claimed to have memorized), Bulwer-Lytton, and Disraeli. Although based on the life of Brummell, *Du Dandysme et de George Brummell* was not intended to be a factual account of the man but more a blend of novelistic dandyism and historical fiction. The essay moved dandyism away from its British, novelistic roots toward its later French life as an aesthetic and philosophical movement. *Du Dandysme* provided the cornerstone for all of the dandyist tradition that followed it, influencing Baudelaire, Huysmans, and the re-emergent British dandies of the late Victorian period.

Barbey's essay offers an unusual mixture of fiction and fact. Since Barbey never knew Brummell personally, he relied upon the only two pre-existing biographies of Brummell, Jesse's and one by a certain Guillaume-Stanislaus Trébutien. Barbey also kept up a correspondence with these authors. However, when a fact did not fit Barbey's conception of Brummell or of dandyism, it was omitted. (Brummell's exile to Calais to escape imprisonment for debt and his eventual madness, for example, do not appear in the essay.) When Barbey asked Jesse for examples of Brummell's supposedly brilliant verbal wit, and the latter could not provide any, Barbey simply decided to render this as the Beau's transcendence of language, his simple, nonverbal elegance: "We will not cite Brummell's words . . . he reigned more by his airs than by his words."[5]

The reputed goal of Brummell's life was to turn his person into a social artwork, and similarly, the goal of Barbey's treatise on Brummell is to turn Brummell's life into a literary artwork. "Writing this history of impressions rather than facts," wrote Barbey, "we soon touch upon the death of the meteor, upon the end of the incredible romance story . . . whose heroine was London's high society and whose hero was Brummell."[6]

In his personal life, Barbey himself was a celebrated dandy who wore rice powder and ruffles well into his eighties. Just as Barbey held up Brummell (whose life he knew only through the texts of others) as the unequalable model of dandyism, later writers saw Barbey as an unsurpassable model of the genre, both for his life and for the dandyist quality of his work.[7] The reproducibility of the dandy is thus always pitted against his singularity; and his historical or biographical status shades off continually into the fictionalized selves of literature. Such blurring of dandyist historical and literary personages occurred throughout the nineteenth century. Balzac's personal reputation as a dandy merged in public opinion with the dandyism of Eugène de Rastignac, or Henri de Marsay.

Baudelaire's dandyism mingled with Samuel Cramer's, Jean Lorrain's with M. de Phocas's,[8] Huysmans's with Des Esseintes's, and Wilde's with Dorian Gray's. And not only were literary dandies linked with their dandified creators, they were often allied in the public imagination with their real-life models, as in the case of Proust's Charlus and his supposed historical model, famous dandy (and notably poor poet) Robert de Montesquiou, or Stendhal's Prince Korasoff and Beau Brummell himself.[9] Many critics have commented upon the contagious mirror-game of fiction and reality inherent to dandyism. "If the dandy is a person who plays the part of himself," writes Jessica Feldman, "how can the real be neatly culled from such fiction?" (2). "Brummell created a myth," writes Françoise Coblence; "he transmitted dandyism as a tradition in which the real and the imaginary are closely joined" (15). Domna Stanton, whose 1980 book *The Aristocrat as Art* focuses more on the literary dandy, agrees that "we cannot say whether it was the social reality that generated the literary formulation or whether real people imitated or dramatized . . . dandies found in literary texts. . . . The truth may lie in a mutually enriching but elusive combination of these two possibilities" (10).

But while critics acknowledge the bleeding of life into art and vice versa in dandyism, no one has studied its cultural implications. What does it mean that a literary movement merged so closely with historical life? This phenomenon is not unique to dandyism; the futurists, the surrealists, the dadaists, all had famous life experiences that seeped into the lore about their art, making the artists themselves into part of their art. And yet no one ever seems tempted to confuse Alfred Jarry with Ubu Roi, or Duchamp with a mustachioed Mona Lisa. Not only was the dandyist movement a blending of historical and literary personages, it actually continues to create a strange confusion or contagion in the criticism it inspires. The main critical studies of dandyism in France and England intermingle chapters and remarks about actual and fictional dandies. Roger Kempf, in his *Dandies*, displays this kind of easy acceptance and mixing of both kinds of dandy: "We . . . imagine the dandy at different hours of the day: Barbey at his *toilette*, Byron practicing his boxing, . . . *Stendhal* or *Marsay* lighting up a cigar" (*Dandies* 13, emphasis added). For the sake of illustration here, Stendhal and Balzac's de Marsay comfortably occupy the same terrain. Michel Lemaire suggests the same parity of the real and the fictional. "From Brummell and Byron up to Mallarmé," he says, dandyism is "a stage upon which appear Baudelaire and Samuel Cramer, Gautier and Fortunio, Barbey d'Aurevilly and the Vicomte de Brassard" (13). And some critics seem to have absorbed (consciously or not) the worshipful tone and melodramatic, purple-prose style of the original dandyist texts. Here, for example, is Barbey on Brummell's gambling at London's Watier's Club:

Drunk on gingered port, these blasé dandies, devoured by spleen, came each night to lull the deadly boredom of their life and to stir their Norman blood. . . . Brummell was the star of this famous club. . . . In his fame as well as in his position there was an element of chance, which was destined to be the ruin of both. Like all gamblers, he struggled against fate and was conquered by it.[10]

And here is critic Patrick Favardin writing in 1988 about dandy Jean Lorrain's sexual practices. The hyperbole and the tone of prurient fascination resemble Barbey's strikingly:

His mind aflame . . . he goes from partner to partner, from body to body. . . . Lorrain's love affairs are like a card game: a machine that absorbs the profound anguish of chance and danger's palpitating insecurity.[11]

Dandyism also conflates textual and human seduction. When Barbey published his essay, he saw it as a kind of textual dandy, designed to seduce with its material, physical appearance as well as with words. He wanted strict control over the size of its cover, its print face, its lettering. Feldman acknowledges the seductive charms of the essay, proving Barbey right.[12] She describes it in particularly vibrant terms, turning the text itself into a mythically seductive sea creature: "The siren-text, sheathed in scales of . . . abstractions, gives way in the notes to a far greater range for the feminine mode of gossip, feelings, personality. Thus the central male text associates with marginal female notes" (91). Dandyism, then, does not just merge the real and the fictional; it creates a contagion of style and seduction. Texts about dandies strive for dandyist appeal; critics writing about dandies or their texts fall easily into dandyist style and succumb to its charms. This is, of course, how all celebrity works; and dandies are among the earliest celebrities. One cannot declare oneself a celebrity any more than one can simply state that one is charming and influential. Celebrity and influence require a vast system of communication, a network of opinion and desire. Emilien Carassus notes, "Rare are those who declare themselves dandies, the majority only obtain the title of dandyism through the opinion of others" (25).

Contemporary examples of such contagion of opinion appear only in popular culture. The same holds true for biographical profiles that mix the real and the fictional. Soap-opera fanzines, for example, easily merge actors with the characters they play. Soap-opera fans routinely write to their favorite characters (not the actors), warning them of imminent disaster or congratulating them on marriages and births. And when we speak of famous actors in their most famous film roles, we refer to them by their real names and not those of their characters, something we do not do for more minor film players: "In *Casablanca*," we are wont to

"*Humphrey Bogart* asks *Sam* to play that song for him." During the golden age of Hollywood cinema, the mark of complete stardom was to be indistinguishable from one's roles. It is a commonplace to say that John Wayne played John Wayne in all his films, or that Katherine Hepburn played Katherine Hepburn. Even now, the fictional varieties of film roles often take a backseat to the celebrity power of the actor. Madonna played herself in *Desperately Seeking Susan*, but, in Abel Ferrara's *Dangerous Games*, she was applauded for not playing a star, for "acting." *The New York Times* reviewer expressed appreciation for her newfound theatrical talents: "[Her] role ... is free of artifice in a way that Madonna's screen roles seldom are. Viewers may have to remind themselves that they've seen this actress somewhere before" (Maslin C14). By putting aside her celebrity, Madonna reseparated the fictional and biographical realms.

But before we discuss how we can trace contemporary (particularly American) concepts of celebrity back to dandyism, we must look at how those concepts changed during Decadence. The Decadent movement crystallized certain concepts of dandyism, making its curious marriage of literature and history much easier to study, sharply defining the roles of spectacle, gender, and theatricality. The English dandies of the Regency and the French dandies up through the July Monarchy all loved *mondainités*: the theater, the court, the public garden. But their dandyism was not yet strongly affected by mass culture and the industrialization of society. Although the typical dandy hero loved to go "slumming" and visit actresses, "ballet girls," and prostitutes, the later decadent dandy experienced such social encounters as they were altered by socially leveled audiences, urban crowds, the rise of media spectacles, and the resulting mechanized representations of the female body. Such additions to the dandyist scenario necessarily tease out of the movement many of its former subtleties, as we shall see in Chapter One, which traces the evolution of dandyism in nineteenth-century France through readings of three key texts: Balzac's *Traité de la vie élégante*, Barbey d'Aurevilly's essay on Brummell, and Baudelaire's *Le Peintre de la vie moderne*.

Chapter Two studies an early confrontation between commercial culture and dandyism by looking at some of Mallarmé's prose texts, including his little-known fashion journal *La Dernière Mode*. In 1874, the poet took over the editorship of this popular women's magazine (which had consisted primarily of fashionplates), producing eight issues over the course of one year. Mallarmé edited, published, and distributed the magazine entirely by himself; he also wrote every article that appeared in it, using a variety of male and female pseudonyms. Under Mallarmé's direction, *La Dernière Mode* was transformed into a meditation on *la femme à la mode*, an elaborate creature whose strange, limbic status raises questions about the cultural body, masquerade, gender, dandyism, and the performance of the self.

Chapter Three moves from the cultural spectacle of Mallarmé's fashionable woman to the mechanical spectacle of Villiers de l'Isle-Adam's *L'Eve future*. The story of a scientist-dandy's experiment in human simulation, this decadent novel recounts a machine-age version of Genesis. The "Future Eve" of the title is a female android designed to replace a young (and human) music-hall performer in the life of a lovesick aristocrat. In *L'Eve future* we can see the moment when the dandy's elaborate construction of his own performance meets and melds with the performance of the popular woman onstage. The result is the first narrative of the mass-media celebrity.

While Villiers's "Future Eve" is a literary depiction of a mass-media icon, Loie Fuller was the first historical example of the genre. Chapter Four is devoted to this American dancer, who captivated Europe—especially decadent writers—for over thirty years, performing her veil dances under rotating colored spotlights. Fuller, who had a genius for mechanical invention, created costumes and stage apparatuses that lent her the illusion of complete immateriality. Onstage, she had no discernible body, but instead dazzled her audience as a series of ephemeral shapes of fabric and light, a protocinematic body. Fuller was also the first cabaret performer to mass market her own image, selling dolls, lamps, and statues in her own likeness in the lobbies of theaters where she performed.

Oscar Wilde's *Salomé*, discussed in Chapter Five, announces definitively the arrival of the camp personality and makes clear its descent from the merging of the dandy and the female performer. Although Wilde wrote *Salomé* in the style of the French decadents, the play narrates the end of the decadent dandy and his metamorphosis into a much more public, overtly gay figure, still deeply connected to female performance.

Chapter One

THE TREATISES OF DANDYISM

THE MOST FAMOUS manifestos of French dandyism are Balzac's *Traité de la vie élégante* (1830), Barbey d'Aurevilly's essay on Beau Brummell (1843), and Baudelaire's *Le Peintre de la vie moderne* (1863). And although it would be slightly forced to claim a neat, chronological progression among the three, in a general sense, when studied together, this trio does narrate the progress of dandyism into decadence. To see how the essays move toward highly charged fin-de-siècle issues (and ultimately modernism), it will be useful to examine the development of a single overarching concern throughout: the question of reproduction. Since dandyism struggles constantly with the problem of how originality can be replicated to create a whole movement, the issue of aesthetic or social reproduction is always present in these three texts. Later on, decadent dandyism will re-pose such questions of replicability and originality through the phenomenon of *mechanical* reproduction, but even in Balzac's text, mechanicity is a discernible subtext.

BALZAC'S *TRAITÉ DE LA VIE ÉLÉGANTE*

The *Traité* is, of course, an early text that predates the phenomena that I shall be talking about later, addressing itself to a purely aristocratic audience. Appearing in installments in the royalist review *La Mode*, Balzac's text coincided with a crisis in that magazine's political identity. The *Traité* was published in five consecutive issues during the autumn of 1830 (between October 2 and November 6), when the directorship of *La Mode* was struggling to define its reaction to the July Revolution and the new government of Louis Philippe. (Balzac would turn what was to have been the essay's final section into a separate article known as *Théorie de la démarche*, which was published three years later in *L'Europe littéraire*.)

That Emile de Girardin—editor of *La Mode*—and his staff generally opposed the new bourgeois liberalism was not in question. Their dilemma lay in deciding whether to *appear* to support the new regime and whether they could allow themselves to express any loyalty to the old aristocracy. Ultimately, despite some concessions to the July Monarchy,[1] *La Mode* decided to remain faithful to its original right-wing leanings and readership.[2] "*La Mode* would show increasing defiance, if not outright opposition towards the new monarchy," writes Roland Chollet, "throughout an October marked by the publication of the *Traité de la vie élégante* and by a clear repolarization of the editorial staff" (312).

La Mode made its political choices especially clear in an editorial published in the November 6 issue, which also contained the final section of Balzac's *Traité*. In melodramatic tones, the editorial laments the void left by the passing of an older, more glorious world: "The world exists no longer," wrote Girardin, "but nothing has replaced it. Or if it exists, it is in an inaccessible, interior exile" (quoted in Chollet 312). Balzac's treatise on elegant living participated, therefore, in *La Mode*'s campaign against the new monarchy and its attempt to maintain ties with its original subscribers in the Faubourg Saint-Germain.[3]

Given the details surrounding its publication, it is not surprising that the *Traité* exhibits upper-class concerns and displays no overt interest in mass culture or urban crowds. And yet, despite its clearly aristocratic tone and context, Balzac's essay contains the germ of many aspects of dandyism that would emerge to dominate the movement in later years. Balzac called his text a "treatise," and like a treatise it makes declarations; it proclaims. In a long series of fragments, the *Traité* offers maxims, aphorisms, and anecdotes. It gives firm advice: "The man of taste must always know how to reduce his needs to the most simple"; "Multiplicity of colors will be in bad taste."[4] At the root of such didacticism lies the crucial dandyist obsession with aesthetic reproduction. To write a dandyist text is to produce more dandies.

But the article that gives such lofty counsel also undermines its potential usefulness, since "a man becomes rich," but "he is born elegant."[5] Despite all the maxims proffered here, there can be no help for those unlucky souls born to be inelegant. Like so much fashion journalism, Balzac's essay contains an element of smug mockery. Fashionable elegance contains within it an essential hopelessness for those who strive for it, since striving is so unbecoming. Readers can try to achieve elegance, but in the end, they will either already have the required *sprezzatura*, or be condemned merely to read about it. The *Traité* suggests paradoxically, then, that elegance can be acquired and that it is unlearnable and unreproducible. Such contradictions, as we have seen, lie at the heart of dandyism—a movement of thousands, of whom only one individual, according to Barbey, could be said to merit the title. ("Indeed, there was only one dandy.")

Unlike Barbey's and Baudelaire's essays, Balzac's text does not confine itself to the biography of a single individual; but it does lean heavily upon a vision of one kind of man—the dandy. Of the three categories into which the young Balzac divides humanity—those who work, those who think, and those who do nothing—the dandy belongs to the third group, the only one that matters. "In order to be fashionable, one must enjoy rest without having experienced work."[6] Beau Brummell, the ur-dandy—whose own remarks on fashion had appeared in three earlier articles in *La Mode* (Chollet 321)—makes an appearance here: "It is useless to add," writes Balzac, "that we owe to Brummell the philosophical inductions by which we have demonstrated how much elegant life is tied to the perfection of all human society."[7] But Balzac does not just use Brummell as a reference; he invites him into the text as a kind of guest celebrity, by means of a fictional interview.

Balzac recounts a conversation he held with the Beau during the latter's exile. Although Brummell had repatriated to Calais, Balzac situates their meeting in Bologna (and compares his fallen grandeur to Napoleon's): "Bologna was his St. Helena, all our feelings merged into respectful enthusiasm."[8] The pages devoted to Brummell purport to be reproducing the Beau's axiomatic remarks on elegance, such as, "Nothing resembles man less than *a man*," or "Actions . . . are never anything but the consequences of our toilette."[9] Balzac also quotes Laurence Sterne's remark that "the ideas of a clean-shaven man are not those of a bearded man."[10]

And then, in a manner very reminiscent of Sterne in its "breaking" of narrative convention, Brummell—a character in Balzac's text—advises Balzac on how best to write that text.[11] At the end of the "interview," Brummell offers his ideas on how Balzac might organize the second portion of the *Traité*, and on what topics he should concentrate. Balzac agrees to take the great man's suggestions; and indeed, the second part of the text precisely follows the advice attributed to Brummell.[12]

By using a historical figure as a fictional character, Balzac plays with the classic dandyist confusion of reality and literature. By keeping Brummell's name and mingling biographical facts about him with whimsical inventions of his own, Balzac goes beyond merely modeling a character on a real individual, to appropriating Brummell's celebrity as an integral part of the text. This move attempts to solve dandyism's aesthetic dilemma of how to reproduce what must remain unique.[13] While getting the most out of Brummell's "box-office appeal," Balzac makes the Beau's celebrity his own by fictionally rewriting Brummell's life and calling it journalism. Presented as a consultant on the writing of the text, Brummell becomes a kind of alter ego for Balzac, the dandyist personification of a writer's inner voice. All dandies, after all, must be part Brummell.[14]

Within Balzac's fictitious, journalistic portrait of Brummell lurks a precursor of an aesthetic sensibility that, while not fully delineated until the end of the nineteenth century, certainly sprang from dandyist roots. I am speaking of camp. Camp style often blends the extratextual, biographical self with the literary or fictionally constructed hero, extending the

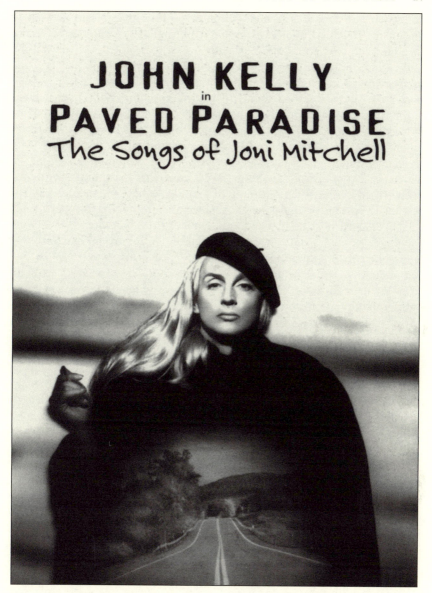

3. Performance artist John Kelly in costume as Joni Mitchell.

boundaries of the latter to include the previously understood identity of the former.[15] Paul Rubens's erstwhile film and television character Pee Wee Herman was an example of camp, as was performance artist John Kelly when he dressed as Joni Mitchell (complete with blond wig) and sang an entire concert of her songs—in eerily perfect imitation of her (Fig. 3).[16] The late actor Glenn Milstead's drag alter ego "Divine" (seen in the films of John Waters) embodies high camp especially well. Divine worked as a base fictional construction upon which all of Milstead's other female characters were built. Divine's and all camp performances challenge the verticality of performance, the structure according to which a "real" person's identity is presumed to exist underneath the "performed" identity, as one rung of a ladder is beneath the next. In the case of Divine, a preconstructed performance animated the performed role, usually surpassing it. The flamboyance of the character "Divine" always overflowed whatever film role (often a suburban matron) was being played. Jonathan Dollimore has addressed this very complexity in camp identity: "[Camp] undermines the depth model of identity from inside, being a kind of parody and mimicry which hollows out from within, making depth recede into its surfaces. Rather than direct repudiation of depth, there is a performance of it to excess: depth is undermined by being taken to and beyond its own limits."[17]

Finally, couched within Balzac's treatise on elegance are two other interrelated topics that presage later nineteenth-century decadent dandyism: mechanomorphism and the reification of the self. Initially, Balzac's view of the machine world appears haughtily and unequivocally dismissive. He sharply distinguishes the worker from the dandy, expressing his disinterest in the coarse world of utility or service. The dull drudgery of "the man who works" is, after all, the antithesis of the leisure required for elegance. Balzac does not, however, distinguish the working man very much from his machine tools; indeed, he sees them as closely resembling each other: "Like steam engines, men regimented by work all look alike and have nothing individual about them. The man-instrument is a sort of social zero."[18] As the opposite of such uninspired sameness and social nullity, dandyism epitomizes elegance, reaching toward human perfection. And yet, paradoxically, dandyism in Balzac's text will later lead right back to the inanimate (although not quite the mechanical) world: "In making himself (*en se faisant*) a dandy, a man becomes a piece of boudoir furniture, an extremely ingenious mannequin, who can sit upon a horse or a sofa . . . but a thinking being . . . never."[19]

The dandy who lives by his "philosophie des meubles, des gilets" ends up conquered by the inanimate world or even aspiring to its condition. A man may turn himself into a dandy by an act of will (*se faisant*), but strangely, he becomes in turn a piece of bedroom furniture. In the boudoir, but not of it, decorating but not acting, the dandy will occupy an erotic arena, but only passively. And though Balzac does not pursue it here, the juncture of sexuality and the object world will come to play an essential role in decadent dandyism, where commodity fetishism becomes a mode of expression for (particularly homosexual) desire.[20]

All dandyism hints at a wish for male autochthony. The dandy, after all, longs to recreate himself as an emblem of complete originality, with no progenitors save other dandies. The society of dandyism reproduces itself through emulation and the following of social dictums, never through familial descendance. Dandies long to establish a nonsanguinary, nonbiological parallel genealogy, a family tree without women. And so, while homosexuality is not a defining quality or a requirement for dandyism, it is an unsurprising adjoining topic. Balzac's text gestures toward, instead of confronting directly, the issues of homoerotic desire, commodity fetishism, and mechanical reproduction that would engage such later writers as Villiers de l'Isle-Adam, Bram Stoker, and Jean Lorrain.[21] As a self-created "meuble de boudoir" or "mannequin ingénieux," the dandy exemplifies the leisured antithesis of the inanimate, mechanized worker, and yet somehow resembles the hapless "man-instrument." Neither exhibits full humanness; both must remain at some level impervious to their surroundings; neither should think. Ideally an automaton, an unthinking mannequin, Balzac's dandy aspires to the condition of the robotic, while insistently rejecting the baseness of industrialized society. What he seems to want is a mechanical coolness minus the mechanical dullness and repetitiveness of assembly-line machinery.

As an early text of French dandyism, the *Traité*—like the novels of Stendhal, for example—still owes much of its focus to the British version of the movement. Its interest in character and dialogue, for example, recalls England's more novelistic dandyism. Its view of elegance as a social (rather than an aesthetic or philosophical) phenomenon similarly harks back to works by Bulwer-Lytton or Disraeli. But at the same time, Balzac's treatise announces the dandyism to come, the dandyism of an increasingly industrialized world, the dandyism that fights off and yet strangely embraces the soullessness of mechanical reproduction, and the decadent dandyism that prepares the way for media spectacles and campy celebrity.

BARBEY'S *DU DANDYSME ET DE GEORGE BRUMMELL*

Next in the trio of French dandyist treatises is Barbey d'Aurevilly's essay on George Brummell, considered the primary source for all dandyist literature that followed. While Balzac's text touched upon issues of biography and dandyism, its official topics were elegance, social life, and social-class divisions—all less precise, less philosophical concepts than dandyism. Later, the dandyist characters of *La Comédie humaine* appeared to follow these early dictates of their creator, using dandyism as a social tool for personal advancement.[22] Barbey's essay, however, removes dandyism from such desultory concerns and devotes itself purely to the dandyist individual—and to only one dandy.[23]

For Barbey, Brummell does not occupy a dandyist milieu; he does not follow dandyist principles; he does not emulate other dandies. For Barbey, Brummell is dandyism, the perfect confluence of person and concept: "He was Dandyism itself" ("Il fut le Dandysme même," *Du Dandysme* 673). Yet while Brummell epitomizes dandyism, Barbey is at pains to explain the essence of this philosophy of self. In fact, dandyism in this text often seems to serve as an allegory for the problem of any kind of descriptive writing, or even of writing itself. Much of *Du Dandysme* grapples with the challenge of describing the ephemeral. Devoted to producing dramatic effect while appearing unconcerned, Beau Brummell defies narrative: "His entire life was an influence," writes Barbey, "that is to say, that which can hardly be recounted" ("Sa vie tout entière fut une influence, c'est à dire ce qui ne peut guère se raconter," ibid., 676).

Brummellian dandyism, for Barbey, resides in the nebulous zone that can exist between two poles of description or two points of reference. Barbey insists, for example, on the essential Englishness of dandyism, and on the impossibility of a truly French dandy: "Let them adopt a disdainful air if they like, and wear white gloves to the elbow, the country of Richelieu will never produce a Brummell."[24] The dandyism that Barbey announces here depends upon its very foreignness for its impact: "[The word 'dandyism'] will remain foreign, like the thing it represents."[25] Yet Barbey does more in this essay than describe Brummell's philosophy; he tries to create his own French version that appropriates and alters British dandyism. More accurately, one might say that Barbey invents a hybrid form of dandyism, which starts with anecdote, social history, and biography,[26] and then spins these rather pragmatic strands into a very abstract philosophical tapestry.

Balzac's *Traité de la vie élégante* appeared in a fashion magazine, and so, however theoretical it may have been, its context was nonetheless journalistic, with other articles on either side. Barbey's essay, on the other hand, though intended for the women's fashion review known as *Le Moniteur de la mode* (for which he had written several articles—under female pseudonyms—in 1843), never completely reached its original destination. The first chapter was published in the review, but shortly before its completion, the editors of *Le Moniteur* decided that Barbey's style was too inaccessible for its readership and fired him. As a result, Barbey published *Du Dandysme* independently, as a small bound book.

Barbey's dismissal from a fashion magazine offers a rather neat analogy for the trajectory of dandyism. The difference between Balzac's treatise and Barbey's is the difference between worldliness and esoterica. Where Balzac offers axiomatic rules, Barbey tries to recreate for the reader something of Brummell's performance, acknowledging that a mere recounting of facts could not convey the Beau's power: "The admiration is not justified by the facts, which perished entirely, since, by their very nature, they were ephemeral . . . it is by manners, by untransmittable manners, that Brummell became a prince of his time."[27] Barbey seeks to reproduce the effects of surprise and uncertainty that he ascribes to Brummell's performance, and to do so requires anecdote.

Of the many anecdotes about Brummell offered in this essay, one is particularly illustrative. It concerns Brummell's self-created royalty—his status as "a prince of his time"—the question of how he acquired this royal status, and how such royalty can be reproduced. Brummell's power sprang from his self-fashioned nobility; his manners alone made him a prince. Yet at the same time, Barbey makes it clear that the real, inherited royalty of the prince of Wales was required for Brummell to achieve his influence.[28] After recounting Brummell's first meeting with the prince of Wales, Barbey explains how the prince's favor brought Brummell into the aristocratic circle that he so needed as his audience: "From that moment on, he found himself ranked very highly in people's opinion. He, the son of a simple esquire, was seen with the most noble of England. . . . So much distinction sent the salon aristocracy flocking to him, on the most flatteringly familiar basis."[29]

But although the most crucial element of Brummell's success was his friendship with the prince, he regularly eclipsed His Royal Highness both socially and physically, and as a consequence courted royal disfavor. Barbey explains Brummell's eventual falling out with the prince in the following passage, especially worth quoting at length for its example of Barbey's own precious and ironic style:

> The regent was beginning to age. His *embonpoint*, that polyp that seizes beauty and kills it slowly in its flaccid embrace, *embonpoint* had overtaken him, and Brummell, with his relentless jesting and that tiger's pride that success can inspire in hearts, sometimes mocked the prince's coquettish and ineffective attempts to repair the ravages of time. As there was at Carlton House a concierge dubbed "Big Ben" for his monstrous corpulence, Brummell had displaced this nickname from the servant to the master. He also called Madame Fitz-Herbert [the prince's mistress; Fig. 4] *Benina*. . . . This was . . . the real cause of the disgrace that suddenly struck the great Dandy. . . . The "Who is that fat man?" uttered publicly by Brummell in Hyde Park, while pointing out His Royal Highness, and a host of other, similar remarks explain everything.[30]

The Marriage of Mrs. Fitzherbert and George IV.   *From a Caricature.*

Charles James Fox is holding Mrs. Fitzherbert's left hand, and Colonel Hanger's
head can be seen between them.   Lord North is seen sitting fast asleep!

4. "The Marriage of Mrs. Fitzherbert and George IV." Caricature from Boutet de Monvel, *Beau Brummell and His Times*.

This passage is typical of Barbey's textual version of Brummell's mordently successful irony. Dandyist irony functions like a pinpoint laser shining through an ornate curtain. Metaphor and circumlocution abound but are occasionally interrupted by one small but effective cutting observation—all the more deadly for its elegant and ornate context. No actual description of the prince's body is needed. His corpulence becomes the allegorical and slightly surreal struggle between an amorous, murderous polyp and its hapless victim. It is the lowly concierge whose body is described as afflicted with "monstrous corpulence," and to whom the nickname is initially applied. The shock comes from the extravagant simplicity of the statement: "Brummell had displaced the nickname from servant to master." Mediation is everything here. The insulting name belongs first to a servant; Brummell merely "displaces" it. Similarly, Bardoes not directly reproduce Brummell's insult, displacing the event himself by narrating it obliquely.

The entirety of Barbey's essay functions in like fashion. From a barrage of historical references, anecdotes, and extremely long footnotes emerges the profile of an individual whose talent lay in indirectness, in influence rather than in action, and hence in the transcendence of reference itself. The anecdote about the prince is also revealing for its handling of the physical world, its discussion of bodiliness. Barbey's interest in the materiality of this essay, and the pains he took to ensure that it was—in its cover, paper, and typeface—a very attractive small book point to the dandyist conflation of material body and performance. The essay tells us that Brummell, while impeccable and elaborate in his dress, insisted upon great simplicity and affected a certain unconcern for his appearance: "He remained dressed in an irreproachable fashion; but he subdued the colors of his clothes, simplified their cut and wore them without thinking."[31] An attached footnote here reads: "A Dandy can spend . . . ten hours at his toilette, but once it is done, he forgets it. It is others who must perceive that he is well dressed."[32]

Brummell's elaborate dress and grooming (he was famous for requiring three different specialists to design his gloves, one each for palm, fingers, and thumb) and his very materiality serve only to dematerialize him, to render him pure presence: "To be well dressed, one must not be noticed" ("Pour être bien mis, il ne faut pas être remarqué," *Du Dandysme* 690). In fact, according to Barbey, Brummell would normally disappear quickly from social functions, adhering to a famous dandyist principle: "In society, as long as you have not produced an effect, remain: if the effect is produced, leave."[33] Toward the end of the essay, Barbey explains why he will not be treating Brummell's last, painful years of poverty and exile: "Why recount them? We are speaking of the Dandy, of his influence, his public life, his social role. What does the rest matter? When one is dying of hunger, one leaves behind the affectations of any society, one returns to human life: one ceases to be a Dandy."[34] Dandyism, then, demands meticulous care of the material self while negating the human body altogether. Hunger, pain, indeed any manifestation of human corporeality recedes under the purely social effect of the dandy. In the same way, the denseness of Barbey's text, all its references and notes, recedes before its central figure, Brummell in all his insubstantiality. Like most premodernist theatrical performance, dandyism requires elaborate control of the physical world but a subsequent negation of it. Actors need their costumes, lines, and stage, but do not, traditionally, refer to them as such. Barbey relies upon hundreds of references and quotations from Lister, Bulwer-Lytton, Sheridan, Carlyle, Milton, Montesquieu, Congreve, Madame de Staël, Mirabeau, Lord Byron, the count d'Orsay, and others, only to insist that Brummell was unique, unquotable, indescribable, and beyond narrative. But the denseness, the references, and the footnotes all form a backdrop necessary to this airy, unseizable topic.

When Brummell calls the prince of Wales "a fat man," he reverses the bodily hierarchy required by a monarchy. What scandalizes in his behavior is the apparent creation of a separate, parallel social universe in which his importance outranks even the prince's, and in which his body can dematerialize while the prince's remains all too material. Brummell's long successful career in England resulted from both his unusual proximity to royalty—itself an accomplishment for a commoner—and the *distance* he kept from his royal friends, his refusal to play his part in the hierarchy. The legend of the Beau narrates the story of royal decay and the creation of a self-generated, independent, and tradition-free royalty of the self. In such a parallel society, the body of the prince, which should be inviolable as symbol of the body of England, can become a corporeal body, the fleshly body of Brummell's remark. It can be as subject to mockery as that of a valet. As Ernst Kantorowicz has observed, the expression "The king is dead, long live the king" contains meaning because the king's physical body can be subsumed by the nonspecific, abstract, allegorical body.[35] When the prince, or the king's successor, can substitute his physical body for that of the deceased, it is because the body is merely the marker or fleshly receptacle of kingly signification. When the regent becomes "Big Ben," he has lost his royal aura. His status as guarantor of the currency of social meaning is gone.[36] Barbey's anecdotes tell the story of an upset in the value of currency and of the emptying out of the royal body's significance.

Françoise Coblence, in her *Le Dandyisme, obligation d'incertitude*, reads dandyism as symptomatic of British and later French anxiety over the death of royal power. The self-sufficiency of the dandified body represents, for Coblence, a breakdown in bodily meaning, a disincorporation of royal power. A void appears in place of this bodily power, and "beginning with this absence, the dandy can reveal himself as the exasperation of a process of individuation and separation unimaginable in an aristocratic society" (36). Relying on Habermas's discussion of the development of the bourgeois public sphere, Coblence distinguishes between the noble, whose entire existence is "dedicated to representation," and the bourgeois, who is what he produces. While life in court is public, "saturated" with representation down to the intimate rituals of waking, sleeping, and resting, life in the rising bourgeoisie creates privacy, where one simply exists, representing nothing, to an audience of no one. The dandy, says Coblence, resembles the noble, since he, too, is dedicated to performing, to representing always in front of an audience. From this analogy comes Coblence's argument that the dandy, in both literature and history, is the anxious response to a declining aristocracy and the rise of the bourgeoisie.[37] "Dandies," writes Barbey, "by virtue of their private authority, establish a rule above that which governs the most aristocratic circles."[38]

When the prince's body can be noted and mocked for its fleshiness, for its sheer materiality, the symbolic power of the royal body, passed from generation to generation, diminishes. In the place of England's royal family tree, its genealogy of kings, Barbey offers a parallel lineage—of dandies. *Du Dandysme* traces the dandy back to his roots in Ancient Greece, the fifth-century B.C. general Alcibiades serving as the Adamic original. The essay mentions Alcibiades twice, once as a contrast to Brummell's unmilitary nature ("Although Alcibiades was the greatest of generals, George Bryan Brummell did not have a military mind"[39]), and once at the end of the essay, in the very last sentence:[40]

> Of double and multiple natures, of an intellectual, undecided sex, in which grace is rendered more graceful by strength, and strength is once more found through grace, Androgynes no longer of Legend but of History, with Alcibiades being the most beautiful example, from the most beautiful of nations.[41]

Barbey understands dandyism as an alternative family tree that springs from ancient roots, the implication being that it bypasses any unworthy ancestors. But what greatly intensifies the power of the Alcibiades reference here is Barbey's description of the dandy as a double-sexed being, as an androgyne of history. Dandies, apparently, reproduce themselves through an ancient process of cultural self-pollination. Help from women is unnecessary because the dandy himself contains a feminine side: "The dandy is a woman in certain respects" ("Le dandy est femme par certains côtés," *Du Dandysme* 710), as Barbey writes earlier in the essay.

Throughout *Du Dandysme*, Barbey raises the topic of women only to insist upon their essential uselessness to the true dandy, despite the social function he admits they perform:

> They were the trumpets of his glory, but they remained trumpets. . . . He was not what the world calls a libertine. . . . To love, to desire, is always to be dependent, to be enslaved by one's desire. Those arms that close most tenderly around you are still a chain. . . . This was the slavery from which Brummell escaped. His triumphs had the insolence of disinterestedness.[42]

Women looked to Brummell for his impeccable taste, prizing it above even a lover's desire: "The woman most madly in love, while pinning on a flower or trying on jewels, thought much more about Brummell's opinion than about her lover's pleasure."[43] Here again, Brummell's cultural power wins out over the corporeal. The pleasure of a woman's lover—sexual pleasure—recedes in importance before Brummell's de-eroticized social power and discernment. The Judgment of Paris has been rewritten as a fashion competition.

Like Balzac's *meuble de boudoir*, Barbey's Brummell inhabits an erotic venue—life at court with all its intrigue and libertinage—but at a cool distance. His lineage is ancient, but his reproduction cultural, or even textual. (Naturally, the subtext of homosexual desire is powerful in such a reference to both ancient Greek soldiers and androgynous, double-sexed beings.) The dandy's social body exhibits artful control and manipulation raised to a virtually maniacal pitch of intensity. Brummell redirects all erotic drive toward the suppression of his physical self, so that the dandified body becomes, again, a kind of mechanical body.[44] Barbey's text, like Balzac's before it, ends with the implication that the dandy is a self-reproducing machine and, at the same time, an almost Promethean figure who dares to steal the spark of life, looking to explore "the mystery of creation," "to give life to inert substance" (Coblence 150).

For Barbey's dandy, then, extreme materiality and concern for the material world lead both to mechanicity or lifelessness and, at the same time, to a curiously disembodied quality. Brummell attends obsessively to his appearance; but the goal of this self-indulgence is total dis-appearance. His excessive interest in his physical, visible self prepares the way, paradoxically, for the social invisibility he desires. Barbey's text mirrors this game of extreme materiality and subsequent dematerialization. The essay's abundance of references, quotations, and notes is a textual analogue to Brummell's elaborate and meticulous toilette, the material coverings of his person. But just as Brummell needs to vanish under his dense and careful persona, so, in a sense, does Barbey's text yearn to escape the web of its own dense and encyclopedic citations. Barbey insists throughout that his subject defies writing, and hence defies both wordiness and referentiality. The text's clear struggle, then, between description and nearly wordless effect replays Brummell's social struggle to pose elaborately while appearing nearly bodiless.

It is not a new idea to suggest that virtuosity or extreme control over one's person leads to a kind of mechanicity; and the question naturally poses itself most frequently in regard to performance. Joseph Roach, in his study of theatrical concepts of the mechanical, finds the essential question to be: "Is the actor's bodily instrument to be interpreted as a spontaneously vital organism? . . . or is it best understood as a biological machine?" (161). Roach looks back to Kleist's 1810 "On the Marionnette Theatre" for an early example of the nineteenth-century fascination with this notion. Kleist's text takes the form of a dialogue between the author and an anonymous dancer, Mr. C., who explains his fascination with the mass-entertainment form of puppet theater. Mr. C. explains that natural grace is often purer and easier to observe in nonhuman form, in marionettes, for example, whose center of gravity animates their limbs flawlessly, and whose weightlessness enables them to soar: the puppets, he says, "are not afflicted with the inertia of matter, the property most resistant to dance" (Kleist 6–7). In this text, the precision, grace, and unself-consciousness of the puppets represent an inevitable extension of the superhuman virtuosity ideally expected of human dancers.

But the explosion of interest in mechanomorphism would have to wait until the late nineteenth and early twentieth centuries, when industrialism and the rise of the factory explicitly broached the issue of the industrialized body.

BAUDELAIRE'S *LE PEINTRE DE LA VIE MODERNE*

Baudelaire's 1863 essay on dandyism, *Le Peintre de la vie moderne*, announces dandyism's transition to the fin de siècle and decadence by dealing explicitly with issues such as the urban landscape, crowds, the slightly macabre beauty in "le Mal," and the languor, the power, and—crucially—the performance of urban women. An examination of this essay, then, will lead out of early dandyism and into this book's major concerns.

Like Barbey's essay, Baudelaire's devotes itself largely to one man's life, in a style that might be called biography-manqué. The title character, the "painter of modern life," is known only as M.G. (for Monsieur G.) throughout the text but was widely understood to be Constantin Guys, an artist whose passion (or mania) for anonymity was respected by Baudelaire, who agreed to use only the artist's initials.[45] He refers to Guys as "the imaginary artist whom we are obliged to call M.G. since from time to time I recall that I have resolved, out of respect for his modesty, to suppose that he does not exist."[46] But this partial veiling of his subject's identity represents more than just cooperative discretion on Baudelaire's part. It will allow him to create, as he says, "an imaginary artist," blurring the factual lines of his text. The imaginary M.G. allows Baudelaire to remove his essay somewhat from the realm of journalism (although it first appeared in installments in *Le Figaro*), and to reconstruct history by means of fiction—both of which are techniques common to dandyist texts. Guys was a commercial illustrator, and his work often appeared, as Baudelaire notes several times, in the British newspaper *The Illustrated News*. But by changing Guys into an imaginary of Guys's life and create a distance between his essay's idealized subject and the quotidian world of business. As we shall see, however, it is a distance that eventually narrows.

Like the dandyism of Balzac and Barbey, Baudelaire's rejects work and condemns the production of anything save one's own carefully tended self. Among the first distinctions made about Guys, for example, is that he is not an *artist*, since that would imply the offensive middle-class status of a provider of services or products, the dreaded *spécialiste*: "The man attached to his palette like the serf to his plot of land."[47] Instead, M.G. is more of a child—*un homme-enfant* or an *éternel convalescent* who sees things in an aura of perpetual newness, "a forgetting or a suppression of anteriority."[48]

Ultimately, Baudelaire settles on the term *dandy* to describe Guys: "I would gladly call him a *dandy*, since the word dandy implies a quintessence of character and a subtle intelligence . . . but on the other hand, the dandy aspires to insensibility."[49] Here again, dandyism is a mark at once of superiority and subhumanness; and Baudelaire's version recalls Balzac's object of bedroom furniture (*meuble de boudoir*) or the mannequin on the sofa. But the Baudelairean dandy has more to contend with than his earlier counterparts, more to resist in his quest for insensibility. In this latest of the three dandyist treatises, the crowds of the late nineteenth century finally appear as an explicit part of the dandy's landscape, creating far more social anxiety than Balzac's salon society or Barbey's version of life at court. This essay, like the art of M.G., addresses itself to the present, not the past: "I wish to devote myself today to the painting of contemporary mores."[50] And the complicated, socially mixed contemporary world outside forces the dandy into a paradoxical relationship with it. Guys is at once a man of the crowds and an impervious onlooker. He may draw inspiration from the teeming, electric life about him, but he must not be touched by it:

> The dandy is blasé, or feigns to be . . . his passion and his profession are to wed himself to the crowd. . . . The observer is a prince who revels everywhere in his incognito . . . he plunges into the crowd as if into an immense reservoir of electricity.[51]

While Barbey saw Brummell as a prince of his times by virtue of his independent royal status while *among* royalty, Balzac's M.G. is a princely observer of city life. The dandy's court has become the crowd.

Despite his interest in the present, Baudelaire seems to yearn for the simple, clear-cut class divisions of earlier times. This nostalgia for a lost era was visible in both Balzac's and Barbey's texts. But here in 1863, after two more revolutions have buffeted French society back and forth between monarchy and republic, such nostalgia emerges as a wistful note within a text otherwise devoted to a fascination with *modernité*.[52] Dandyism may reinvigorate or even improve upon a waning aristocracy, refashioning it as pure meritocracy, but Baudelaire recognizes that even this brand of elitism is something of a last gasp in a world where aristocracy is stumbling, but democracy has not completely taken over: "A type of new aristocracy . . . based upon heavenly gifts conferred by neither work nor money. Dandyism is the last burst of heroism in the decadent period."[53]

Unlike the other dandies in the tradition, however, Constantin Guys produces something other than his own carefully tended self, however impassive he may have been. M.G. is an illustrator, he creates art to be reproduced and seen. Although a dandy, M.G. has a profession, just as Baudelaire does. Such a parallel relationship between an author and his biographical subject is common in dandyist literature, recalling, for example, the connection between Barbey and Brummell in *Du Dandysme*.

Of the three treatises examined here, Baudelaire's text is alone in staging the essential contradiction of the dandyist artist, the contradiction between espousing an antiutilitarian philosophy of pure, ephemeral performance and producing written or painted permanent, material objects. Anything so public as literature or painting would violate the required solipsism of dandies, whose performances are supposed to remain a purely social phenomenon. But M.G., like Baudelaire, at once embodies dandyism and portrays it in his work, becoming, therefore, a doppelganger for the author. In writing of Guys, then, Baudelaire also manages to write a fictionalized autobiography, using a historically real artist as a stand-in for himself.

Section 7 in Baudelaire's essay, "Les Annales de la Guerre," blends world history, dandyism, and the established Romantic tradition of the *voyage en orient* in its descriptions of M.G.'s illustrations of the Crimean War. By combining standard motifs of Eastern exoticism and sensuality with Western motifs of urban dandyism, this section announces the arrival of that peculiarly Baudelairean decadent dandyism that would so powerfully influence all who followed. This section describes with delectation the dandyist figures who populate these drawings and their ornate, orientalist context:

> Here we are in Schumla . . . Turkish hospitality, pipes and coffee . . . King Othon and his queen . . . are dressed in traditional costumes. . . . The king's waist is cinched like that of the most coquettish palikar, and his skirt flares out in the exaggerated manner of the national dandyism.[54]

Dandyism here resides not in the person of Guys, but within his depictions of the Orient. If to be a dandy is to turn one's life into a work of art, this section of *Le Peintre* takes the idea rather literally. And it is not only dandyist style of dress that appears in these figures. Certain other aspects of dandyism seem to be embodied in different ways by various personages in Guys's canvases. Barbey's oblique notion of the dandy's "undecided sex," for example, becomes explicit here in the androgynous figure of the eunuch who appears in Guys's illustrations of Turkey:

> The heavy, massive carriages . . . from which emerge sometimes some oddly feminine glances . . . the frenetic dances of the performers "of the third sex" (never has Balzac's comical term been more applicable . . . since . . . beneath the flaming makeup of cheeks, eyes and eyebrows . . . and in the long tresses that float down the back, it would be difficult, if not to say impossible, to perceive their virility).[55]

Like the dandy, the eunuch is a creature of theater, disguise, and rerouted sexuality. Like that of the dandy, the eunuch's inner nature—his virility, in this case—remains indecipherable to an audience, concealed by artful arrangements of manner and dress. If the eunuch resembles the dandy in the orientalist world of these war drawings, he resembles the women just as much. In fact, Baudelaire places his description of Guys's eunuchs directly before his description of Guys's "femmes galantes," who come from a variety of Eastern countries—"des races opprimées" (Fig. 5):

> Among these women, some have preserved the national dress, embroidered vests . . . flowing scarves, wide pants . . . striped or gilded gauzes . . . others . . . have adopted the main sign of civilization, which, for a woman, is invariably the crinoline, while nonetheless keeping . . . a slight souvenir of the Orient, such that they have the look of *parisiennes* who might have wished to disguise themselves.[56]

In keeping with other aspects of Guys's Oriental works, the women depicted represent a melding of East and West. Like both the dandy and the eunuch, these women disguise themselves elaborately; and if the eunuchs represented a theatrical obscuring of sex, these women suggest a theatrical obscuring of race, becoming pastiches of Oriental and Parisian types.

M.G.'s *femmes galantes* are familiar to a reader of Baudelaire since they strikingly resemble the *femmes fatales* of *Les Fleurs du mal*, such as la dame créole, la passante, or the languorous owner of the "chevelure." In including this passage of description devoted to Guys's Oriental courtesans, Baudelaire indirectly points to his own most famous work, and hence furthers the implicit connection between himself and Guys, and between their two oeuvres, reminding the reader of the vertiginous layers of biography, art criticism, and autobiography at work here.

The essay increases this confusion of fact and fiction, self and other, by virtue of its curious treatment of M.G.'s artworks, its reluctance, that is,

5. Egyptian women. Detail from "Donkey Races in Alexandria," by Constantin Guys, *Illustrated London News*, August 1855.

to acknowledge that what is being described is artworks and not life. Though the essay's title promises a discussion of a person—the painter of modern life—it turns out to be the artist's work that is discussed almost exclusively, with the inevitable dandyist implication that persons and artworks are somehow interchangeable. Baudelaire concentrates so heavily upon the realism—the *effet de réel*—of Guys's painted figures that their status as representations is all but forgotten. The long passages about the various scenes and characters leave only rare clues that artworks are being described. In fact, so few are the overt reminders to the contrary that a reader could easily be led to believe that these descriptions come from Baudelaire's own personal experiences. Only the infrequent mention of a title, or a rare remark about Guys himself, interrupts the smooth and absorbing flow of description and jars the reader. And with each passing section, Baudelaire includes fewer such references,[57] until, in Section 9, "Le Dandy," no overt trace of Guys or his art remains, save for a single mention of the artist's initials, at the very end of the section. The framework discussion of Guys's artwork, then, disappears almost entirely in the very section devoted to the figure who embodies just such a collapse of distinctions, the figure who turns self into art.

In earlier sections of the essay, Baudelaire discussed the art of self-transformation or disguise. The eunuchs and prostitutes of Section 7 and the soldiers of Section 8 all shared a certain doubleness of nature. The eunuchs embodied a dual sexual nature, the women dual nationalities, and the military men, Baudelaire tells us, exhibited "a singular mixture of placidity and audacity" (*Le Peintre* 1176)—a double nature necessary for their hazardous occupation. Now, in this discussion of the dandy, such theatricality or obfuscation of self becomes a quality of the text itself, which reproduces on its own the elements it had been narrating. Curiously, the dandy's status as part of Guys's artwork disappears. No mention is made of where these remarks of dandyism come from; they just begin with no warning. Sections 6, 7, and 8 all began with one sentence explicitly indicating that the topics to be described came from M.G.'s universe. Section 9, however, disavows the identity of its subject, just as its subject—the dandy—habitually disavows his own provenance, preferring his self-created aristocracy. No mention of M.G. is made in the opening sentence: "The rich, idle man, who has no occupation other than running after happiness . . . will always enjoy a distinctive physiognomy."[58] Once again, dandyism proves to be a topic that coincides with highly performative texts.[59]

"Le Dandy" reads most like a treatise or manifesto, performing a kind of variation on Balzac's and Barbey's earlier essays. Guys has all but disappeared, and so have his artworks; and what is left is a series of recognizable statements, such as "Dandyism is a vague institution, as bizarre as dueling; very ancient, since Caesar, Catiline, and Alcibiades provide the most dazzling prototypes. . . . Dandyism, which is an institution beyond laws, has its own rigorous laws. . . . These creatures have no occupation save cultivating the idea of beauty in their persons."[60] These remarks seem out of context. Baudelaire has done nothing to introduce them or to explain why he has chosen to focus here on the dandy. Only in the penultimate paragraph does Baudelaire acknowledge the anomalous character of this section: "What might have seemed to the reader a digression is not one," he writes ("Ce qui a pu paraître au lecteur une digression n'en est pas une"). On the contrary, this philosophical detour has been inspired by Guys's own dandies: "Considerations and moral reveries . . . rise up from these drawings. . . . Need I say that M.G., when he sketches one of these dandies on paper, always lends him his historical, even legendary character?"[61] The historical or legendary character of dandies was a constant topic, of course, throughout the nineteenth century. Baudelaire's reference to antiquity (Caesar, Catiline, and Alcibiades) looks to the dandyist tradition of tracing its lineage back to classical times. In referring to these ancient dandies and in providing this manifestolike treatise on dandyism, Baudelaire not only suggests but also en-

acts the purely cultural form of reproduction and transmission associated with dandyism, since this section as a whole reproduces traces of
dandyism's *textual* ancestors—the essays of Balzac, Barbey, and also
Théophile Gautier, whose 1858 essay *De La Mode* clearly influenced
Baudelaire.[62]

But in addition to classical Greece and Rome, Baudelaire's essay introduces another, more surprising dandyist homeland: North America—
a part of the world with which the French decadents would be at once
fascinated and repulsed. Directly after mentioning Caesar and Alcibiades, Baudelaire remarks that Chateaubriand believed he had found a
version of dandyism among Native American tribes: "Chateaubriand
found it in the forests and around the lakes of the New World"
("Chateaubriand l'a trouvé dans les forêts et au bord des lacs du Nou-
veau-Monde," *Le Peintre* 1177). A bit later, Baudelaire goes on to jux-
tapose explicitly the New World dandies and Decadence:

> Dandyism is the last burst of heroism in Decadence; and the type of dandy
> found by the traveler in North America in no way weakens this argument:
> nothing prevents us from assuming that the tribes we call *savage* are the last
> vestiges of great civilizations that have vanished. Dandyism is a setting sun. . . .
> But alas! the rising tide of democracy, which invades and levels all things, day
> by day drowns these last representatives of human pride.[63]

These remarks hint at the role that America, Yankee businessmen, and
American-style democracy would play in turn-of-the-century Decadence.
The United States was becoming the symbol of vulgar new money, au-
tomatonlike workers, and worst of all, a scientific progress that threatened to level all the necessary fine distinctions of society.[64] In this passage on Chateaubriand, not only is dandyism ancient—the debris of a
lost civilization—it is the lost, non-Western, non-European underside of
the New World, a kind of orientalist, dandyist subconscious.

Baudelaire, who normally condemned what he saw as the "American-
ization" of Europe, did have great respect for one American, Edgar Allan
Poe, whose poetry he had translated. But for Baudelaire, as for the
French decadents in general, Poe was not a typical American, representing rather the antithesis of New World coarseness, a prisoner of genius,
condemned to "a great barbarism, lit by gas" ("une grande barbarie
éclairée au gaz," *L'Art romantique* 153). Poe was "the inverse of American society" (Lemaire 30), much like Chateaubriand's lost dandyist
tribes. For Baudelaire, Poe was a true dandy, "an aristocrat in a democracy."[65] Later in the century, though, such dandyist disdain for things
American would circle back to the decadents' fascinated obsession with
America, and the automated, mechanical eeriness suggested by entertainment and technology in the United States.[66]

With *Le Peintre de la vie moderne*, Baudelaire clearly pays homage to several dandyist predecessors, and with Sections 10, 11, and 12, which return to urban Paris, he doffs his hat particularly to Gautier's *De la Mode* and Balzac's *Théorie de la démarche* (the 1833 addendum to *Traité de la vie élégante*). These sections, "La Femme," "Eloge du maquillage," and "Les Femmes et les filles," concern themselves with Parisian life and style, and with the subtleties conveyed in the minute details of dress, posture, facial expression, and demeanor—in women.

Baudelaire was famous for having insisted upon women's incapacity for dandyism, and their repugnant naturalness: "Woman is 'natural,' which is to say abominable, therefore she is also always vulgar, which is to say the opposite of a dandy."[67] But the women in these final sections of *Le Peintre* are far from natural; they are creatures of disguise and social manipulation, suggesting that Baudelaire might be closer than he admitted to Barbey's opinion that dandies were "in certain respects women."

The women described here spring from Guys's illustrations, but as in the section on dandyism, no titles of illustrations appear. Unlike the section on dandyism, however, from time to time this one mentions M.G.'s status as artist-creator of these women. The painterly context has fallen away somewhat, but since, unlike the dandy, the urban woman cannot be entirely her own creation, M.G.'s presence remains visible. Women, it appears, are a grand spectacle produced by a collectivity of forces. The urban woman is *une divinité, un astre,* whose dazzle is due in part to her parure—"Everything that adorns a woman . . . is a part of her" ("Tout ce qui orne la femme . . . fait partie d'elle-même," *Le Peintre* 1182–83)— and in part to her status as inspiration to male artists: "This creature . . . for whom, but above all *with whom*, artists and poets compose their most delicate gems" ("Cet être . . . pour qui, mais surtout *par qui* les artistes et les poètes composent leurs plus délicats bijoux," ibid., 1181).

The women in these pages offer Baudelaire an occasion to espouse the philosophy at the heart of both dandyism and "art for art's sake,"[68] which insists upon the creative power and modernity of surfaces, artifice, and theatricality. Like his earlier novelistic protagonist La Fanfarlo (1847), Baudelaire's modern woman depends upon her toilette for her success and for her very existence, to the point that she is virtually inseparable from her dress:

> What poet would dare, in depicting the pleasure caused by the appearance of a great beauty, separate the woman from her dress? What man . . . has not taken pleasure . . . in an artfully composed toilette and has not taken away with him an image of it inseparable from the beauty of the woman to whom it belonged, thereby making of the two, of the woman and the dress, one indivisible totality?[69]

As a champion here for artifice, Baudelaire draws force for his argument by debunking the notion of any virtue in naturalness. "Eloge du Maquillage" sings the praises of makeup in all forms, praising the mystical transformation achieved when rice powder grants a woman's face marblelike perfection, "an abstract unity . . . [that] immediately brings the human being closer to the statue" ("[Une] unité abstraite . . . [qui] rapproche immédiatement l'être humain de la statue," *Le Peintre* 1185). Here, Baudelaire is quoting nearly verbatim from Gautier's *De la Mode*, which preached the acceptance and embrace of cosmetics such as powder, "that fine dust," which, Gautier said, lends the face "a marbled sheen . . . [that] approaches that of statuary" ("un mica de marbre . . . [qui] se rapproche ainsi de la statuaire," quoted in Godfrey, "Baudelaire, Gautier," 80).

Gautier's *De la Mode* addressed itself to painters, reproaching them for their reluctance to paint contemporary dress and parure; the women it discussed, therefore, occupy the position of objects of representation. Of course, Baudelaire also bases his discussion of women upon an initial assumption of their status as artworks, as part of Guys's urban landscape. But very quickly his essay lends these women a strange kind of independence. Section 12, "Les Femmes et les filles" begins with an acknowledgment that the women belong to M.G.'s work: "Thus M.G. . . . willingly depicts women very adorned and embellished by all manner of artificial display" ("Ainsi M.G. . . . représente volontiers des femmes très-parées et embellies par toutes les pompes artificielles," *Le Peintre* 1186). As the section progresses, however, the reader is left in the middle of urban Paris, and the framework of Guys's drawings is abandoned. "We see [the women] walking nonchalantly down the paths of public gardens," writes Baudelaire.[70] "Little girls . . . play at hoops"; "actresses from the little theaters" emerge from buildings; someone's mistress sits beside him in a café window. Eventually Beauty itself emerges for Baudelaire out of these (often debased) creatures, a beauty, as he says, "qui . . . vient du Mal" (ibid., 1187), a beauty that he finds even in the lowliest prostitutes, "those slaves confined in those hovels" ("ces esclaves qui sont confinées dans ces bouges," ibid., 1188). The world fills up with women, glimpsed from all sides and belonging to all walks of life. Guys's drawings have become the flaneur's universe, but though the women's status as representations diminishes, they never attain the level of self-possession or self-control attributed to the dandies or the soldiers of earlier sections. The last section on women (Section 12) ends with a description of "nymphes macabres" and "poupées vivantes," whose eyes flash sinisterly, and whose beauty comes from cruelty and evil; and again, they resemble strongly the women of *Les Fleurs du mal*. The women, then, do not manage to escape from Guys's control to the macabre reality Baudelaire granted the dandy earlier in this essay; into have been transferred from Guys's artistic universe to Baudelaire's own. Like dandies, these carefully soignée women are modern artists of the self; but unlike dandies, they ultimately depend for their ontological status upon an exterior creator—a painter, a poet, or whoever else might translate the monstrous beauty they unwittingly embody.

Up until its last section, "Les Voitures" (Fig. 6), Baudelaire's essay invites the reader into Guys's universe while sidestepping the fact that these are but drawings being discussed. Strangely, though, the final section ends this fantasy abruptly. M.G. is omnipresent here; his artist's brush—his *pinceau*—is a constant presence, the exactitude of his renderings and his technical skill very much emphasized by Baudelaire. In this section, Baudelaire brings the reader out of the reverie of Guys's drawings and reminds us of the technical aspects of art, of the effort it takes to create such lifelike illustrations. "Les Voitures" details M.G.'s drawings of horses, riders, races, and elegant carriages. These final pages insist upon Guys's obvious expertise, his "remarkable knowledge of harnesses and carriage-building" ("connaissance remarquable du harnais et de la carrosserie," *Le Peintre* 1191). Baudelaire praises the realistic rendering of carriages: "All of his carriages are perfectly authentic, each part in its place" ("Toute sa carrosserie est parfaitement orthodoxe; chaque partie est à sa place," ibid.).

Suddenly, the realism of Guys's drawings becomes a technical accomplishment, no longer an uncannily absorbing force. Baudelaire seems to have awakened from the dream that sent him traveling through an alternative universe. He speculates that Guys derives his artistic pleasure not from any given object he chooses to paint but from "the series of geometric figures that the object, already so complicated, ship or carriage, engenders successively and rapidly in space" ("la série de figures géométriques que cet objet, déjà si compliqué, navire ou carrosse, engendre successivement et rapidement dans l'espace," ibid.). The very objects that had held an almost magical reality for Baudelaire are now reduced to their shapes and contours. And what had posed as a credulous enjoyment of an artist's realism ends up sounding very much like an explanation of modernism—with its emphasis on shapes, surface, and paint (or even futurism, with its fascination with speed).[71]

Section 12 further emphasizes the painterliness of Guys's works by putting them in an art-historical context, by placing Guys, that is, in a list of artists Baudelaire deems equally praiseworthy: "His works will be as sought after as those of Debucourt, Moreau, Saint-Aubain, Carle Vernet, Lami, Devéria, Gavarni" ("Ses oeuvres seront recherchées autant que celles des Debucourt, des Moreau, des Saint-Aubain, des Carle Vernet, des Lamis, des Devéria, des Gavarni," *Le Peintre* 1191–92). Just as Baudelaire has pulled his critical focus back from the objects depicted to

6. Horse-drawn carriage. Detail from "Street in Alexandria, by Night," by Constantin Guys, *Illustrated London News*, August 1855.

the shapes they describe, so has he relaxed his gaze upon Guys himself, who becomes at the essay's end one in a series of contemporary artists. With these final pages, Baudelaire undoes somewhat the magical fusing of artist and work that so much of the essay strove to establish. Why would this last section strike such a different chord? And what are the ramifications of this?

Throughout this essay, it has become increasingly clear that, although Baudelaire draws heavily from the dandyist tradition he has inherited, he alters it significantly as well. From the beginning, by deciding to devote this essay to a productive and commercial artist, he has confronted the dandyist taboo on work or production. He has, furthermore, announced himself as a partisan of the contemporary, choosing to lionize not a distant dandy of the past, but a living artist.

And within his discussion of both Guys and his illustrations, another significant change appears. Despite his sitings of dandies within Guys's work, Baudelaire does not view dandyism as a quality embodied uniquely in dandies. Or, to put it another way, dandyism here looks less like a goal to be pursued by a single type of individual, and more like an attribute that can be found in a variety of persons—found, perhaps, in the crowd.

As the descriptions of Guys's various characters mount, the quality of dandyism begins to distribute itself over many different individuals, from Oriental kings, to eunuchs, to soldiers, and finally, to women. The unity of the dandyist figure begins to break down, its integrity is compromised. This is analogous to what happens in Baudelaire's concluding remarks about Guys's technique. When the formal or technical aspects of the drawings overtake their depicted content, their integrity also begins to break down. Guys's talent is revealed as the product of a slightly mechanistic, scientific process, the product, that is, of work and training, and not the magical production of a dandy's sheer panache.

Baudelaire's essay takes both the iconic personality of the dandy and the mimetic power of Guys's work and dismantles them, spreading the pieces out over characters and scenes from both urban and Oriental landscapes, in much the same manner that the impressionists fragmented light, painting the process of illumination rather than persons or objects. "Guys is . . . shattered by otherness," writes Leo Bersani, "penetrated . . . shaken by the spectacle of external life" (*Baudelaire* 11).[72] Personal magnetism and artistic power are now narratable as the products of given *processes* rather than static fact.

This reading of *Le Peintre de la vie moderne* is, of course, consistent with Benjamin's interpretation of Baudelaire as a poet reacting to commodity culture, reacting to the transformation of self into exchange item: "The *flâneur* is someone abandoned in the crowd. In this he shares the situation of the commodity" (*Charles Baudelaire* 55). Benjamin saw the commercial, capitalist underside of Baudelairean aestheticism and the doctrine of *l'art pour l'art*,[73] and read even the trademark nonchalance and impassivity of the dandy as a quality borrowed from commercial life, specifically from the demeanor of merchants:

> To Baudelaire the dandy appeared to be a descendant of great ancestors. . . . It pleased him to discover in Chateaubriand a reference to Indian dandies—evidence of a past flowering of those tribes. In truth it must be recognized that the features which are combined in the dandy bear a very definite historical stamp. The dandy is a creation of the English who were leaders in world trade. The trade network that spans the globe was in the hands of the London stock exchange people; its meshes felt the most varied, most frequent, most unforeseeable tremors. A merchant had to react to these, but he could not publicly display his reactions. The dandies took charge of the conflicts thus created. They developed the ingenious training that was necessary to overcome these conflicts. They combined an extremely quick reaction with a relaxed, even slack demeanor and facial expression. (Benjamin, *Charles Baudelaire*, 96)

The similarity that Benjamin observes between the dandy's insouciance and the merchant's studied calm implies the dandy's close relationship to the mechanical, replicable process of the commodity's creation. But in

Baudelaire's essay, there is a curious device that mediates between the clearest, most overt discussions of the dandy and those of process or technique. Reviewing the sections of Le Peintre in order, we see that between Section 9, devoted to the dandy, and Section 12, where technique or process emerges, are the three sections that detail the world of urban women.

Not only are these three sections positioned textually between the dandy and the artist's process, they are positioned *rhetorically* between the two sections as well. Whereas the discussion of dandyism suppressed virtually all mention of Guys's artistry or presence, the discussion of carriages and horses spoke of little else. In between, as we saw, were the sections devoted to women, sections that hinted at a kind of ontological uncertainty. Not uncannily independent creatures like dandies, the women of Guys's world (and Baudelaire's text) need male intervention for their existence. But at the same time, these women certainly detach themselves from the context of the illustration; they become denizens of the Parisian scene, strolling in gardens and sitting in cafes, bedecked in crinolines and painted with eyeliner. The suppression of titles for these illustrations frees these women textually from the confines of their original tableaux; and Baudelaire's depiction of them as self-created artworks (of dress and parure) attributes to them a certain independence. Yet they are also the raw material out of which male poets fashioned their bijoux. The women's relationship to the artist's *technè* is, therefore, ambiguous, neither fully detached nor fully enmeshed.

And when at last Baudelaire emerges from his *mundus muliebris*, the subject with which he decides to conclude his essay is carriages—lifeless objects, conveyances, machines. It is as if the section on women served as the mediating term between the dandy-artist's implacable, mechanical, objectlike identity and his activity or expertise vis-à-vis mechanical objects exterior to himself. While the dandy is an "ideally closed consciousness" (Bersani, *Culture*, 80), the expertly technical artist must be permeable, open to the images that confront him. In between these two figures stand the women who are at once paintings of modern life and painters of modern life. They can openly display all the contradictions inherent in the stance of the dandy who produces art. They are human, but somehow not too human; artists of the self, but not to the same extent as dandies. They reflect modernity in their poses and contexts, but they also produce it with their self-styling.

The role of the women here is both instrumental and exemplary. While acting as so many Ariadnes leading the dandy-subject out of his labyrinth of self-enclosure, they also resemble the display object or social spectacle that the dandy longs to be. Sartre saw the deep connection between Baudelaire's dandy and women, noting that like women, the dandy depended greatly on a public, on opinion. "What recovers the myth of dandyism, " he wrote, "is not homosexuality, it is exhibition-ism" (Sartre, *Baudelaire*, 178). What dandies and women have in common is spectacle; but the dandy's spectacle is disavowed by him, while the women's admits its artistry. For this reason, the urban women of *Le Peintre de la vie moderne* serve as mediators, negotiating the transition—a kind of debiologized birth—from *le meuble de boudoir* to the artist of the crowds and commodities, while remaining themselves in a curious state of ontological liminality.

That the women here serve a mediating function between dandies and machines becomes especially clear when the final section of *Le Peintre* is read alongside its predecessor, Balzac's *Théorie de la démarche*. According to Balzac, one of the supreme tests of poise is the act of descending from a carriage. Section 10 of his essay offers an anecdote, reminiscent of fairy tales, about the Princesse de Hesse-Darmstradt, her three daughters, and the empress who had to choose which girl would marry the grand duke. Without even speaking to them, the empress decides upon the middle daughter because her grace in descending from her carriage had been impeccable.

In Balzac's tableau of aristocratic life, it is the noblewoman's movement that matters, the shapes described by her ankles and skirts. Thirty years later, this scenario has changed; Baudelaire ends his own dandyist treatise with carriages, but not the ladies within. No longer backdrops for princesses, Baudelaire's carriages are worthy subjects all by themselves. The movement in question is not human but mechanical, found in the geometry of equipment, not in female limbs. And yet, a shadowy female presence lingers over the final section of *Le Peintre de la vie moderne*, since it both follows three sections entirely devoted to women and conjures up earlier dandyist scenes of women and "high life." The conclusion of *Le Peintre* summons up these various female figures only to refashion their grace and social performance as speed and mechanical motion; the earlier, Balzacian dandy who once sat back and judged them is now an active artist. Such transformations of the dandy's relationship to women will be replayed and developed further throughout the fin de siècle, as we shall see.

Idols and Effigies: Jean Lorrain's *Une Femme par jour*

In *La Fanfarlo*, Baudelaire's 1847 novella about a dandy's love affair with a *danseuse* of many theatrical charms, the dancer winds up removing her makeup permanently, growing fat, and having children, thus losing all her allure. Himself also condemned to bourgeois respectability, Samuel Cramer must abandon his dandyist ways. "He fell very low," writes the narrator, "I learned recently that he founded a socialist news-

In this mid-century tale of dandyist love, the woman of the stage is an attraction for the hero; but she does not draw him into her spectacle of self-creation. While Cramer's dandyist identity finds a subtle parallel in Fanfarlo's elaborate and theatrical self-construction, the connection between the two characters stops there. Cramer's dandyism draws him irresistibly to the world of greasepaint and theater ("He will always love rouge and makeup. . . . He would happily repaint the trees and the sky," *La Fanfarlo* 274), but his identity is not *mise en cause* or dismantled by Fanfarlo. When she abandons the stage, he abandons his dandyism; and the unmistakable parallelism suggests a deep similarity between the two identities. But Cramer's dandyist self and Fanfarlo's onstage appeal are separate.[74] When the dancer gives up her elaborate accoutrements, Cramer's identity is not revealed as any kind of process; it is, rather, abandoned—and for that debased world of political journalism.

Le Peintre de la vie moderne alters and complicates this relationship between the dandy and the performing woman.[75] In this text, there are, of course, no women *characters* in the sense that Fanfarlo is a novelistic heroine. No "real" or potentially bourgeois women lurk beneath their painted surfaces in *Le Peintre* for the very good reason that the women exist here only as paintings. Artifice has won out completely; and as Baudelaire acknowledges in his discussion of fashion, the woman and her artifice should not and cannot be separated.[76] (And again, such a notion looks forward to a camp aesthetic.)

With their rice-powdered skin and kohl-rimmed eyes, the Parisian women of *Le Peintre* acquire the flat, decorative immobility of religious statuary, which is appropriate given the essay's claim that dandyism is "a kind of religion." These women are painted into urban fetishes: "Woman has every right . . . to try to appear magical and supernatural; . . . an idol, she must adorn herself to be adored."[77] These fetishes then mediate between the static dandy and the more active urban artist. Unlike Samuel Cramer, who enters the fray of external, urban life when deprived of the theatricality of his dancer-mistress, the later Baudelairean dandy somehow reassumes agency and mastery of the external world *through* the theatricality of the women.

Idols or effigies are familiar background images in the literature of dandyism, since dandies themselves aspire to a condition of impassivity that resembles a statue's calm. (Balzac's *meuble de boudoir* is a kind of idol.) As Decadence overtook dandyism, however, the dandy and the idol separated; and the fetish object became at once more a material object and more a part of the protagonist's inner psychological life. Often, in decadent literature, the appearance of mystical objects coincides with a fascination with the material, almost cratylic power of language itself. Decadence takes up the earlier, Romantic motif of the supernatural (such as Olympia in Hoffmann's *Der Sandmann* or the monster in Shelley's *Frankenstein*), and blends it with the psychological and social identity of a dandy-hero.

As I said earlier, the dandyist treatise relies upon a biographical fiction: it takes a life and turns it into art, which is exactly what the dandyist credo demands. The texts I have examined in this chapter mimic both the dandies of whom they ostensibly write and those whom they address. These three texts are special in that, as treatises rather than novels, they occupy a genre closer to performance. Like the manifestos of Breton or Marinetti, they perform what they describe. Baudelaire's in particular demonstrates as well as narrates the movement of the dandy's performance toward the public space—with the necessary intervention of the woman, whose own social spectacle is on the rise.

As the end of the nineteenth century approached, dandyism could no longer maintain the self-enclosed, elite nature of its artistic and historical performances because powerful performances of quite a different kind began to dominate the cultural landscape. The explosion of mass culture in the 1880s and 1890s in France made possible a new, very public cult of personality that was distinctly at odds with the rules of dandyism. In the first place, mass culture showcased women especially, a fact at odds with dandyism's masculinist focus; the first "household name" celebrities were such female stars of the music hall as Jenny Lind, La Goulue, Nini Patte-en-l'air, and Loïe Fuller. The mass-cultural personality was, furthermore, necessarily an active part of a new social leveling, and therefore posed a contradictory model to dandyism's elitism; at the music hall, workers enjoyed the same shows that aristocrats and the bourgeoisie attended. Moreover, images of the newly emergent star culture, in their endless replicability, dismantled the unreproducibility at the heart of the notion of the dandy. What brought celebrity to the new artists of mass culture was, in large part, the replication of their likeness through the new inventions of lithography, photography, and eventually, cinema.

Decadent dandyism is paradoxical in that it turns sharply away from the external world while nonetheless being deeply aware of the new, changing, and largely urban landscape. The desire to escape the world and its bourgeois dreariness is visible in a Baudelairean fascination with drugs and alcohol, a fascination that becomes more prominent during this period, particularly in the writings of Lorrain and Huysmans. At the same time, the crowd—so important as a backdrop for Baudelaire's dandy—becomes a key, menacing presence for the decadents.[78]

The 1871 Paris Commune and its bloody suppression, the increasing number of workers' strikes (made possible by the reinstatement first of the right to convene publicly in 1881, then of the right to unionize in

1884), and the charismatic General Georges Boulanger's disturbing manipulation of thousands of people[79] all combined during the turn of the century to make the small-scale social spectacle of the earlier dandy seem impossible, and to transform the crowd into a frightening, potentially dangerous entity. This development appears in the literature of decadent dandyism as the protagonists' attempts to define their lives against those of the masses, and the sequestering of much of the literary action within felted, ornate, and remote interiors.

And yet, the crowded world of the factory, the streets, and the music hall was compelling to the decadent dandy, and crept resolutely back into his work. The realm of mass culture was particularly alluring, in large part because the artists onstage so resembled dandies, offering spectacles of elaborately constructed, highly stylized selves. It is, therefore, easy to understand why the decadent dandy, despite his hermeticism, was drawn to the female star of the late nineteenth and early twentieth centuries. Writing of the performances of these women, the decadent dandy cannot help encountering the same issues that surround his own performance of the self.

But these old issues are confronted in a new way. The decadent texts that deal with mass culture no longer claim to be part of a discrete movement, nor are they manifestos of any kind. The new female *vedette* draws the dandy into her world, attracting him as a strange female doppelganger, and making much more explicit many of formerly latent subthemes of dandyism. One such subtheme is the blasphemous rivalry of man with God for the power of creation. While the dandy sought, as we have seen, a parallel lineage of cultural genealogy, the decadents—inspired by the new possibilities suggested by electrical inventions—toyed with the very explicit subject of technological simulation of life, putting a more scientific, mass-cultural spin on the earlier tales of Hoffmann or Shelley.[80]

The scenario of the decadent dandy and the spectacle of women, or the female artist of the popular stage, appears in the work of authors such as Mallarmé, Villiers, Huysmans, Arthur Symons, Max Beerbohm, Jean Lorrain, and Oscar Wilde, and painters such as Toulouse-Lautrec, Degas, and Manet—all of whom grappled in some way with the decadent dandy's new social challenges. Later chapters will treat the complexities of this confrontation in the work of Mallarmé, Villiers, and Wilde, but here I would like to speak briefly about someone I think I can safely call a lesser writer, Jean Lorrain, whose obsessive yet relatively uncomplicated treatment of women in the mass-cultural space makes his work an excellent introductory example.

Heavily rouged, powdered, openly gay, and an aficionado of hallucinogenic drugs, Lorrain was, in true dandy fashion, hard to distinguish from his literary heroes. Like his characters, for example, he was known as an *ethéromane*; and his *Confessions d'un buveur d'ether* (in a collection entitled *Histoire des masques*) reinterpreted the famous De Quincey work. Even while insisting upon his own nobility of birth, Lorrain was fascinated by "the rabble," by *la canaille*. And of particular interest to him were women performers, especially the often lower-class *artistes* of the music hall.

Lorrain's 1890 *Une Femme par jour* is a collection of 300 impressionistic sketches that appeared originally in serialized form in the *L'Echo de Paris*. The editor of *L'Echo* announced the series as "a portrait of the contemporary woman. . . . The examples chosen randomly from the highest society as well as the lowest."[81] Of the various women described, many were actual stage performers; the rest were viewed as "performing" in the drama of daily life.

Lorrain's "femmes par jour" are miniature biographical accounts woven together with the author's own aestheticized fictions. They resemble earlier dandies' descriptions of celebrated dandies of yore, but insert a new, feminine subject. Narratives about lives dedicated to performance, Lorrain's mini-essays themselves become, in turn, textual performances, playing the same *mise-en-abîme* mirror game that we saw in the work of Balzac, Barbey, and Baudelaire.

Like Barbey, Lorrain often disguised his own identity when he wrote for the press, inventing various fictional personae for himself—many of them female. (Even the name "Jean Lorrain" was a creation; he was born Paul Duval.) Between 1885 and 1890, for example, Lorrain called himself "Mimosa," "Stendhaletta," and "Alelquine"; somewhat later he would call himself "Mme Baringhel" and write about current events as a self-proclaimed "femme du monde" (Jullian, *Jean Lorrain*, 87–92). For the run of *Une Femme par jour*, Lorrain used an aristocratic name (this time masculine) of his own invention, "Restif de la Brettonne"; and under this fictional cover he even made third-person references to a writer of his acquaintance known as "Jean Lorrain." Such free and varied use of fictitious identities obviously complicates the dandyist masquerade, for not only is the text of uncertain facticity, the writer is as well. That Lorrain reserved these pseudonyms for his journalistic career underlines the relation we have already seen between the mass production of journals and newspapers and the replicability of the dandyist self.

The descriptions of women in *Une Femme par jour* can be brutal; they are indeed "mordant sketches," as the editor of *L'Echo* dubbed them. Addressing himself, in one of the collection's portraits, to a young actress who has tried—apparently unsuccessfully—to imitate Sarah Bernhardt, Lorrain can find no words of praise or encouragement other than the scathing advice: "Take better care of your fingernails" (*Une Femme* 53).

Female players from the other side of the footlights receive similar treatment. Lorrain is fascinated by "les clientes du docteur miracle," the morphine-dependent courtesans whose dramatic nightly appearances as audience members amount to a kind of "performance." In their drug-induced stupors, these courtesans hover between life and death, between the animate and inanimate worlds. Described as "ghouls and vampires . . . who have nothing alive in their appearance" (ibid., 138), whose eyes resemble "open wounds," they recall Baudelaire's *nymphes macabres* and *poupées vivantes*. One courtesan, "La belle Madame G.," is particularly uncanny, existing in the "immobility of a ghostly doll" ("une poupée spectrale"), no more than a compilation of artificial luxury items:

> Hair of silk and teeth of real mother-of-pearl, as for her bosom, she is enameled down to her navel to accommodate her ballgown . . . she says "Papa," "Mama," and "Good day, Your Excellency," thanks to a spring mechanism hidden in the silk of her bodice and which Monsieur knows how to work . . . an export: she comes from America, knows how to work a fan, flutter her eyelids and gives the appearance of breathing like a real human being. I was remembering Dr. Coppelius's beautiful Olympia.[82]

Hoffmann isn't the only literary predecessor Lorrain is invoking here. Balzac, in *Théorie de la démarche*, also imagined springs hidden inside women, albeit in a less literal way: "Have you never laughed . . . at those women who offer their hand to you as if some spring mechanism were operating their elbow?" (*Théorie* 59). While Balzac was merely expressing dandyist disapproval of graceless women, Lorrain, with his limbic *morphinées*, approaches a literal vision of mechanical femininity.[83]

The passage on Madame G. brings together, in very condensed form, most of the issues that appear in decadent treatments of the performing woman. First among these is the explicit constructedness of the woman's body. Like Baudelaire's and Gautier's fashionable women, Madame G. is virtually indistinguishable from her collection of adornments and cosmetics. But Lorrain's version of such fashionability adds the morbid tones of Decadence, offering a rather explicit illustration of Benjamin's observation that "in relation to the living [fashion] represents the rights of the corpse" (*Charles Baudelaire* 166). Like the dandy, Madame G. artfully assembles a kind of social performance. Unlike the dandy, however, she is animated not by her own genius but by the work of others: both the "miracle doctor" and the lover, the "monsieur" who controls her mechanism, allowing her those three (snidely amusing) phrases.

Madame G. further recalls the women of *Le Peintre de la vie moderne* in her need for masculine artistry or intervention. But while Baudelaire's essay only hinted at the proximity of female performance to the fragmentation and mechanicity of urban modernism, Lorrain's makes this notion explicit. Artistry, such as Constantin Guys's expert renderings of carriages, has now become overtly scientific or medical knowledge—expertise in drugs and the manipulation of machinery (the spring hidden in the courtesan's ball gown). Given her mechanical nature, it is not surprising that Lorrain's latter-day Olympia comes from America, the country that embodied for the decadents all the dangers (and charms) of technological advancement and commodity fetishism.

Not all the portraits of *Une Femme par jour* are so scathing or morbid as Madame G.'s. Some simply revel in the new *étoiles* of mass culture. A sketch of cabaret star Yvette Guilbert, for example, lauds the singer's "exquise silhouette." An essay on "Jessica," an acrobat at the Folies-Bergère, rhapsodizes about "her moon-colored costumes and fabulous leotards." Jessica, says Lorrain, brings "cruelty and malaise to the involuntary pleasure one feels in beholding the aerial torture of a svelte female body" (*Une Femme* 203).

Lorrain's style oscillates, then, between sinister preciosity and the rhapsodic. The music hall and the theater fascinated him; but his writing also contained the anxious misogyny of the dandy who finds his terrain invaded, the spectacle-personality who sees an unexpected rival in women of the stage. His response was to take textual control of these female performers and remake them in the decadent image—to turn them into frightening, moribund dolls.[84]

But Lorrain only went so far; and the majority of his work is not devoted to spectacle or to women of the stage. The decadent writer who, without a doubt, wrote the most essential texts on the confrontation of dandies and female spectacle was Mallarmé, who devoted several complex prose pieces to the topic.

Chapter Two

MALLARMÉ: CROWDS, PERFORMANCE, AND THE FASHIONABLE WOMAN

Two Prose Pieces and Decadence

WHILE MALLARMÉ is usually labeled a symbolist rather than a decadent, the distinction between the two camps has never been clear, connected as they are—especially in the case of Mallarmé—by the concept of *l'art pour l'art*.[1] Both movements deal with ostensibly apolitical interests: ornate, jewel-encrusted domestic interiors in the case of Decadence, the crystalline interior of language itself in the case of symbolist writing. Both rely upon a pantheon of recognizable characters—often culled from mythology, Shakespeare, or the Bible. And in the case of visual art, paintings that treat the classic themes of Decadence—works by Redon or Moreau, for example—are generally known as symbolist.[2]

Mallarmé had an ambivalent relationship to the decadent-dandyist literature of his era. Though in his youth he had tremendous admiration for his mentor Villiers de l'Isle-Adam, for example, he later expressed disapproval for Villiers's typically decadent use of wordy, colorful descriptions and heavy reliance upon anecdote.[3] Mallarmé, of course, shunned such devices, choosing instead to pare down his language to a studied and ascetic brevity. Nonetheless, decadent themes do appear in his work; and sometimes, a dandyist tone—a playful, even precious quality—creeps in as well. This should not surprise us, since what could be called Mallarmé's personal dandyism—his brilliant conversational style, his wit, and the famous Tuesday night salon performances—figures prominently in the poet's reputation.[4] What is surprising is that so little of his famed chattiness ever spilled over into his work, and that what did emerge of this decadent-dandy side is so rarely studied. We can find this little-known aspect of Mallarmé in some of his prose texts.

For my purposes here, I turn to two prose pieces in which Mallarmé grapples with the classically decadent topic of public female performance: the woman who acts as spectacle before a crowd. We have seen how Baudelaire and Jean Lorrain use the social and theatrical performances of women as a mediating force between the dandy and the potentially threatening urban world. And we have seen how the carefully

constructed persona of the dandy finds a counterpart—at once reassuring and menacing—in the equally elaborately constructed woman onstage. Baudelaire's *poupées vivantes* and Lorrain's immobilized *poupées
spectrales* resemble the dandy observer, but, unlike him, they require
(male) intervention and control for their performances.

In confronting the female performer, these dandies begin a process of
dismantling that will lead, ultimately, to the transformation of the nineteenth-century dandy into the contemporary iconic personality of the
mass media. Mallarmé's early prose poem *Le Phénomène futur* (1864)
and his eight editions of *La Dernière Mode* (1874) take another explicit
step in this process of transformation. Both texts treat the worldly issue
of the woman onstage before a crowd, a woman who offers up her performance for the private aesthetic appreciation of a lone, male genius.[5]
The two texts, however, are very different.

Le Phénomène futur is stark and allegorical. It depends upon virtually
none of the usual trappings of Decadence, and contains no overtly
dandyist character. Nonetheless, this prose poem partakes thematically
of decadent dandyism and occupies a special position within Mallarmé's
oeuvre, a position that, as we shall see, grants it an important relationship to the descriptive and narrative world of Decadence.

La Dernière Mode, on the other hand, is quite manifestly a decadent-
dandyist text. Here, in a journal originally aimed at the bourgeois
woman, Mallarmé's dandyist interests in spectacle, fashion, performance, and self-disguise take shape, unobscured (although clearly influenced) by the poet's normally rarefied poetics. In *La Dernière Mode*,
Mallarmé's poetic, authorial voice blends with frivolous, stagy parodies
of lady journalists and society columnists. The result is a proto-camp
document that offers an unusually clear example of dandyism taking
apart and examining its own social and sexual subtexts, as well as an example of the dandy's curiously specular relationship to the commodity.

A Phenomenon of the Future

A pale sky, over a world ending in decrepitude, will perhaps disappear with
the clouds: faded purple shreds of sunsets dying in a sleeping river on a horizon submerged in light and water. The trees are weary and beneath their
whitened foliage (from the dust of time rather than that of the roads) rises the
tent of the Showman of Things Past: many a streetlamp awaits the twilight
and reanimates the faces of an unhappy crowd, vanquished by the immortal
malady and the sin of the centuries, men accompanied by their wretched ac-
complices pregnant with the miserable fruits by which the earth will perish. In
the troubled silence of all those eyes supplicating the far-off sun plunging beneath the water with the despair of a cry, here is his simple patter: "No sign
will treat you to the spectacle within, since there is now no painter capable of
rendering even the merest shadow of it. I bring you, living (and preserved

throughout the years by sovereign science) a Woman of yore. Some kind of primal and naive madness, an ecstasy of gold, I know not! That which she calls her hair, curves with the suppleness of fine cloth about a face lit by the blood-red bareness of her lips. In place of useless clothing, she has a body; and her eyes, which are like precious gems, cannot match the gaze that emerges from her happy flesh: from the breasts engorged as if full of eternal milk, their tips tilted toward heaven, to the silken legs that still wear the salt of the primeval sea. Recalling their poor spouses, bald, morbid, and full of horror, the husbands press forward: their melancholy wives, driven by curiosity, also want to see.

When they have all gazed upon the noble creature, the vestige of an age already accursed, some, indifferent (for they will not have had the capacity to understand), but others, brokenhearted and with eyelids wet with resigned tears, will look at one another; while the poets of those times, feeling their extinguished eyes lighting up once again, will make their way toward their lamps, their brains momentarily drunk with an obscure glory, haunted by a Rhythm and forgetting that they exist in an age that has outlived beauty.[6]

LE PHÉNOMÈNE FUTUR

Crowds and a Spectacle

Although less linguistically sophisticated than much of Mallarmé's later works, Le Phénomène futur is striking in its complicated play of gender, event, and history, and in its distillation of the problematic of female performance and the urban spectator. The poem establishes a typically decadent scene: a gray, moribund world; and a typically decadent subject: the bleakness of the future. Within this barren landscape, a lone performing woman—a sideshow attraction at a carnival—returns hope and poetry to the few poets in the crowd who can correctly interpret her. Though a carnival is certainly an older form of entertainment and not identical to a mass-cultural space such as the music hall, the poem is filled with the kind of anxiety typically expressed by the decadents toward mass society. We are in a future, debased world; dulled and witless crowds predominate; they sit hypnotized by a spectacle. The clarity and simplicity with which these themes appear and the poem's spare, allegorical quality make Le Phénomène futur a perfect example with which to study Mallarmé's relationship to the encroachment of mass culture as figured by female performance.

The sideshow woman is a living anachronism, a visitor from another age, "une Femme d'autrefois." The beauty of the woman is set off by a postapocalyptic landscape that implies the demise of poetry itself. The sunset, that classic topos of romantic poetry, is worn out and lies under water: "Faded purple shreds of sunsets dying in a sleeping river on a horizon submerged in light and water." The spectacle of a former poetic ideal, the only real woman left, is a scientifically preserved relic. Yet although *la Femme d'autrefois* is beautiful, her beauty is entirely defined by the hideousness of the "bald, morbid" other women of the crowd, defined, that is, against imminent decay. This woman brings a *memory* to men; she is a *souvenir*, representing an earlier poetics, a Baudelairean ideal now understood only by an elite few. Whether sphinx, cat, or dream of stone, the fatal, dehumanized beauties of *Les Fleurs du mal* always conjure personal memories for the poet/narrator. But while *la Femme d'autrefois* is recognizable as a composite of those early Baudelairean female types, she communes with her poet through public spectacle and the crowd, bringing back a collective cultural past rather than a personal one. In this respect, she resembles more the women of the later Baudelaire, the women of *Le Peintre de la vie moderne*, whose theatricality filters and transmits the urban landscape for the male artist-observer, rather than isolating him in private reverie. (Although Mallarmé seems to feel none of Baudelaire's exhilaration in the "electricity" of crowds.)

Le Peintre ends, as we saw, with Baudelaire shifting his focus from urban women to the pure geometry of the inanimate world, to the shapes and movements of carriages, and, most important, to the artistic and technical process, figured by the artist's *pinceau*. *Le Phénomène futur* suggests a very similar shift, but within a condensed, poetically dense scenario. Preserved by "la science souveraine," by the masculine realm of knowledge and process, *la Femme d'autrefois* lends meaning to the crowd for the worthy few subtle enough to understand.[7] She is a poem that has yet to happen, a nameless entity waiting to be named, the cultural body rendered sterile, mute, and unaware—entirely dependent upon male knowledge and artistry for her existence.[8] *La Femme d'autrefois* is pure, liminal, female theatricality, preserved by men of science to inspire men of poetry. The barker claims her beauty to be beyond any artist's capacity—"There is now no painter capable of rendering even the merest shadow of it"—thereby insisting upon her status as challenge to and potential product of artistic process. Her challenge to representation is further suggested by the fact that *la Femme d'autrefois* does not appear directly in this poem. She is described, that is, only by the barker outside, never by the poem's primary narrator. And the barker speaks of her only from his distant position outside the tent.

The "scientific" nature of this woman's beauty—its "preserved" quality—further underscores her relationship to artistic *technè* and to male process. In this, she resembles not only the women of Baudelaire's *Le Peintre* but also Jean Lorrain's *morphinées*, or *poupées spectrales*, those bizarre and medicalized beauties glimpsed at the theater. Like them, Mallarmé's woman onstage is a scientific oddity, a medical miracle. Though *Le Phénomène futur* is an earlier text, and predates Lorrain's typically fin-de-siècle fascination with drugs and hypnotism, it clearly participates in the "technologization" of femaleness and responds to the increasingly "scientific" or mechanical nature of mass entertainment.

Although *Le Phénomène futur* tells a story of privileged understanding and private poetic creation, like other decadent texts that treat popular performance, it necessarily touches on larger, more political issues. The wretchedness described here, for example, cannot be dissociated from the crowd: indeed, the sickness seems located in the body politic.[9] In his rather dyspeptic essay of 1862, *L'Art pour tous*, Mallarmé had proclaimed the masses unfit for any sort of literary education: "Let the masses read works on moral conduct, but please do not give them our poetry to ruin" ("Que les masses lisent la morale, mais de grâce ne leur donnez pas notre poésie à gâter," *Oeuvres complètes* 260).[10] And here in *Le Phénomène futur*, two years later, the poet once again lambastes "la foule." Anticipating the conservative pessimism of "crowd psychologists" Gustave Le Bon and Gabriel Tarde,[11] Mallarmé depicts a crowd that is miserable and dull, uncomprehending and wretched—"profanateur" of all it touches.

The Women

"Bald, morbid, full of horror," the women of this future world are hideous; and their repugnant aspect seems inextricable from the public nature of this performance and the social decrepitude of its audience. A political anxiety, then, allied with the horror of women, must be remedied by masculine knowledge, by "la science souveraine." This science both preserves the lone ideal woman from the gruesome fate suffered by her female spectators and spares the poets as well. With the adjective "souveraine," Mallarmé effectively removes from "science" its undesirable, populist connotation of progress,[12] giving it instead an aura of private, royal privilege. This privatized science confers a man-made, superior fecundity that supersedes natural fecundity, escaping the confines of time itself.

The women of the crowd can no longer give life. Their reproductivity will only destroy the earth; their wombs enclose only death: "the miserable fruits by which the earth will perish."[13] This is a world that has forgotten or lost its ancestors—an alienation linked to the crowded, debased nature of society. The scene recalls de Tocqueville's warning that democracy would estrange men from the genealogical order: "Democracy make[s] every man forget his ancestors . . . it hides his descendants and separates his contemporaries from him" (397). Generational succession in Mallarmé's future world breeds only death. The bourgeois young poet predicts—with aristocratic anxiety—a socially leveled populace that, like de Tocqueville's democracy, can no longer connect past to present. "Man can be democratic," writes Mallarmé in *L'Art pour tous*, "the artist ... must remain aristocratic" ("L'homme peut être démocrate, l'artiste ... doit rester aristocrate," *Oeuvres complètes* 259).

That reassuring symbol of generational cycles, the maternal body, is replaced by *la Femme d'autrefois*, whose uplifted breasts only appear to contain milk: "The breasts engorged as if full of eternal milk, their tips tilted toward heaven." Theirs is the milk of metaphor, of the "comme si," a white ink offered up to the male poet to color with his writing. It is mother's milk removed from temporality, destined for no human baby. The women of the crowd reproduce nature; and nature—indeed, time itself—is clearly decaying: "The trees are weary ... beneath their whitened foliage (from the dust of time)." But *la Femme d'autrefois* reproduces culture, having been herself transported from another age via the cultural knowledge, the science of men. She is the ancestor on no family tree, save the one redrawn by the poet. The audience members who rush home to write, "feeling their extinguished eyes lighting up once again," are correcting their *poetic* sterility. Mute and motionless, nameless and insentient, *la Femme d'autrefois* spurs the masculine creative work of poetry by recalling the past. Her beauty arouses only the solitary eros of writing, an antidote for a perceived sense of abortive sexuality and paternity.[14] She renews the cultural, individualizes science, and figures the suppression of the natural—all goals of the decadent dandy.[15]

Memory, Temporal Play, and the Performance

The lone poets of Mallarmé's crowd "translate" the beauty of *la Femme d'autrefois*, who acts as a private technology of memory, incarnating another age for the crowd. To understand this woman and to be prompted by her to write is essentially to use the performance of a woman as a memory device. Richard Terdiman has written on what he sees as a "crisis of memory" in nineteenth-century France. Terdiman argues that French society of this time lost the sense of events as "natural occurrences," and that France underwent an estrangement of history and cultural memory that resulted in the nineteenth century's becoming the first age "whose self-conception was defined by a disciplined obsession with the past" (*Present Past* 31). Terdiman attributes this "crisis of memory" not only to the political and military upheavals of the period, but also to the "quantum leap in the productive power of human labor: the coming of the machine." The machine's "rapid, virtually endless replication and dissemination of objects" altered the very perception of time, according to Terdiman, turning history into an obsession with seizing and holding onto the past:

> For the nineteenth century . . . history increasingly became the discipline of memory.
>
> Positively, history systematized the memory problem. By interrogating it through its own paradigms, it created the preconditions for uncovering the crisis that disconnection with the past inevitably entailed. But though history thereby became guarantor and registrar of the past, its locus when "natural" or "organic" memory became problematic, its sedimentation as "discipline" had a subtle negative resonance. For history simultaneously became the place to which the mnemonic crisis determined by such evacuations could be *displaced*—at the limit, it became the tomb in which it could be concealed. By taking on the function of "preserving" the past, history hid the individual *dispossession* of the past. (*Present Past* 31)

Terdiman's remarks offer us an interesting context for *la Femme d'autrefois*. For Terdiman, history becomes a technology of memory for a century estranged from its past. This technology is, at the same time, something of a burial site, a crypt for an artificially preserved memory. We can see such commingled images of death, preservation, and artifice in the figure of *la Femme d'autrefois*. A creature from the historical past, a woman of yore, her performance and her strangely preserved body function much like Terdiman's vision of history: as remedies for what appears to be a tenuous grasp on temporality itself. But at the same time, *la Femme d'autrefois* represents only selective memory and incomplete temporality, for she also plunges her poet spectators into a necessary forgetfulness: an oblivion of existing in an era that has outlived beauty ("l'oubli d'exister à une époque qui survit à la beauté"). While reminding them of their cultural past, she also makes them forget their present. Again, this is a typically dandyist concept: a nostalgia for the past turns history into a fetishized discipline for an elite few. But within this masculinized and private vision of history, a female performer is somehow necessary. And though she is, like the dandy himself, a reified and debiologized entity, brought to life, like Athena, through the agency of men alone, she represents a step toward the dismantling of the dandy's seamless persona.

In earlier times, the selective cultural legacy of the dandy was transmitted far beyond the reach of either crowds or common sideshow girls. But in the case of *Le Phénomène futur*, however idealized *la Femme d'autrefois* appears, however spare and obscure Mallarmé's text may be, there is no escaping the fact that this poem is about a naked woman in a carnival tent. A peep-show attraction leads these men to salvation. The erotic fascination of performance has shifted from the superior dandy to this socially debased woman. The elitist dandy-poet must now pay to see her in the hope that her common and sordid spectacle will actually raise him above the urban chaos.

Form and Time

Who tells a tale like *Le Phénomène futur*? The play of temporality in this poem calls into question the stance of its narrator. Is he someone who has seen the future and traveled back in time to tell us of it? Or do we, the readers, travel forward in time in the act of reading the poem? Are we perhaps eavesdropping on the future with the narrator's help? Since the poem's last line narrates the writing of new poetry, the possibility arises that the text we are reading is the product of one of the poets in the crowd, in which case the poem would itself be the time traveler, sent back to us from the future. Such logic suggests the clear and obvious analogy between *la Femme d'autrefois* and the text of the poem: both are anachronistic, detached from their own eras upon their presentation to an audience. The performing woman's identity melts into that of the poem, a standard motif of romantic, decadent, and symbolist literature (for Samuel Cramer, La Fanfarlo was "poetry with arms and legs"), and one that has received a great deal of critical attention.[16] Perhaps the narrator is also a carnival barker, a "montreur de choses futures." In this case, it is up to us to decide who among us are the wretched masses witnessing such a spectacle, and who are the knowing few who will find inspiration in it. If the poem is a theatrical happening, its place in time is indeterminable. Furthermore, time is no longer a trustworthy method of calibration here, for it is itself aging—the cycle of renewal has disappeared, a white dust covers the trees. The indeterminability of time in the poem implicates both reader and text in a curiously unsettling game of mirrors.

Le Phénomène futur divides into two paragraphs, the first written entirely in the present tense, the second in the future anterior. This disparity creates further temporal confusion. The use of the present tense implies a narration taking place in the future. The use of the future anterior implies a turning away from the future, a movement back into a prophetic present. This change in narrative point of view occurs around a blank, the space between the two paragraphs. Given the supreme significance that Mallarmé attributed to such moments in a text, what could be happening in the space of silence between the poem's halves?

The first half of the poem describes the promised spectacle of the woman "à l'intérieur," the condition of the crowd, and its desire to see the show. The second half of the poem describes the effect of the spectacle upon its audience. Nowhere, however, is there a direct description of the woman or of the actual moment of *watching*, of audience and performer together. Mallarmé suppresses the event of the performance, refusing to allow the body of the woman into the body of the text, following his own dictum to paint "not the thing, but the effect it produces" ("non la chose, mais l'effet qu'elle produit").[17] The blank space in the text, surrounded by "before" and "after" descriptions, must therefore represent the moment of the woman's appearance, suggesting that no writing could be adequate to it. This blank resembles strongly the blank space that Mallarmé sees in the performances of pantomimist Paul Margueritte, whose work is described in the prose poem *Mimique*. Like *la Femme d'autrefois*, the mime in *Mimique* proffers his performance for the "translation" of the poet/audience member: "A phantom as white as a still-unwritten page" ("Le fantôme blanc comme une page pas encore écrite," *Oeuvres complètes* 310).[18] As performance studies scholar Peggy Phelan has observed, "Performance's only life is in the present. [It] cannot . . . participate in the circulation of representation of reproduction" (146). The performance of *la Femme d'autrefois* hovers just beyond the limits of linguistic reference and, in this, shares the ineffable quality that defines the performance of dandyism in Barbey d'Aurevilly's essay.

Enframed by two halves of the poem, the blank space is a spectacle presented to an audience. The event of the spectacle alters and confuses the temporal frame of reference, just as the female performer sends certain members of her audience into forgetfulness of their epoch through her figuring of the past. One might say, then, that temporal upheaval results from both the spectacle of the woman and the blank space in the text, or perhaps that these two elements are collapsed into one, with the mute whiteness of the text being analogous to the mute woman who must be turned into poetry. And of course, the withered state of the described future world seems itself to be related to temporal confusion and unreliability. This is a world in which the sunset, that "natural" sign of regular temporal flow, fades beneath the river; and people seem to suffer from an illness that is itself immune to time: "la maladie immortelle." The cyclical nature of time has broken down, replaced by something resembling what Guy Debord has labeled "spectacular time." "Temps spectaculaire" is consumable and only "pseudo-cyclical," reversible and no longer subject to any natural rhythms. For Debord, this "time of the spectacle" is the alienated time of capitalism and mass culture, the time, certainly, of the crowds (Debord 121–25). We can see its precursor in the curiously reified temporality of Mallarmé's poem.

The Prose Poem and the Ornament of Legend

If the text seems caught between two temporal realities, a future and a past, its very genre suggests a similar duality. As a poem in prose, *Le Phénomène futur* straddles two worlds. This is clearly not Mallarmé's obscure verse style, but neither is it the prose of *reportage* for which he expressed so much disdain.[19] The prose poem mediates between these two realms. It bespeaks a desire to personalize and elevate the vulgar and to vulgarize the personal. And of course, the poem narrates just such a vacillation. The scenario of huddled masses who face the dazzling *Femme d'autrefois* lends itself easily to the comparison of prose facing poetry. The inspired man in the crowd who later sits down to write has not witnessed the same show as his prosaic neighbors. He sees a spectacle within a spectacle, a secret show that he alone can decode. This secret spectacle that inspires poetry amid decrepitude and dulled senses shares certain characteristics with the genre of the prose poem itself. Richard Terdiman has described the prose poem as "counterdiscourse," that is, text that harnesses a dominant discourse—prose—to achieve its own, subversive ends. In the prose poem, Terdiman sees an attempt by the avant-garde to appropriate an instrument of the masses and individualize it.[20] This is what the poet in the crowd does with *la Femme d'autrefois*. He participates in and witnesses a spectacle for the rabble, but attempts later to decontextualize the spectacle, just as a prose poem by Mallarmé strives to co-opt the prose of *reportage* for the poet's own, rather hermetic ends.[21]

Naturally, the prose poem cannot entirely shake off the dust of the streets, nor can it honestly claim such purification as its goal. This genre remains perpetually suspended between two realms, at once evoking and suppressing the common or popular, much like *la Femme d'autrefois*, who stands between past and future, a public yet private performer. *Le Phénomène futur* is clearly devoid of all particular referent; like *la Femme d'autrefois*, this text wears no costume and speaks nothing about its own origins. And yet the text has a particular relation to the "exterior" world of Mallarmé's oeuvre.

In 1864, Mallarmé, teaching at a Tournon lycée, was struggling to complete his dramatic poem *Hérodiade* (which he would eventually put aside for nearly thirty years). Turning away from that task in exasperation, he wrote *Le Phénomène futur*, a story of poetic inspiration triumphing over sterility.[22] The female carnival performer of *Le Phénomène futur* does, in fact, appear to be an interpretive turn on *Hérodiade*. Both women emerge, of course, from the past. Both are seductive and powerful performers.[23] And yet they are so different. *La*

Femme d'autrefois is blank, naked and mute, her performance unconscious, as well as suppressed by the text. She comes from another time and place, appearing to have been violently ripped from her original context; indeed, this strange liminality, this blankness, is her primary characteristic. Hérodiade, on the other hand, figures nothing more strongly than referentiality itself. In *Hérodiade*, Mallarmé tries to recontextualize legend, refashioning an ornate, orientalist—and typically decadent— story into his own spare and cryptic verse.[24] It is not hard to see *la Femme d'autrefois* as an extreme version of this refashioned Herodias, a bare, cool, idealized princess of pure poetry—the perfect Mallarméan turn on an overworked topic. It is precisely through her highly emphasized simplicity, her "pared-down" quality, that *la Femme d'autrefois* refers to the usual trappings of performance and costume. She conjures all the accoutrements of the classic nineteenth-century Salome through her conspicuous lack of them (much as she invokes the problem of representation by being beyond artistic rendering). Instead of golden anklets or seven veils, for example, it is her *hair* that gleams in an "ecstasy of gold," floating around her "with the suppleness of fine cloth." Her body replaces rather than wears a princess's robes: "In place of useless clothing, she has a body."

In trying to write *Hérodiade*, a potential spectacle, Mallarmé occupies the position of a "montreur de choses passées." With *Le Phénomène futur*, he suppresses the heavy ornamentation of Hérodiade's story and substitutes a corrective or remedial narrative. In place of the autobiographical story of a poet struggling to capture and write a performance, to write the spectacle of a woman, *Le Phénomène futur* tells the rather hopeful story of a young poet's sudden inspiration while confronting a performer. With *Le Phénomène futur*, Mallarmé puts aside the woes of a frustrated playwright and indulges in a reverie of being just an audience member, someone on the other side of the performance. And instead of grappling with the dense trappings of *Hérodiade*, the poet in this dream sequence can face a spectacle of blankness, pure inspiration that melds perfectly with poetic genius.

In attempting *Hérodiade*, Mallarmé chooses to enter a very public literary domain; he acknowledges as much in the preface to his 1898 *Noces d'Hérodiade*: "I have kept the name Hérodiade in order to differentiate her from the Salome I will call modern or exhumed, with her archaic *fait-divers*."[25] He joins the crowd that has written of Salome, struggling with the story's complex attachment to literary and biblical history. "I wish to make of her," he wrote, acknowledging this struggle, "a purely dream-like creature, absolutely independent of History" ("Je tiens à en faire un être purement rêvé et absolument indépendant de l'Histoire").[26] In *Le*

Phénomène futur, the poet, a member of a crowd, distinguishes himself by virtue of his private relationship to the public spectacle. The analogy is clear: the "public" spectacle of the Hérodiade/Salome story will be rendered private by Mallarmé; *la Femme d'autrefois* will be used privately by the poet, rescued from History and the sordid realm of the *fait-divers*.[27] In the movement from playwright to prose poet, Mallarmé stages the scene of his own inspiration. He strips Hérodiade/Salome of her performance, her name, her legend and adornments; the result is *la Femme d'autrefois*, a streamlined, vulgarized Hérodiade—princess turned peep show. In order to "paint not the thing, but the effect it produces"—the goal, he claimed, of writing *Hérodiade*—and in order to stage his own effective transcendence of the popular, the frustrated playwright needs, perhaps, to be a spectator at a public event.[28] "The idea will be created . . . in a sort of pubic epiphany," comments Jean-Pierre Richard (98). A prose poem is an appropriate medium for this sort of transcendence or epiphany: Hérodiade at a carnival sideshow could be read as another analogy for a poem in prose.

The only words spoken in *Le Phénomène futur* are those of *le Montreur de choses passées*, who tells the crowd of the impossibility of representing this woman, "There is now no painter capable of rendering even the merest shadow of it"; and going back to these words, we can read them in the context of the poet's struggle with his *Hérodiade*. In *Le Phénomène futur*, Mallarmé stages a bifurcation of the poetic self. Writing *Hérodiade*, he grapples unsuccessfully with the material of literary legend; *Le Phénomène futur* turns that frustrated poet into a carnival barker, popularizing (vulgarizing) the role. Hérodiade becomes a sideshow again, a socially debased version of the dancing princess. And the successful poet recreates himself as aristocrat, distinguishing himself from the crowd through his renewal of poetry.

Le Phénomène futur renders explicit the problematic element of performance contained within *Hérodiade* and suppresses the consciousness of the performing woman. Later, Mallarmé would give up entirely on the idea of staging *Hérodiade*, and in *Les Noces* he goes so far as to remove any mention of the princess's dance from the body of the text, leaving it only as a brief stage direction.[29] As the performance is stripped away from the carnival woman, she becomes an inspirational blank between past and present, a draft of necessary Lethe for the earthbound poet of a wretched world.[30] Through *la Femme d'autrefois*, the poet rises above the crowd and enters into private communion with his cultural past, for she represents a collective past while enabling the poet to shun the collectivity. She promises an ideal held very dear by decadent dandyism: a private genealogy, exempt from generational decay.

LA DERNIÈRE MODE

The Performance of Fashion

Ten years later, Mallarmé would interrogate the poet's relation to temporality and the public cultural arena when he assumed the role of sole editor, publisher, and writer of the (already extant) fashion magazine *La Dernière Mode*. And though Barthes believed that fashion, with its democratic replicability, killed dandyism,[31] *La Dernière Mode* proves that fashion was actually a little gentler in its approach, offering dandyism a path toward its twentieth-century incarnation: the iconic media personality. Reading this text by Mallarmé, we see the nineteenth-century dandy take an important step down this path.

Clearly, the ideals of "la mode" and "dandyism" are strikingly similar. Both depend upon "phases of newness, foreignness, surprise and scandal."[32] Both concern the aesthetics of performance; both strive to grasp the present, existing only in an unnarratable "now." "The today of Fashion," writes Barthes, ". . . destroys things all around it, refutes the past . . . censures the future . . . tames the new even before producing it."[33] Individual objects of fashion must be caught at just the perfect moment in order to be worth mentioning at all: "There are no dancing slippers," writes Mallarmé, "save those of future balls" ("Pas de souliers que ceux des bals futurs," *Oeuvres complètes* 716). In his famous essay on the time consciousness of modernity, Habermas acknowledges the dandy's kinship with fashion:

> The modern work of art is marked by a union of the real or true with the ephemeral. This character of the present is also at the basis of the kinship of art with fashion, with the new, with the optics of the idler, the genius, and the child, who, lacking the antistimulant of conventionally inculcated modes of perception, are delivered up defenseless to the attacks of beauty, to the transcendent stimuli hidden in the most ordinary matters. The role of the dandy, then, consists in turning this type of passively experienced extraordinariness to the offensiveness in demonstrating the extraordinary by provocative means. The dandy combines the indolent and the fashionable with the pleasure of causing surprise in others while never showing any himself. He is the expert on the fleeting pleasure of the moment. (*Philosophical Discourse* 10)

To create a mise-en-scène of this "fleeting pleasure" was Beau Brummell's task when he appeared at a social gathering; it was Barbey d'Aurevilly's task in writing of Brummell; and it was the task of the poet of *Le Phénomène futur*, in which the elusiveness of the moment coincides with a female, theatrical apparition. Writing—virtually in their entirety[34]—eight issues of *La Dernière Mode*, Mallarmé creates for himself a project that combines all three of these tasks, while adding a new one. Not only will he attempt to render in words the ineffable spectacle of female fashionability, he will write about it under many pseudonyms, in a series of theatrical, literary guises—many of them female. In other words, Mallarmé will occupy both sides of the footlights; he will play at being at once dandified audience member and the woman onstage.

Twentieth-Century Critics of La Dernière Mode

Virtually all of the criticism focused on *La Dernière Mode* interprets it as a highly coded symbolist poem, so cryptic that it masquerades in its form (prose rather than poetry) and in its content. Critics tend to fold this text back into the body of Mallarmé's oeuvre, seeing its real-world, mass-publication status only as an ingenious disguise for its "true" function as commentary on Mallarmé's overall project, in particular, his literarily utopian idea of "Le Livre." Jean-Pierre Richard writes: "*La Dernière Mode* . . . purports to be an account of a purely contingent, absolutely mortal life. . . . But upon close examination, does this exist in *La Dernière Mode*? Is the journal anything other than a wish? than a utopia?" (302). Jean Moréas declares that Mallarmé "knew how, with his animated words, to render an actress's leotard a subject worthy of Plato" (quoted in Rhodes 10). Barbara Johnson focuses on the close, metaphoric relationship between femininity and poetry, writing of *La Dernière Mode*: "It is as though Mallarmé's interest in writing like a woman about fashion was to steal back for consciousness what woman had stolen by unconsciousness, to write *consciously* from out of the female unconscious, which is somehow more intimately, but illegitimately connected to the stuff of poetry" (128). Finally, Roger Dragonetti calls *La Dernière Mode* "this sibylline text, in which the present mingles with the past and with the future" (91) and asks, "According to the theory of *Variations*, is this journal not written in the image of The Book?" (88).

But it is not enough to read *La Dernière Mode* only within the limited context of Mallarmé's poetry. To do so is to ignore that by taking on this project, Mallarmé is, quite deliberately, engaging with the world beyond his own poetic enterprise. Naturally, his linguistic and philosophical investigations did not stop when he began editing *La Dernière Mode*. Naturally, *La Dernière Mode* differs profoundly from the many other fashion magazines that were published during this period.[35] But to turn this text into just another example of Mallarmé's verse, finding in it a secret code, "une écriture piégée," in Dragonetti's words, leading right back to familiar Mallarméan themes such as "Le Livre," is to set out on a rather dull treasure hunt. A more interesting task is to resist what Jean-Pierre

Lecercle has aptly named the "integrating reflex" ("le réflexe intégra-teur," 46)[36] and look at *La Dernière Mode* as the anomalous endeavor that it was for Mallarmé, asking how his poetic sensibilities melded (or clashed) with the spheres of mass-produced fashion and real-world jour-nalism.

The Journal and Its Audience

Of course, the audience of fashionable bourgeoises (and Mallarmé's fel-low artists) to which *La Dernière Mode* was addressed should not be confused with the socially heterogeneous mass audiences that, I am ar-guing in this book, eventually transmuted the dandy into the contempo-rary media star. But *La Dernière Mode* does rely—far more overtly than even the prose poem—upon a dominant form of discourse. And the fact that Mallarmé seriously meant to write journalism (for him a debased genre) for a very large number of nonliterary (and therefore, for him, de-based) readers of the rising middle class[37] makes the magazine an ap-propriate text with which to study the effect of increasingly leveled soci-ety upon the aristocratic sensibilities of dandyism. As Rachel Bowlby notes in her discussion of *La Dernière Mode*: "Fashion is placed along-side high culture. . . . The frivolous and the serious can no longer be held apart" (195). In other words, poetically speaking, Mallarmé is slumming here. The same poet who expresses such contempt for newspapers con-descends to write for a crowd, however select—and even includes an en-tire advertising page, a section for which he had elsewhere expressed par-ticular disdain.[38] *La Dernière Mode*, furthermore, did take mass culture as its subject occasionally, as when culture critic "Ix" (often called Mal-larmé's *porte-parole*) recounts the Grand Duke Constantin's attendance at the Folies-Bergères for a performance of "L'Homme-Tatoué."[39]

One-Man Show

La Dernière Mode is a one-man show of considerable virtuosity. Mal-larmé takes on a large variety of fictional identities and thoroughly en-joys the journalistic and theatrical gymnastics that the task requires of him. The characters developed in this display of versatility vary not only in sex, but in nationality and race as well; they include "British" society reporter "Miss Satin" (who drops many English words into her column, while actually being, we are told, "une parisienne connue" and therefore a doubly fictive character); fashion and culture critic "Marguerite de Ponty"; "Le chef de bouche chez Brébant"; and a Creole woman who signs her recipe column "Olympe, négresse." As this sample illustrates, however, Mallarmé's various characters do not stray far from the the-

ambiguity, the relationship between England and France, and orientalism. Mallarmé tailors the pseudonymous "journalists" of *La Dernière
Mode* to fit his diverse rubrics, among them "La Chronique de Paris,"
commenting on the social gatherings of "le high-life"; "la Gazette de
fashion"; "Correspondance avec les abonées"; "Les Voyages"; and
"Conseils sur l'éducation," for the mothers of young children.

Certainly, interest in a magazine like *La Dernière Mode* was not un-
heard-of for a writer like Mallarmé. Balzac, Barbey d'Aurevilly, Gautier,
Jean Lorrain, and Oscar Wilde (to name just a few) all dabbled in fashion journalism or women's magazines;[40] some, such as Barbey and Lorrain, even used female pseudonyms occasionally. But Mallarmé's experiment diverges from his compatriots' efforts in one very crucial way: *La
Dernière Mode* was not just a publication to which the poet contributed
individual articles; it was a magazine that he took over completely, in-
habiting it from the inside, essentially "performing" the entire publication, start to finish (including all attendant administrative duties, even
the letters to the editor). *La Dernière Mode*, therefore, provides Mallarmé with more than discrete opportunities to alter his identity; it grants
him a whole series of theatrical, textual costumes, which he dons and removes with great aplomb, one of those costumes being the whole magazine itself. Rather than any one mask, it is this alternating series of fictive identities that comprises the performance here.

But as in any such self-conscious spectacle of virtuosity, perfect seam-
lessness is neither possible nor desirable. What we marvel at is not that
the actor disappears completely inside his role, but that he almost does.[41]
The pleasure and discomfort of this disjunction between author and textual voice make *La Dernière Mode* an early step away from pure dandyism—with its goal of seamless performance—and toward a modern
camp aesthetic—with its goal of a noticeable distance between actor and
role. The preciousness of tone and the theatricality evident as Mallarmé
puts on and takes off his journalistic masks make *La Dernière Mode* a
precursor of a modern drag performance, in which one actor costumes
himself as a series of commodified personalities (such as Marilyn Monroe and Judy Garland).[42]

Symbolism, Dandyism, and Irony

The fact that I am arguing for a larger perspective on *La Dernière Mode*
should not be construed as a dismissal of its relationship to Mallarmé's
other work. Indeed, only when the symbolist subtexts of the publication
are recognized can its commentary on larger issues be studied. The critics of *La Dernière Mode* are not wrong when they maintain that Mallarmé the fashion journalist speaks on several levels at once. It could not

be otherwise: such a linguistic purist and poetic genius could hardly abandon all his principles for this one text. Instead, Mallarmé does at least three things simultaneously. First, he indulges in some unmistakable and rather hermetic symbolist poeticizing (to which the ultimate failure of his editorship has been attributed). Second, he includes some perfectly useful journalistic information of unsurprising content (fashion advice, theater schedules, recipes, book reviews). Finally, Mallarmé produces a very deft parody of the genre he has chosen. In other words, he camps it up. Of course, his ironic excesses in *La Dernière Mode* were not meant to be perceived by the *lectrices*,[43] but rather were intended for the enjoyment of his literary friends and, perhaps, future literary critics. But what is curious is that so few of Mallarmé's critics have ever taken notice of it. S. A. Rhodes, Sylviane Huot, and Jean-Pierre Lecercle have all remarked on how "overelevated" the prose style of this magazine was; but no one seems willing to acknowledge that this "over-the-top" quality might be deliberately funny or parodic.

Frequently, Mallarmé's characters fairly swoon with appreciation for the luxury items that they treat in their columns. Gushing with admiration for some satin ballgowns, carried away by their colors and fabrics, fashion editor Marguerite de Ponty struggles to rein in her prose in this passage:

> Satin ballgowns . . . veiled in white illusion tulle fastened gracefully on one side by masses of flowers, others entirely trimmed with real feathers and lace . . . many golden white ones beaded with white jet. . . . Thousands of ravishing styles. . . . Turning away from the many adorable details that I long to describe, I will continue with strict brevity. . . . All the colors: tender mauve, gray-green, twilight, czarina gray, scabious blue, emerald, golden chestnut . . . but I must stop.[44]

Overwhelmed by a desire to write more, longing to report every detail, Madame de Ponty certainly appears to be the antithesis of Mallarmé's usual poetic persona. Her staged struggle to keep herself from adding more text is comically at odds with Mallarmé's famed restraint. But, at the same time, Mallarmé's interests hover closely above this passage. The dress in question is for dancing, and is veiled in "tulle *illusion blanc*" (emphasis added), recalling the classically symbolist (and especially Mallarméan) fascination with the dance, as well as Mallarmé's attraction to the "illusions" he could create with "le blanc."[45] The list of largely jewel tones, described with such delectation, furthermore, leads us back to the poet's frequent comparison of words and precious gemstones.[46]

Within this passage, then, Mallarmé manages to report on a ballgown for his readers, travesty a female magazine writer, and experiment with the relation between fashion and his own hermetic brand of poetry. The hieratic power of words within the Mallarméan poetic universe is at once recalled and parodied by Madame de Ponty's breathless description. Through this playful irony, we can see Mallarmé's high cultural world of letters begin to expand its boundaries, merging with the more democratic world of fashion and journalism, as his dandyism begins its evolution into camp. It has been suggested that Mallarmé mocked his female readers by raising the level of language in *La Dernière Mode* beyond their comprehension. While I would not argue with this (Mallarmé was not especially fond of women), the passage above hints that the poet may also have been making fun of himself, reformulating his "art-for-art's-sake" poetics into a campy masquerade.

The Mechanized, Externalized Self

We have been tracing the development of dandyism from the early social phenomenon of the late eighteenth and early nineteenth centuries through the decadent version of the movement, where we can see the externalization of the dandy's elaborate self-construction in the phenomenon of female performance. Beginning with the last sections of Baudelaire's *Le Peintre de la vie moderne* and moving through Lorrain's and Mallarmé's interpretations of feminine theatricality, we have observed the self-enclosed, fetishized self of the earliest dandies being slowly taken apart by and reinterpreted through the theatricality of women, with, at the same time, a new emphasis upon the artistic and technical expertise of the dandy spectator—his *pinceau*, his *science souveraine*.

In the case of *La Dernière Mode*, once again the dandy spectator is partially creating a female spectacle, the fashionable woman; and once again the text emphasizes his technical agency. Indeed, one could say that much of the magazine is devoted to creative and technical *process*, since *La Dernière Mode* contains lengthy descriptions of the components of fashion—objects of dress, coiffure, and jewelry—and instructions on their proper use. What makes this text so unusual, though, is that even as it focuses on the dandy spectator's creative intervention in a female spectacle, *La Dernière Mode* implies a melding of the creator and his creation—the dandy *becomes* the female spectacle. Throughout *La Dernière Mode*, Mallarmé alternately constructs and then inhabits the woman of fashion, sporadically wearing a kind of textual drag, since the "journalists" who describe and exemplify fashion are often themselves female characters. Neither totally independent from nor the unequivocal product of Mallarmé's prose, the fashionable woman functions here more like the poet's new, public alter ego, heralding the end of the purely privatist dandyist aesthetic while being still attached to it.

Françoise Coblence has remarked that dandyism was a daily process of self-reification or self-mechanization. Of the ur-dandy Beau Brummell, she writes: "Daily the process of self-objectification is replayed for him . . . he works at becoming rigid, starched, petrified, devitalized, a thing. . . . In becoming himself an artifact, [he] produces a smoothly mechanical simulacrum, perfect and impassive" (151). In *La Dernière Mode*, the dandified Mallarmé externalizes this practice, using it not for self-creation, but for the creation of his fictive journalist characters, and, by extension, for the creation of the fashionable woman—who is, in turn, a perfect and impassive artifact. What distinguishes *La Dernière Mode* from other dandyist texts involving performing women is that Mallarmé allows us to watch as his own persona is continually dismantled, absorbed, and rearranged by the slightly mechanical *femme à la mode*, whose physical aspect is, furthermore, known to the reader via the fashionplate, a mechanically reproduced illustration.[47] Just as the dandy appeared to be the product of a debiologized birth, so will the ideal fashionable woman. *La Dernière Mode* invites us to watch as the dandy contemplates the female spectacle within himself and then turns it outward toward the public space in a kind of literary mitosis. Unlike the technologized star of later years, whose descendance from the dandy remains only dimly visible, both Mallarmé's personae in *La Dernière Mode* and the entire magazine itself reveal the close relationship between the male dandy and the female spectacle.

The mechanical or instrumental quality of *La Dernière Mode* exists as well in its relationship to women's apparel. On the metaphoric level, Mallarmé often discusses the journal as if it were itself an article of clothing. Unlike Barbey d'Aurevilly, for example, who wanted to turn his volume *Du Dandysme* into a precious art object, Mallarmé sees his magazine more as an article of clothing. He worries over its being wrinkled or wilted, like a badly laundered blouse. In the issue of September 20, 1874, the editor addresses a reader who has written to the magazine: "Mme la Marquise M. de L. . . à Rennes: We regret deeply that our issue arrived at your home in a faded and wrinkled state: but postmen so rarely wear gloves, and to fit the journal into the mailboxes, they often fold it into four parts. . . . What can one do?"[48] On October 18, 1874, the editor cautions his readers to take proper care of their collected issues of *La Dernière Mode*:

> Our journal is a luxury publication, and according to the custom adopted today by our devotees, at the end of the season or the year, each issue must be bound with its cover . . . we implore . . . all our subscribers to start now keeping the journal in good condition; as for the creases found in those delivered abroad or in the provinces, they will disappear with binding.[49]

Beyond this implied, metaphorical identification of the journal with actual clothing, *La Dernière Mode* functions on a more literal level like female apparel, actually helping to clothe its readers. This is because the first issue of every month included a separate, full-scale dressmaker's pattern that allowed readers to reproduce one of the journal's lithographed toilettes. "Today's pattern . . . when unfolded," writes Madame de Ponty in the edition of December 6, 1874, "immediately displays (without its being necessary to read it here) a charming winter confection."[50] These patterns lend a very direct, instrumental quality to *La Dernière Mode*, for not only does the journal speak of *la mode* and compare itself to fashionable items of clothing or decor, it actually intervenes in the production of fashion, in the dressing of women. The unfolded pattern, always "de grandeur naturelle," makes both *La Dernière Mode* and the reader into something of a female simulacrum. Essentially, a life-sized pattern is a dress made of paper. The journal arrives, then, with its own clothes on; the fashionable woman appears here on paper; and this image is accompanied by a paper garment. Furthermore, in sending along patterns with the journal, *La Dernière Mode* helps its reader transform herself into the lithographed woman of the fashionplates, the woman who displays the various outfits. The reader who receives the pattern and has it sewn for her steps into the illustrated pages of the magazine. Like *la Femme d'autrefois*, who receives her name and identity from the poet in the crowd, the *lectrice* receives her "fashionability," her visual meaning, from the dandified male artist. This proffering of a pattern literalizes the relationship of dandy spectator and female performer: she enters into his fiction—in this case, his fashion illustration.

Certainly, this scenario recalls both Baudelaire's and Lorrain's suggestions of male technical control over female spectacles. As we have seen, both of those artists hint at a process of *mechanical* (as well as purely artistic) intervention on the part of the dandy spectator. Here, in *La Dernière Mode*, Mallarmé goes beyond merely describing the woman performing "la mode"; he even goes beyond intervening in this performance via his fashion journalism. Mallarmé actually offers his reader physical tools—her own *pinceau*, as it were—with which to construct herself along the lines of contemporary fashion—fashion, that is, represented to a vast public by mechanically reproduced lithographs, circulated by the thousands. In this small way, Mallarmé enters the realm of production. His private, hermetic realm has opened out to confront the widening public commercial arena.

The Dandy, the Commodity, and the Fashionable Woman

The most important relationship for the classical dandy is that between himself and the inanimate world. Striving to become an art object, the dandy dehumanizes himself in order to create his social spectacle. In *La Dernière Mode*, however, the spectacle in question belongs no longer to the male dandy but to the fashionable woman; and it is she, furthermore, who achieves the status of art object. While the dandy's performance of the self was strictly solipsistic and designed to suppress all traces of the effort or technique involved, in *La Dernière Mode* Mallarmé lets us see the system at work, making the process more public. He does this by enumerating and describing the objects required to achieve fashionability, and by using his pseudonymous voices as his own textual *parure*, dressing himself in a variety of fictions, with the result that his authorial voice winds up wearing a mutating series of drag costumes. And while the dandy longs to be an unreproducible art object, the modern fashion magazine instructs its public to imitate the highly reproducible objects that comprise "la mode." If the dandy longs to be a one-of-kind *meuble de boudoir*, the middle-class fashionable woman can only hope to be department-store furniture. Both are fetishized selves, but the fashionable woman's self-reification occurs more overtly through the commodity. By extension, the multiple selves of Mallarmé turn the unique dandy persona into an identity just as public and changeable as that of the fashionable woman, whose look follows the seasons. Following the analogy between author and woman of fashion, we shall see that the entire text of *La Dernière Mode* takes on the character of multiple commodities giving shape to Mallarmé's voice while pointing to the end of Mallarmé's genre of hermetic poetry.

Luxury items create the women of *La Dernière Mode*. But while they must appear to grant a one-of-a-kind status, they must at the same time be readily available to all readers. These objects are commercial commodities, available in department stores. The commodities constitute the very condition of visibility itself, filling the implicit, female void considered to lie beneath all fetishized surfaces. And just as the fashionable commodity lends shape to the void that is woman, the fashion magazine lends words to the blank textual space implied by the spectacular moment of fashion. Whereas Mallarmé leaves a blank space between the stanzas of *Le Phénomène futur* to indicate the space of female performance, here he tries to fill that space with items such as "the new cashmere," which, as Madame de Ponty instructs her readership, ". . . is worn in the evening . . . but through this wrapping . . . the woman will appear, visible."[51] Although the relationship here between the woman and fashion resembles the circular rapport between the dandy and the inanimate world, it differs in its addition of the dandy himself as a third element, as well as the elements of public purchase, mass production, and advertising.

Like so many of the female characters we have been looking at (especially *la Femme d'autrefois* of *Le Phénomène futur*), the implied female reader of *La Dernière Mode* is neither entirely human nor entirely alive, but hovers in a middle space dependent upon male artistry and objects to lend her life, corroborating Benjamin's observation that "fashion prostitutes the living body to the inorganic world" ("Paris" 166).[52] The highly constructed quality of *La Dernière Mode*'s fashionable woman indeed lends her a deadened, marionettelike quality.

The idealization and fetishizing of the female body is, as Nancy Armstrong has pointed out, part of any fashion magazine's agenda: "A woman's magazine like *La Dernière Mode* illustrates how parts of the body, like objects that make up the household, were detached from the whole and then fetishized as they came to represent an idealized version of the whole" (16). But *La Dernière Mode* offers an extreme example of this; within its pages, the living body who wears the clothes and attends the balls often disappears entirely from the description, leaving a series of nearly verbless adjectival phrases connecting commodity to commodity. "The phrases contain very few verbs," writes Lecercle. "No hand is guiding them. Any trace of work or effort, that might trouble the *jouissance* of appearance . . . is erased. The woman who receives these decorations . . . is immobile, statuelike" (63). We can see the immobility of the prose in a description of a wedding gown: "Pleated tunic attached at the skirt; at the hem of the tunic, fringe with white pearls. Large satin belt on one side, glides over the tunic and ties in a bow at the train: this bow is fastened to the skirt by a wreath of orange blossoms."[53] Not only is the prose static here, but it makes no mention of any female body parts. The individual elements of the gown emerge from one another. Instead of the relationship, for example, between the dress and the bosom, waist, or legs underneath, Madame de Ponty shows us a tunic that leads to a skirt, then to fringe, a belt, a train, a bow, and finally flowers. This alternative, fabric body supersedes the human, eliminating all trace of the fleshly body beneath it.[54]

Mallarmé acknowledges fashion's (and his text's) dehumanizing effects when he suggests a comparison between his readers and inanimate objects of fashion, including the journal itself: "Once her toilette is complete, a lady, alone, in her isolation from politics and morose concerns, has the leisure to feel a need to bedeck her soul as well. Let this volume remain half-opened for a week upon silks adorned with dreams, upon cushions, like a perfume flacon."[55] The journal, like the woman of leisure, reclines upon silks and cushions in political isolation, resembling both the feminized bibelot ("un flacon") and the *lectrice* herself. Both magazine and reader are female curios, indistinguishable from their luxurious surroundings. The journal does not need to be read; it is merely displayed "entr'ouvert"—suggesting the presence of a titillating and provocative spectacle between its covers.[56] Fashion is itself portrayed as a female spectacle, described in issue number 8 of the magazine: "Fashion, half parting its curtains, suddenly appears to us, metamorphosed, brand new and of the future."[57] This female performance of fashion can be usurped by a male spectator. Indeed, in Mallarmé's presentation, the text of *La Dernière Mode* itself plays the role of a languid, half-dressed woman, a woman of leisure at home perhaps. Eleven years later, in a letter to Verlaine, Mallarmé writes, "The eight or ten issues of *La Dernière Mode*, when I strip them (*dévêts*) of their dust, still serve to set me dreaming."[58] This is perhaps the most frequently cited reference to the fashion magazine, found in nearly every critical discussion of this work.[59] What is so interesting here is Mallarmé's use of the peculiar verb "dévêtir" to describe the action of dusting off a book jacket. He must undress *La Dernière Mode*, for once it is again naked, it serves to stimulate poetic reverie. This is the very function served by *la Femme d'autrefois* in *Le Phénomène futur*, whose pure nudity reinspired the poets' deadened imaginations. Magazine and reader take part in an uncanny and recognizably decadent game in which inanimate objects are humanized (*La Dernière Mode* as woman, or female spectacle) and individuals are reified (reader as apolitical knickknack). The difference is that unlike, for example, Jean Lorrain's reified *morphinées* or Baudelaire's painted café women, the female spectacle includes the participation of a much larger audience: the readership of a magazine, as well as the intervention of the realm of the mass-produced, fashionable commodity.

Advertising, Fashion, and the Dandy

Nineteenth-century fashion was an arena in which the new mass production of clothes slowly overtook the invididual dressmaker's trade.[60] *La Dernière Mode* stages the dandy's confrontation with the newly massified nature of fashion by replacing the prosaic story of mass production that lurks behind each individual object with elevated poetic description. One method of doing this is to equate the fashionable with the royal, as "Ix" does: "The rhythm of winter dances will bring you back . . . before that impartial mirror in which you will seek out the queen of the ball with a gaze that will lead directly back to your own reflection, for truly, what woman, being always this queen for someone else, is not also a queen for herself?"[61] (The queen of the ball before her mirror here clearly conjures Mallarmé's princess Hérodiade, who also contemplates her own reflection.[62])

For her part, Madame de Ponty royalizes *la mode* by linking the period's most celebrated couturiers with the queen of Babylon. Fashion, she writes, sits upon "its royal dais, made of the fabrics of the centuries (those worn by Queen Sémiramis and those fashioned with genius by Worth or Pingat)."[63] While Worth and Pingat certainly established international reputations for genius and innovation in fashion, Worth in particular was known for his markedly *un*royal popularization or vulgarization of *la mode*. It was Worth, in fact, who invented prêt-à-porter, and who was first to put his creations in the department stores.[64] The alliance of Worth and Sémiramis returns the commercial, mass-produced goods to the realm of private hedonism and—importantly—exclusive privilege. "The poetics of fashion," writes Lucienne Frappier-Mazur of *La Dernière Mode*, "occults the production process of which it conserves only the result: the luxury item" (55). The described object of luxury appears out of all context, no longer the product of human labor; the now-fetishized commodity floats freely away from the history of its own creation. In decontextualizing the commodity, however, Mallarmé manages only to accomplish precisely what was one of fashion's biggest tasks: to occult the history of production, "[prescribing] the ritual by which the fetish commodity wished to be worshipped," as Benjamin has said ("Paris" 166).

As the items described in *La Dernière Mode* appear to exist apart from their unglamorous origins, the texts themselves acquire a similarly detached quality. This is because one of Mallarmé's editorial innovations for the magazine was the complete suppression of "continued" articles. All texts, that is, fit entirely within their frames, with no "envois" or continuations of an article on a nonconsecutive page (Lecercle 31). Each text floats, therefore, in its own space, complete and unconnected to the rest of the journal, as compartmentalized as Mallarmé's distinct, pseudonymous voices throughout. The spatial compactness and detached quality of each article underscore the ambiguity of the word "article" itself, as Richard Terdiman has observed: "Newspapers trained their readers in the apprehension of detached, independent, reified, decontextualized 'articles,' and the ambiguity of the term (which might mean either an element of newspaper format or 'a commodity') is itself significant" (*Discourse/Counter-Discourse* 122). The fashion chronicler, who writes of the magical objects that create the woman of "high life," enters into a relationship with that woman similar to the dandy's own relationship to himself. In *Le Phénomène futur*, the blank performance of the woman becomes the poetry of the male spectator; he adorns her naked body with his own creation. Her mysteriously absent history invites him to offer his poetry in its place. In authoring *La Dernière Mode*, Mallarmé resembles the dandyist male spectator in that prose poem, adding his poetic narrative to the blank space left by the suppression of commercial realities.

Under the control of its previous editors, *La Dernière Mode* had been itself a kind of textual blank, composed solely of fashionplates with virtually no text to accompany the illustrations.[65] Mallarmé, however, decided to give words to those pictures, and invented various editorial rubrics along the lines of many similar magazines of the period.[66] In adding text to *La Dernière Mode*, Mallarmé added words to pictures of objects, inserting his own narrative where one was missing. Rather than the tale of the production history of fashionable items, *La Dernière Mode* offers a poetic replacement to fill the silence of the image. Substituting his own poetics for the narrative of the commodities described and advertised in the pages of *La Dernière Mode*, Mallarmé offers a myth of origin, and, as Jennifer Wicke has shown, advertising provides commodities with their missing narratives.[67] Mallarmé fills the void necessarily created by commodity fetishism. The performing woman of fashion figures this void, suggesting to Mallarmé an origin in need of a myth. The poet finds this alternative myth in orientalist images of ancient queens and princesses.

Like advertising, *La Dernière Mode* stages a vacillating game in which the history of objects, their production, and their mechanical underside are alternately suppressed and revealed. The women on both sides of the text—reader and "journalist"—perform a parallel game, sometimes celebrating their connection to massified society, sometimes denying it. As I have mentioned, Mallarmé expresses a clear disdain for advertising, insisting that the "fourth page" is one of the few realms in which poetry cannot flourish. And yet, as Rachel Bowlby has shown, *La Dernière Mode* owes a real debt to the world of department-store advertising. Bowlby examines a publicity device known as the *agenda*, invented by *Le Bon Marché* department store. Printed to look like personal datebooks or calendars, these advertising circulars endeavored to create a natural, household vocabulary of necessity for the luxury items they promoted. The store's ingenious and highly successful advertising campaign turned on the notion that the bourgeois home not only needed the objects advertised, but actually depended upon these objects to define its very existence, especially the existence of the woman of the house. In addition to being outright advertisements, the *agendas* were usable calendars that calibrated the passage of time using the yearly cycle of sales and special events at *Le Bon Marché* instead of the usual religious holidays. In distributing them to their customers, *Le Bon Marché* encouraged the *bourgeoise* to view her life as one with the life of the store. She could jot down her appointments and organize her day on a temporal grid whose axes were established by the store. The desired message was that the housewife's movement through the world, and her entire existence, took shape through her relationship to the commodity. Shopping and owning goods lent her identity.[68]

Bowlby is correct in seeing the highly commercial quality of *La Dernière Mode*, whose text—quite apart from the section overtly devoted to advertising—overflows with commercial references: the dates of department-store sales, merchants' addresses, even train schedules and hotel information. The vacillation between the hermetic and the public, the worldly and the rarified is nowhere more clearly displayed than in one particular item, appearing in *La Dernière Mode* of October 4, 1874. In the regularly appearing section "La Mode," Marguerite de Ponty informs her readers of "the adornment of the hour," a diamond choker or dog-collar necklace. The necklace consists of a black velvet ribbon that serves as backdrop for a complex arrangement of precious stones:

> A thousand diamond letters glitter with the captivating sparkle of a secret that appears but does not reveal itself: the first and last names of the woman who wears the necklace are interlaced with those of the man who gave it to her as a gift. Legend has it that only one jeweler makes these necklaces and varies their mystery, now, to give his address here, even among women, would be an act of high treason: useless, since it is not ours to buy them. . . . I will add however . . . that the necklaces are made in colored gemstones and in pearls.[69]

The text goes on to tell us that for a long time, nothing has succeeded in surpassing the appeal of this necklace, not "months spent gazing at the sea" ("les mois employés à regarder la mer"), nor "weeks occupied hunting on the estate" ("les semaines occupées déjà à chasser sur les terres"). The dog-collar choker inhabits the realm of aristocratic pleasures, an exclusive, fashionable world of seaside vacations and hunting. The appeal of the necklace combats or resists the temporality of this world, for neither the months (at the sea) nor the weeks (at the hunt) can dull its attraction. This object, while being part of "la dernière mode," the adornment of the hour, also transcends this worldly temporality: in other words, it remains the very latest fashion despite the inevitable elapsing of fashionable time. Unlike other fashionable items, the necklace is both new and old.

This dog-collar's poetic, even symbolist appeal for Mallarmé is obvious. By deciphering a secret meaning—the hidden names spelled out by the diamonds—its wearer or beholder would resemble the crowd poet of *Le Phénomène futur*, who decodes the special significance of *la Femme d'autrefois*, distinguishing himself from the rabble. The necklace offers the kind of *écriture piégée* with which Mallarmé scholars habitually compare all of *La Dernière Mode*, seeing the journal itself as a kind of diamond-studded velvet ribbon that conceals the encrypted, authentic, symbolist identity of the poet Mallarmé.

While the *collier-de-chien* is indeed a typically Mallarméan conceit, what interests me even more here is the place of this object in the exterior world of Paris in 1874. Jean-Pierre Lecercle has discovered that another fashion magazine of the time shared Mallarmé's interest in this particular necklace. *La Vie Parisienne* described the very same diamond dog-collar in its issue of August 22, 1874, two months prior to *La Dernière Mode*'s article. In its rubric "Choses et Autres," *La Vie Parisienne* states:

> A new fashion, inaugurated in Trouville during an intimate evening: a dog-collar necklace in black velvet with the name of the woman who wears it mingled with the name of the happy mortal who gave it to her, such that the two names are illegible. The little diamonds glitter on the black velvet with the troubling sparkle of a mystery that appears but cannot be penetrated. . . . Only one jeweler makes these necklaces, varying them infinitely, turning the letters about with a cabalistic art, and owing his immense success to his discretion. They absolutely refused to give us his address. One has to be one of the initiated. These necklaces are also made in little colored gemstones and small pearls.[70]

What does it mean that Mallarmé's description so clearly derives from this earlier one? First, of course, that Mallarmé was not above making use of other magazines' articles for his own. It means that he not only read *La Vie Parisienne*, but was serious about inserting his own fashion review into this genre. As esoteric and rarefied as parts of *La Dernière Mode* are, the journal positions itself as a member of a group.

Of course, the *réflexe intégrateur* might lead a critic to interpret these twinned passages as a symbolist allegory of the necklace itself. According to such a reading, the poetry of Mallarmé's description would hide by being intermingled with the description from *La Vie Parisienne*. One would have to be among the cognoscenti, to be "in the know," in order to perceive the similarity. But in this case, even such a forced "symbolizing" or elitist reading is thwarted. In this case, to be "in the know" means to be outside the hermetic, poetic universe, to read other fashion journals, to partake of the dominant discourse of the exterior world.

Both passages suppress the name of the jeweler who fashions these collars. Marguerite de Ponty tells us that it would be treason to reveal this name, since only gentlemen ought to buy the necklace. *La Vie Parisienne* says that it was unable to obtain the name, its queries having been rejected: "On a absolument refusé." No human creator, then, can be attached to this necklace, which floats, decontextualized. In both cases, its provenance, the history of its production, is raised as a question and then suppressed. While the names of the wearer and recipient are the *secret irritant* of the necklace, the creator's name is explicitly excluded from this game. The description of the dog-collar necklace in both publications becomes, then, a kind of anti-advertisement. While *La Vie Parisienne* claims to have tried and failed to obtain the jeweler's name, *La Dernière Mode*'s article suggests that Madame de Ponty deliberately withholds it. The dog-collar necklace can only come to a woman through love. Desire for a certain product is created, but to satisfy this desire a personal relationship must intervene to mediate the commercial transaction. The public ritual of purchase becomes bound up in an intimate ritual of courtship, another example of an attempt to render the public private. The necklace particularly illustrates what Theodore Zeldin has called the bourgeois double bind: "Do as others do . . . do not be common." It tells the story of commodity fetishism in microcosm. The condition of production—both social and technical—must be effaced; and the object becomes a detached article with no past, inserted instead into the discourse of romance and fashion. The story that Mallarmé writes for the necklace is analogous to the classical dandy's "private genealogy" of self, which rewrites his family history as literary adventure. Unlike that of the earlier dandy, though, Mallarmé's recreated history is not autobiographical; it belongs to a commodity and not to himself.

Painted Ladies

Just as *La Dernière Mode* offers alternative narratives for the commodities it describes, so does it construct fantastic, alternative identities for its *lectrices*. Persistently conflating the bourgeois reader and fashionable items, the journal manages to suggest that, like the fabrics that evoke Sémiramis, for example, Parisian women live in secret, ennobling rapport with poetic, mythic, or orientalist counternarratives to their daily existence. It offers them a substitutive genealogy. The best example of this appears in the "Chronique de Paris" of August 1874, in which "Ix" reports on the Baudry paintings decorating the new Opéra. More precisely, he describes a scene of narcissistic female self-recognition in the paintings, detailing the female patrons as they look upon such allegorical paintings as "la Tragédie," "la Comédie," "la Mélodie," and "Salomé dansant." These bourgeois women read themselves into the allegorical and biblical paintings, experiencing them as mirrors.[71] Amid "the rustling of fabric," "the clatter of jewelry," and worldly chatter, the ladies exclaim, "That face, but it's Madame X!" or "Darling, did you pose for this other portrait?" "That forehead, that expression, whose are they? I recognize them, noble, pure."[72] "Ix" writes: "I pass the visitors who, mentally, are recognizing themselves" ("Je passe les visiteuses qui, mentalement, se reconaissent elles-mêmes," *Oeuvres complètes* 735).[73]

  In fact, the women are not completely wrong to see themselves in these paintings. Baudry was famous for employing local female celebrities, performers, and courtesans as models for his work.[74] The bourgeois matrons' pleasure in recognizing their idealized, painted images is tainted, therefore, by the distinctly vulgar worlds of show business and prostitution. Unlike the dandy, who takes pleasure in likening himself to ancient

Greek generals, these women of the haute bourgeoisie can only view themselves as "Melody," or Princess Salome, if, at the same time, they accept an unsettling proximity to socially debased worlds. With a commercial *clin-d'oeil*, Baudry's portraits disrupt the process of self-recognition in an art object or idealized figure. High culture merges with low as Mallarmé's and Baudry's worlds of poetry and fine-arts painting collapse into a fashion magazine gossip column.

When Baudelaire chronicles Constantin Guys's paintings of urban women, he does not include a scene of the models confronting their own portraits. On the contrary, his illustrations are faits accomplis, worlds in themselves. But in Mallarmé's Opéra account, Baudry's models stand in front of their portraits, explicitly calling attention to the issues of aesthetic reproduction and behind-the-scenes secrets. These women exist at three different levels of representation: in "Ix's" description of them, as figures painted by Baudry, and in their possible third role as celebrities worthy of Baudry's transformative talents. At the same time, the author himself is masquerading as the journalist "Ix." While resembling the dandyist scenario in which the self acquires a second, purely cultural identity through art or history, then, this section of *La Dernière Mode* fragments that scenario's essential components, models stand next to their portraits, and the narrator wears one of his many textual disguises.

"Ix" makes it clear that these bourgeoises are slightly pathetic and absurd in allowing the paintings to confer a desirable identity upon them, be it luscious call-girl or biblical seductress. And within Mallarmé's contemptuous description of the matrons lies his ironic view of the relationship between *La Dernière Mode* and its readers. The Opéra scene is, in fact, a compact *mise-en-abîme* of this relationship: the ladies accede to fashionability and beauty by identifying themselves in the paintings, just as the reader of a fashion magazine receives her identity as "fashionable" through the editor's dismantled and idealized reflection of her.

La Dernière Mode repeats scenarios resembling the Baudry episode, journalistic vignettes in which bourgeois women are encouraged to interpret narcissistically, and to see their own self-portraits in art, often orientalist art. In his "Chronique de Paris" of November 15, 1874, "Ix" reviews a new collection of poetry by d'Hervilly—"Le Harem":

> *The Harem*: the title given by M. d'Hervilly to his latest book of poetry may be a bit shocking for some French ladies. But let no startled fan flutter over this: for so long as it is imprisoned in its volume, this gyneceum will remain closed upon your bookshelf. . . . In barbaric nations, women are held captive behind walls of cedar or porcelain, but by dint of our own superior law, the Poet (whose authority in matters of vision is no less than that of an absolute monarch) enjoys dominion only over his imagined visions of women. Yellow

or white or black or copper-colored, he needs their grace when he sets to work; it forms the floating images that animate his books, especially this cosmopolitan album. . . . The secret, charming readers, now divulged, of those hours suddenly empty without reason, and of those half-absences of the self, to which you succumb sometimes in the afternoon: somewhere a poet is dreaming of you or of your type of beauty.[75]

The passage at once lauds the liberty of the Western woman and redeposits her into the confines of a poetic harem. "Ix" encourages his *aimable lectrice* to see herself as a potential harem girl, and furthermore, to see this role as a remedy for a strange affliction: "ces quasi-absences de vous-mêmes." These absences of the self create the necessary precondition for the required narcissistic interpretation. Before reading herself into the poetic harem, before metamorphosing into an orientalist phantasm, the reader must undergo a loss of self; she must relinquish part of her identity. The void that results is then filled with the voluptuous fantasy of the poet who employs her beauty for his own ends. The final bit of reassurance, "Let no startled fan flutter over this," smacks of the same ironic condescension of the Baudry/Opéra scenario. "Don't worry ladies, this lush, erotic realm will not overtake your living room," says "Ix"; but it is too late. The *lectrice* is already a part of this orientalist fantasy, a harem girl who remains just slightly, and ridiculously, bourgeois—like the Opéra patrons who were both dreamy incarnations of Salome, and gossiping matrons.

In the same "Chronique," "Ix" reviews *Les Princesses* by Théodore de Banville. Here again, a list of fantasy characters is offered to the reader as a kind of idealizing reflection:

[Banville] has resuscitated the body and soul of Sémiramis, Ariadne, Helen, Cleopatra, Hérodiade, the queen of Sheba, Mary Stuart, the princess of Lamballe, and the Princess Borghese. . . . *Ladies, now you may delve into these profound portraits as if they were mirrors always somehow reflecting your own image*, for there exists no little girl . . . who does not carry within her a drop of that eternal, royal blood that created the great princesses of yore.[76]

These resuscitated "femmes d'autrefois" are no longer just princesses in a story, nor are they even the mythological creatures that Baudelaire, for example, sees in everyday women. These women represent the desired result of a modern woman's metamorphosis, achieved through a reading of Banville by way of a fashion magazine. The mass-produced publication interposes itself, becoming the tool with which the woman herself enters this decadent scenario of male poet and femme fatale.

The substitutive genealogy offered to the reader by these passages relies upon other artists—Baudry, d'Hervilly, and Banville—to provide the context for the transformation. While Baudelaire employed Guys as his alter ego, and concentrated solely on Guys's painted subjects, Mallarmé includes a third party, his female reader, who is invited to step into these artworks via her experience of *La Dernière Mode*, replacing her own identity with one acquired through this multilevel process of reading, which mixes "high" culture with "low," ancient princesses with modern matrons.

A New, Collaborative Performance

With its elaborate descriptions, its conflation of women and commodities, its orientalist fantasies, its vexed but intimate relationship to the world of popular culture, and the transmuting identity of its author, *La Dernière Mode* narrates and enacts the move by which the dandy transferred some of his highly constructed persona to the late-nineteenth-century performing woman. In this text, the dandified poet breaks apart his own persona and disperses it among many journalistic voices, thereby rendering visible the formerly hidden nuts and bolts of dandyism. Mallarmé displays the dandyist self as the elaborate, multilayered, theatrical construction it always was, and then, in a surprising twist, offers up a new, equally complicated construction: the fashionable woman—who is both the magazine's reader and its *product*. The dandy behind *La Dernière Mode* meticulously creates his own female counterpart, a woman whose status as ornate bibelot mirrors the dandy's own identity, while tranforming it. Through its abundant advice, explicit instructions, and long lists of required accoutrements, *La Dernière Mode* reveals the fashionable woman's identity to be the compilation of a thousand minute details, a performance as dependent as the dandy's upon slightly dehumanized theatricality and self-consciousness, but, unlike the dandy's, exuberantly proud of its artifice, and highly public.

Like light fragmented by a prism, the dandy's seamless performance seems to break apart when it confronts the popular, feminized, commercial culture of late-nineteenth-century France. A new performance is created out of this confrontation, one that does not strive for isolation, or disdain the popular stage, the marketplace, or technology. This new spectacle will never be seamless; rather, it will revel in its hybrid nature, its mechanicity, and its celebration of the commodified personality.

Chapter Three

ROBOTIC PLEASURES, DANCE, AND

THE MEDIA PERSONALITY

MALLARMÉ'S *La Dernière Mode* is a dandyist project that conflates women, popular bourgeois culture, and the inanimate realm of the commodity. In his various textual disguises, Mallarmé invites his reader to succumb to "quasi-absences" of the self, and then to fill that absence with a new, imagined identity, being reborn as a kind of "Femme d'autrefois," ancient queen, or allegorical figure. *La Dernière Mode* decomposes both the dandy's persona and the performance of female fashionability into a heap of fetishized details, revealing an uncanny play between the realms of the animate and the inanimate, and suggesting a new partnership between the dandy and the female spectacle, the fashionable woman onstage.

Villiers de l'Isle-Adam's 1886 novel, *L'Eve future*, develops this partnership to its natural conclusion, turning the story of the dandy and the performing woman into a science-fiction tale of human simulation. Villiers takes up the Baudelairean themes of a dandy's fetishizing gaze, the female body, and a fascination with urban machinery and melds them with the fascination with female accoutrements, fashion, and detail that we saw in *La Dernière Mode*.[1] Let us first turn to the dandy's side of this new process, and examine Villiers's central male protagonist.

EDISON: CELEBRITY AND THE TECHNO-DANDY

> That [Edison] had some of the spirit of the actor and the
> showman was plain enough; like Barnum he was
> not afraid to advertise his wares.
> *(Matthew Josephson)*

In 1876, Villiers de l'Isle-Adam began work on a novel he first entitled *L'Eve nouvelle*, later changing it to *L'Eve future*. In it, a scientist dandy creates a perfect simulacrum of a woman, using electricity. The scientist of the novel is named Thomas Edison and lives in Menlo Park, New Jersey. Accordingly, any discussion of Villiers's place in fin-de-siècle literary interpretations of dandyism, femaleness, spectacle, and celebrity must first examine the author's choice of Edison as a protagonist.

Between the years 1876 and 1881, one of the most famous men in the world was a young American scientist who seemed to be rivaling God in his ability to reproduce the very essence of human life: the breath, the voice. Soon after Thomas Alva Edison presented his new phonograph machine in 1876, he became a living legend. Thousands of tourists traveled to his home in Menlo Park, New Jersey, to witness the astonishing phenomenon of sound recording. Enjoying the adulation (although later he would tire of the strain), Edison led tours of his laboratory and patiently explained his inventions, which included a variation on Bell's telephone and the "aerophone"—a kind of electric public-address instrument. To demonstrate the wonders of the phonograph, or "talking machine," he would whistle popular songs, ring bells, even cough or sneeze into the recording tube and then reproduce the sounds for the crowd's amazement. Mail to Edison's household was delivered in several bushel baskets daily; newspapers and magazines from all over the world clamored for interviews. He became a figure in fables told to children about the benefits of hard work and serious study.

Edison's genius (as well as his talent for self-promotion) sparked both big business and public narrative. In 1878 a group of venture capitalists formed the "Edison Speaking Phonograph Company" to support and promote his research; and several years later, the monumental invention of the light bulb led to the "Edison Electric Light Company." The ramifications of this lone scientist's work were extensive. When news of the creation of the Electric Company reached London, for example, the value of Chartered Gas Company stock plummeted, and a serious stock-market panic ensued.

In short, Edison was an international phenomenon, a hero, almost a literary character. "[He was] regarded," remarked one of his laboratory assistants, "with a kind of uncanny fascination, similar to that inspired by Dr. Faustus of old" (quoted in Josephson 170). Cartoonists of the period depicted Edison as a medieval magician, in black flowing robes and a conical cap, pouring steaming potions into mysterious bottles, "extracting sparks from the air" (Simonds 120).[2]

Beyond America, one country that had warmed especially to Edison's brilliance and personality was France, where he was regarded as the embodiment of America's recent grand-scale technological advances, but also as a refined European spirit. In much the same way that Baudelaire insisted upon seeing Edgar Allen Poe as a rare and Europeanized American, the French press hailed Edison as the "New Jersey Columbus," turning him from New Worlder into Old Worlder, while offering a chilling suggestion of the imperialist use to which electrical inventions would ultimately be put.[3] In 1878 the Exposition Universelle of Paris featured a stand of Edison's inventions, displaying eight telephones, an aerophone, and a phonograph. Edison himself was elected Chevalier de la Légion d'Honneur that year and was quoted regularly in the French press.

As we saw earlier, the tradition of dandyist literature begins with stories of individual men—biographies that are then liberally slanted and rewritten until they become something else, hybrids of fiction and history. Beau Brummell's life blended into Barbey d'Aurevilly's fantasies; Constantin Guys's oeuvre offered Baudelaire a realm in which to play out his aesthetic philosophy. In "casting" Edison in the starring role in *L'Eve future*, Villiers partakes of this tradition. Much as Balzac did with Beau Brummell in the *Traité de la vie élégante*, Villiers uses a highly recognizable historical figure and "borrows" his celebrity to make a fictional or literary point. And, as in the case of Balzac's text, Villiers's novel looks forward to certain aspects of a camp aesthetic in its mixing of journalism and fiction to celebrate a famous individual whose exterior fame supersedes the boundaries of his fictional character. Villiers goes further than Balzac did in his reliance upon the real, extraliterary facts of his protagonist's life. In creating dialogue for Edison as well as some plot elements, Villiers borrows extensively from the scientist's own pronouncements, and even from statements mockingly attributed to Edison by the European and American press.[4]

But unlike those earlier dandyist writers, who exploited the legends surrounding other dandies—individuals whose celebrity was restricted to an elite audience—Villiers chooses to write a fictionalized account of the man who practically invented the mass media and consequently destroyed the possibility of "private celebrity." *L'Eve future* makes a dandy out of someone whose life was completely at odds with dandyist aesthetics: one of the founders of mass culture, and an American at that.

Earlier dandyist writers grappled in their work with issues of celebrity and the reproduction of style and personality. The very essence of dandyism involves, as we have seen, a kind of generational transmission of cultural cues and postures, an implicit investigation into the artificial or nonbiological creation of life. To write a decadent-dandyist novel about Thomas Edison is to acknowledge overtly that the entire dandyist movement was always about reproduction, and to acknowledge as well the inevitable progression from strictly high-culture, elitist, and European heroes to a more socially leveled, American star personality. Even before it begins, Villiers's novel recognizes that the logical next incarnation for the dandy is the mechanically reproduced, popular American celebrity; and how better to signify this than by using the man singlehandedly responsible for nearly all the techniques with which celebrity is perpetuated?[5]

L'Eve future begins with an "avis au lecteur," in which Villiers seeks to distinguish between Thomas Edison the man and Edison the literary hero: "In America and Europe, a LEGEND has been awakened in the popular imagination around this great American citizen. . . . The Edison of this present volume, his character, his residence, his language, and his theories are—or had to be—at least passably distinct from the real man."[6] Such a preface to a novel immediately raises several issues, first among them the question of Villiers's place in the *avis*. The author is peering out from behind the fictional curtain, the "real" Villiers addressing his reader before officially beginning his story in a narrator's voice. The content of the *avis* mirrors this play of identities since it treats the problem of distinguishing the "real" Edison from the fictional Edison. To the world outside, Edison is a legend, a crowd-pleaser, particularly beloved of the crowds of America and France. Within the world of Villier's novel, Edison is defined *against* the crowd—as a private, literary creation who springs only from the author's imagination. But the distinction falters. Villiers admits that his Edison will manage to be only "passablement distinct" from the real Edison.

That Villiers equivocates in his distinction between the real Edison and the fictional one suggests how much *L'Eve future* as a whole will struggle with the difference between the world outside and the world within, between the socially leveling crowds and the private realm of genius—an old dandyist dilemma. The problem this time is that the genius, Edison, belongs to the wrong side of the equation; he is a legend not of ancient Greek military glory, like Alcibiades, but of the contemporary crowd. In fact, Edison belongs to the masses to a far greater degree than does any French literary protagonist before him, including even Baudelaire's urban flaneur.

In *L'Eve future*, not only Edison but also the female android (called "the Andreid") will mediate between the realms of decadent dandyism and mass culture. With its lengthy description of the android's construction—a machine-age story of Genesis—Villiers's novel elaborately recounts how the late nineteenth century merged the iconic, male personality of the dandy with the machine-age female, performing personality. In other words, it tells the story of the emergence of the industrialized "star" and the commodification of the body (especially the female body) within mass culture.[7]

The Story: Old and New Worlds

Written between 1876 and 1885, *L'Eve future* is, in many respects, a classic text of the Decadent movement. The prose, densely detailed and ornate, relies heavily upon orientalist and antique motifs. References to ancient legends, Egyptian royalty, tropical birds, rare plants, and lavish furnishings all figure in elaborate descriptive passages, just as they do in works by Huysmans or Gautier. But of course, in this novel, New Jersey, not Paris, is redesigned as a remote, Oriental landscape—an inherently less plausible premise, but one that sets the stage for the novel's confrontation of New World and Old World cultural spectacles.

The story is quintessentially decadent as well. Villiers attempts to transform Thomas Edison from the Barnumlike celebrity he was known to be into something resembling more a modern Merlin—a genius working in seclusion for the benefit of only one other person. Edison's astonishing wizardry will either salvage or destroy the life of his protégé, young Lord Celian Ewald, visiting America from England. Edison's physical characteristics, dress, and demeanor all mark him as the typical decadent-dandy hero. His face, though framed by "tempes grisonnantes," is somehow ageless; like Constantin Guys, he is described as "an eternal child" (*L'Eve future* 769).

Lord Ewald is a wealthy young dandy from an ancient and noble English family. True to his genre, Ewald is lovesick over a small-time but exquisite actress, Alicia Clary, whose face, inexplicably, is an exact replica of the "Venus Victrix"[8]—a plot element that foretells the novel's preoccupation with women as reproduced art objects, a common dandyist theme.[9] But—and this is the tragedy—despite her sublime beauty, Alicia's soul offers nothing more than bourgeois platitudes. She is at once *sotte* and *déesse*, the perfect division of form and content:

> Now, between Miss Alicia's body and soul, there was not a disproportion which disconcerted me and troubled my reason: there was a disparity! . . . the contours of her beauty seemed alien to her, her words seemed out of place and embarrassed in her voice. Her intimate being stood out as if in contradiction with her form . . . in the Limbo of Becoming this woman had strayed into this body and . . . it did not belong to her. (Villiers, *Future Eden*, 33–34)[10]

Convinced that he can love truly and deeply only once in his life—a trait he believes he inherits from his aristocratic male ancestors—and unable to master his despair over Alicia's vulgarity, young Ewald has decided to take his own life.

Edison, we are told, owes all his fame and success to Ewald, who, traveling in America many years earlier, had met the elder scientist and salvaged his business from bankruptcy. (Here Villiers transforms, in true decadent style, the American capitalism that supported and promoted the real Edison into a private system of contributions from European aristocracy.) To prevent his friend's suicide and to pay back the old debt, Edison offers to design a "replacement" for Alicia. As a structural base for this replacement, Edison intends to use the mechanical "Hadaly," a female android of his own engineering, who lives in a secret, lavishly furnished cave beneath his laboratory. Alicia's replacement promises to be a physically perfect simulacrum whose beauty will reproduce the original's point for point. But this newer model will not contain Alicia's shockingly average mind and soul. Instead, the android will speak only brilliant and suggestive prose—chosen from among Edison's favorite literature and philosophical works and prerecorded unwittingly by the real Alicia—words that will be played endlessly on golden phonographs placed within Hadaly. Edison explains: "The songs and the speech of the Andreid will be forever those that your very lovely friend will have dictated to her . . . the accent, the timbre and her intonations . . . will be inscribed on the plates of two phonographs of gold . . . which will serve as Hadaly's lungs . . . pure, virgin gold."[11] In response to Ewald's concern that this new creation will not be the same woman with whom he has fallen in love, Edison remarks that Ewald is not in love with Alicia but with his own reflected image:

> It's this shadow that you love. . . . It is that alone that you recognize, absolutely, as *REAL*! In fact, it is this objectified vision of your own mind that you call forth, that you see, that you create in your human living girlfriend, *and which is none other than your own soul reproduced in her.* Yes, that is your love.[12]

Edison's observation places Ewald in the category of such decadent heroes as Huysmans's Des Esseintes or Wilde's Dorian Gray, young dandies who live primarily narcissistic, autoerotic existences. But while *L'Eve future* depends upon some recognizable plot mechanisms of the decadent period,[13] it also introduces a radical new element to the genre. Though it is true that Ewald prefigures both Des Esseintes and Dorian Gray,[14] there is another point of ostensible resemblance among the novels that actually distances *L'Eve future* from the other two. This is the resemblance between the decadent dandy and Hadaly.

HADALY AND THE DECADENT DANDY

Like the decadent dandy, Hadaly[15] is eternally young and attractive, lives suspended between the worlds of human beings and inanimate objects, and occupies a lavishly decorated, orientalist interior. Hadaly shares in particular an essential aspect of the dandy: sexual invulnerability. Androgynous and nonreproducing, the dandy never loses himself to an erotic encounter. His sexual experiences serve only to reaffirm his imperviousness to others: "Do unto others what you do not wish them to do to you," proclaims Des Esseintes (Huysmans, *A Rebours*, 95). But though she will occupy a sexual space in Ewald's life, replacing his lover, Hadaly does not have a functioning sexuality—a fact that Ewald accepts willingly, telling Edison he is happy to transcend mere physical "posses-sion" in order to achieve ideal love. Ewald must love his android "only as she deserves" ("comme elle le mérite, seulement," *L'Eve future* 840), says Edison, and this means chastely, making Hadaly more of a doppel-ganger for the dandy than his lover. Like Balzac's *meuble de boudoir*, Hadaly inhabits an erotic arena while remaining coolly distant from it, recalling Françoise Coblence's description of the dandy as "a mechanism . . . whose life is absent, like a well-ordered artifact" (148). But at the same time, Hadaly also suggests the eventual dismantling of the male dandy, for she encroaches upon the most essential element of his life: his solipsism, his self-containment.

Threatened by a world of infinite exchangeability and mass produc-tion, the dandy steps neatly aside, content to contemplate that world from a distance. He exists in a self-created space *ailleurs* where his only creative product is himself, transformed into a nonreproducible and pre-cious object. The dandy watches the stylized performance of this other self as a detached spectator. More precisely, the dandy is the incarnation of this spectator/performer relationship in one individual.

Indeed, there are many spectator/performer pairs in the novel. Ewald is captivated by Alicia's performances; Edison and Ewald each play au-dience to Hadaly; Sowana, the somnambulistic widow (of whom more later), performs clairvoyant feats for Edison; and Edison clearly "per-forms" his science for Ewald. There is a major difference, though, be-tween these pairs and the decadent scenario of a dandy in love with a performer. The love affairs of Des Esseintes or Dorian Gray are merely ancillary to their relationships with themselves, and in no way undo the autospecular nature of the dandy. In those texts, the fact that the women are performers serves primarily to dissociate them from reproduction. But the dandy/performer relationship in *L'Eve future* announces a kind of reproductive partnership, for the focus of the spectator is Hadaly—an emblem of the science of reproduction, although she is herself sterile.[16]

When Barbey d'Aurevilly fills his treatise on Beau Brummell with dense allusions to history and legend, the encyclopedic nature of his prose serves as a textual analogue for the densely constructed nature of the dandy himself. Villiers produces much the same effect by creating an extremely dense text here, filled with encyclopedic references to contem-porary theories on biology, engineering, and machinery.[17] This time, however, the analogue within the novel's plot for the emphatically con-structed nature of its narrative is a *female* figure, the android, rather than one of the male dandies in question. Like Mallarmé's fashionable woman, Hadaly is the nonbiological product of her dandy creator. But, of course, the notion of human simulation through robotics takes the re-productive subtext of *La Dernière Mode* to a new, more literal level.

MECHANICAL PROCESS AND DANDYIST CONSTRUCTION

Like the traditional male dandy, Hadaly is a creature "apart," making her home in a cave and traveling, vampirelike, in a closed coffin. (Ewald learns that to reanimate her when removing her from her coffin, he must press certain jewels worn around her neck.) Like the dandy, Hadaly is a carefully created, precious object, defined against a common, middle-class world. But she represents a rupture with a cardinal rule of dandyism, for Hadaly takes over the role of "performer" in the dandy's self-contained, one-man show. By choosing to fabricate an android, Ewald and Edison abandon the dandy's devotion to creating only himself. However much Hadaly will function as Ewald's reflection, she is nonetheless separate from him. The creation of Hadaly externalizes the dandy's process of self-reification, completing the transition suggested by Baudelaire in *Le Peintre de la vie moderne* and by Mallarmé in *La Dernière Mode.*

For Baudelaire, Constantin Guys's dandyism existed in the subject matter of his art and not in personality or social performance. By the end of *Le Peintre*, Baudelaire's interest moves even further away from Guys as an individual, focusing instead on artistic *process* and its relation to pure geometry and the intricate workings of carriages. The text of *La Dernière Mode* does not even presume to be about any one real individual, addressing itself instead to *la femme à la mode*, who is nothing more than a lifeless, somewhat mechanical compilation of trinkets and technical tours de force. *L'Eve future*, with its admittedly science-fictional quality, takes the final step in this process, literalizing the notion of a dandyist construction of an exterior entity. The novel devotes itself entirely to a story of process, artistry, and technological marvels, the story of Hadaly.

As the tale of a dandy's manipulation of mechanical reproduction, *L'Eve future* narrates the final shattering of the dandy's hermetic, specular shell. The focus of attention for Villiers's male protagonists shifts from the performance of the self to the performance of a female creature who appropriates, and then reformulates, some of the dandy's essential qualities. Hadaly represents the intrusion both of women and of a multiclass, mechanized society into the dandy's closed circle of spectator and performer, a change suggested but not fully developed in *Le Peintre de la vie moderne* and in Lorrain's "Clientes du docteur miracle."

Perhaps the most illustrative example of the novel's staged clash of an elitist, private aesthetic and mass culture is its reliance upon various wonders showcased by nineteenth-century World's Fairs. While exotic and precious furnishings surround Hadaly in her subterranean home, for example ("The narrator of *The Thousand and One Nights* [would] pale with envy!" exclaims Ewald [*Future Eden* 113]), the cave's lavish decor and the many accoutrements required for Hadaly's transformation turn out to be borrowed not from any remote Eastern milieu, but from the expositions of 1867 and 1878. When Edison first takes Ewald down into Hadaly's home, the young lord is struck by the melodious beauty of many rare birds that fly free in the oddly tropical cave: "There, as if beneath the caress of an imaginary breeze, undulated a myriad liana and oriental roses . . . a flock of birds from the Floridas, the rarest breeds of the South of the Union, shimmered upon this artificial flora. Its multicolored arch flowed in this part of the room with sparks and prisms."[18] Edison explains that, like Hadaly, the birds are all mechanical recreations, animated not by life but by electricity. Tiny phonographs inside their bodies produce their songs: "Hadaly's birds are plumed condensers," Edison tells Ewald (*Future Eden* 108). Such an invention surely suggests the decadent dandyist desire to "privatize" that new goddess of the masses, electricity,[19] since Hadaly's birds are decadent bibelots kept far from the eyes of the vulgar public that might enjoy musical recordings at the cabaret.[20] But at the same time, it turns out that Villiers borrowed his concept of the mechanical birds from the rather vulgar, public context of the 1878 Paris World's Fair, which featured a display of exactly such birds. Like Hadaly's, the electrical birds at the fair met the visitor at the entrance to an exhibition of technological wonders.

Throughout the novel, many of the elaborate objects used by Edison for Hadaly—hairpieces, dental appliances, corsets—as well as several of the scientific processes described—robotics, record-making, and "photosculpture," for example—are reminiscent of popular displays at that same exposition. The secrets of Edison's dandyist art are, therefore, recognizably borrowed from the very un-dandyist realm of popular, mechanized entertainment.[21]

La Femme fatale: A Subplot

The story behind the desire for an artificial woman begins in the subplot of the novel, uncovered and explained in Book 4. This story-within-a-story will intensify and render more explicit the interconnection of performance and reproduction. The presence of the metallic Hadaly proves, of course, that Edison had been experimenting with human simulation long before Ewald's arrival; and the narrative within Book 4 explains why. Edison recounts the story of another friend of his, a wealthy young married man named Edward Anderson who suffered a disastrous, ultimately murderous affair with a *danseuse*. Anderson amassed his fortune, just as Edison did, through his own intelligence: "He was an inventor . . . his business being cotton textiles, he had found a way to size and press cloth very economically . . . he made a fortune" (*Future Eden* 117). Anderson can, therefore, claim membership in the meritocracy of genius so applauded by both Edison and Villiers—the sort of genius that can allow even an American to approach dandyist status.[22]

But Anderson loses his fortune, destroys his family life, and eventually commits suicide as a result of his liaison with Evelyn Habal,[23] a dancer he meets when, after her performance, his friends encourage him to walk onto the stage itself. Villiers renders with some drama this fatal moment of stepping onto the actual performance space: "During intermission, he could hardly get out of following his two friends. The effect of the sherry prevented him from realizing one thing: they were going onstage" (*Future Eden* 118).

The chapter entitled "Danse Macabre" (after Baudelaire's voluptuous and grotesque poem) explains how the happily married Mr. Anderson falls prey to a dancer's ruses. Although appearing to be a teenaged girl, with hair "like burnished gold" (*Future Eden* 134), Evelyn Habal is in reality an aging (thirty-four-year-old) enchantress of entirely artificial charms. Edison explains to Ewald how Mr. Anderson dashed his life and his marriage in pursuit of this chimera, the creation of a hideous, scheming hag. To prove his point, Edison shows Ewald two films of Evelyn dancing, that is, two mechanical reproductions of a performance. In the first film, Evelyn appears in all her glory:

> A transparent vision . . . danced in a sequined costume, a kind of Mexican folk dance. The movements were as lively and sharp as life itself, thanks to the process of successive photography, which can capture ten minutes of movement on a film strip of six cubits. . . . Suddenly, a flat, dull-witted, harsh voice appeared, the dancer was now singing. (*Future Eden* 133–34)[24]

Viewing this first film, Ewald is unable to understand the horror of Anderson's fall. "This pretty girl dances better than she sings," he concedes. "However, I can imagine that, confronted with so many charms, your friend—if sensual pleasure was enough for him—would have found this young woman most adorable" (ibid., 134). To disabuse him, Edison then shows him a second film, this one very different: "A vaguely feminine, bloodless creature, with stunted limbs, and hollow cheeks, toothless mouth nearly without lips, a nearly bald skull.—'What is this witch?' asked Lord Ewald."[25]

This is, of course, the real Evelyn stripped of her elaborate and various cosmetic trickery, all of which Edison has retrieved and now displays to Ewald, piece by piece, in a chapter entitled "Exhumation." From out of a special drawer Edison, with great disgust, pulls out each item of Evelyn Habal's witchcraft: a wig, "a horrible tail of faded, false braids," which Edison sarcastically refers to as "the gleaming tresses of Hérodiade"; pots of theatrical makeup, "the roses of her virginal modesty," says Edison; a set of dentures, "the beautiful, fresh little luminous teeth"; two mounds of cloth padding, "the beautiful firm breasts of the Nereid"; and even "the ballerina's legs," preformed, stuffed dancing tights, now just "two heavy, fetid stockings" (*L'Eve future* 901).

In a strange reinterpretation of texts by Balzac, Gautier, and Baudelaire, Villiers creates here a fetishistic enumeration of female artifice, devoid of any appreciation for the artistry. Those magical effects lauded by Baudelaire in his "Eloge du maquillage," or Gautier in "De la Mode," become here the deadly result of nefarious manipulation. While Balzac, in his *Théorie de la démarche*, insists that female grace could not be simulated (only one of the three princesses descends properly from her carriage), Villiers is not so sure. Displaying a pair of Evelyn's high-heeled shoes designed to make the foot look smaller, Edison declares: "And here is the posture of the stride, the arching, the svelte rigor of a female foot where no scheming, servile, common blood intrudes" (*Future Eden* 138).[26] Throughout most of the novel, Edison appears to be a benign, avuncular genius, filled with compassion for his friend Ewald, expressing no anger of any sort. It is only in the "Exhumation" chapter that Villiers allows Edison to speak with such viciousness and sarcasm, only when a woman's skill in the process of self-creation, her "sartorial autoreification,"[27] is being discussed.[28]

Edison's demonstration offers another instance of resemblance between a female character and a decadent dandy. "To *appear* to be is *to be* for Dandies, as it is for women" ("*Paraître*, c'est *être* pour les Dandys comme pour les femmes"), writes Barbey d'Aurevilly in *Du Dandysme* (703n), and as a self-created, totally artificial woman, Evelyn Habal is pure "paraître," something of a female dandy. She represents a threatening usurpation of self-control and self-awareness. Like Alicia, Evelyn displays a division of form and content, interior and exterior. And yet, she is quite conscious of this distinction—in a sense, she is her own Edison. When Ewald sees the second film of Evelyn, he exclaims, "What is this witch?" a phrase that recalls Edison's sobriquet "the wizard of Menlo Park" (a term used in *L'Eve future* to refer to the scientist). It is precisely this point of resemblance between Evelyn and Edison, their wizardry, that is so menacing to the latter. The myriad electrical gadgets and orientalist bibelots surrounding Edison in his laboratory are the masculinized, scientific counterparts to Evelyn's accumulated objects of parure.[29]

The dancer's extreme artifice gives Edison the idea of creating a totally artificial woman, one who could not endanger men, "since, in short, woman herself gives an example of renovation by artifice, let's spare her that task" (*Future Eden* 140).[30] Many chapters follow that detail the secrets of the future android's lifelike components, from hair and skin to digestive apparatus. From the early dandy's careful construction of his social performance, we have moved, through the intervention of a performing woman, to a dandy's construction of a truly mechanical being.

TECHNO-*BLASON*

> [*L'Eve future*] is the logical conclusion of a century of
> fetishization of the female body.
> *(Naomi Schor)*

The novel moves, therefore, from a catalogue listing of a woman's deceptive toilette practices to a catalogue listing of the scientist's attempt to recreate and improve upon these items, a kind of mechanized "Eloge du maquillage."[31] Ross Chambers has said that the new Hadaly displays "the perfection of the void" (*L'Ange* 471), the perfection of the tabula rasa onto which a male intellect projects his creative impulses. And at this point in the novel, this appears to be true. Edison intends his android to reflect only her owner's consciousness. He instructs Ewald to chose his words carefully when speaking to Hadaly, in order to give her conversation the appearance of meaning: "It will be up to you," says Edison, "to lend it depth" (*L'Eve future* 913). Hadaly's form and content appear to depend upon the agency of her male creator and owner. Edison believes that he has created a new, harmless version of the wicked Evelyn Habal, a creature deprived of any consciousness, a creature of pure exteriority. "I promise you," continues Edison, "that this metal object that walks, talks, responds and obeys, contains no one inside of it" (ibid., 830).[32] Hadaly is meant to be pure "spectacle" minus the agency of the performer. When Ewald, speaking of Alicia, cries to Edison, "Who will remove that soul from that body for me?" (*Future Eden* 49; "Ah! Qui m'ôtera cette âme de ce corps?" *L'Eve future* 814), Edison is ready. He needs only to adjust and cover Hadaly's components to fit the specifications of Alicia's physical self. Ewald's clever enframement of the result will take the place of her soul.

Hadaly, or the New Eve, is meant to be the perfect simulacrum, an exact replica of a woman. However, in all the descriptive pages that follow, one element is noticeably missing: although the subplot generating the entire novel depends upon the attractions of a dancer, no mention is made of dance or performance of any kind. Evelyn's talents in this area are even acknowledged by Ewald: "She dances better than she sings"; and Alicia's singing voice enthralls all who hear her. Yet Edison says nothing about his ability to create a dancing or singing android.[33] Indeed, the very passage that describes that first film of Evelyn contains a peculiar elision, or *escamotage*, of her dance. Rather than recount the dance itself, the narrator marvels at Edison's technological powers of reproduction: "The movements were as lively and sharp as life itself, thanks to the process of successive photography, which can capture ten minutes of movement on a film strip of six cubits" (*Future Eden* 133). Edison's performance seems to overtake Evelyn's in importance. Any element of interest or appeal in her Mexican dance has been replaced by fascination with the movements of mechanical reproduction. But here we see more than just the insistence upon Edison's creative control of the android. This slippage from cabaret dance to filmic or photographic procedure announces the conflation of women's bodies and the mechanical, cinematic images that will come to characterize mass culture. Indeed, the fascination of film overrides the appeal of both Evelyn's *and* Edison's abilities. And though Ewald admires Evelyn's dancing, it is the narrator who expresses admiration for the process of photography, as though the power of this medium were such that it bursts through the level of fictional dialogue. Cinema is the star here.

La Danseuse and the Commodity

The motif of the female performer, particularly the dancer, appears constantly in symbolist and decadent literature, and much critical attention has been focused on it.[34] The dancer is generally thought to represent a poetic ideal, the perfect fusion of interior and exterior. Jean Starobinski interprets the motif of the *danseuse* as "an inaccessible Eldorado, the primal unity that civilization could not destroy" (69). Evelyn and her dance do suggest this kind of indestructible, primal unity, for while Edison may be able to separate Evelyn Habal's exterior and deceptive toilette from the body beneath it, she is inseparable from her dance. Her dance is therefore unreproducible for Edison, uncommodifiable. It is the only one of Evelyn's many charms that cannot later be exposed for its artificiality and pulled from a box. With Hadaly, Edison attempts to control the dancing body, to retrieve, perhaps, the idealized, Romantic topos of the *danseuse*. But of course, mechanical simulation can never lead back to this ideal. The story of Hadaly's genesis figures instead the loss of this ideal and its replacement by the prurient fascination with mechanized action. This fascination, furthermore, leads to the production of a reproducible commodity—the android—which exhibits, as we shall see, an additional magical, indefinable element. This special quality, although analogous to the earlier Romantic enchantment of the dance, is, in fact, the magic of commodity fetishism.

Villiers's novel casts a starkly cynical light on the Romantic purity of the dancing-girl topos. From the outset, the story is told as an example of an economic exchange gone awry. For Ewald, Evelyn Habal represents a loss of purchasing power. While he believed the mistress he was supporting to be a lovely young dancer, she was, in reality, a painted hag. The real Evelyn was not the product on which Ewald meant to squander his fortune; she causes him to question the value of his financial transactions with her. Evelyn's connection to deceptive purchasing practices is reinforced by the novel's frequent comparisons of her beauty to false gold. Although she is bald, for example, her hairpiece allows her to appear "rousse comme l'or" (*L'Eve future* 897). Edison compares her to the deceptive "upa" tree, whose worm-covered, rotting leaves only *appear* "gilded by the sun" ("dorées par le soleil," ibid., 895). If gold can be imitated or counterfeited, its value is no longer stable and predictable. Therefore the paying spectator is deprived of knowledge and control.

The creation of Hadaly is an attempt to regain control over the economic transaction by mechanizing the dancer-as-commodity, depriving it of self-mastery and self-consciousness. Unlike Evelyn, Hadaly is made with reassuringly real gold—"l'or vierge" of her phonograph-lungs. This gold has never circulated—it is virginal—and it never will, for it is locked away inside of Hadaly. Its purity and value are to remain unsullied by the marketplace. Hadaly's value is meant to be precisely calculable, for she is Edison's repayment of the gold lent to him by Ewald. When Ewald agrees to accept her, Edison exclaims "Quitte!" and his debt is canceled.

THE MARKETPLACE AND ADVERTISING

But the very notion that Edison wishes to repay Ewald intimates that the scientist cannot escape the realm of exchange. Ewald does not see his donation to Edison's business as a loan; noblemen do not practice money-lending. Edison's exclamation of "Quitte!" immediately marks the new android as a commodity on the market, distinct from a private gift between dandies.[35] In this way, Hadaly is as much a commodity as Evelyn Habal herself was.

Even the minor trickery in which Edison engages in order to enlist Alicia's aid in the creation of Hadaly bespeaks his proximity to the marketplace. Needing to convince Alicia to pose for photographs and to record long passages of dialogue (to be inserted into Hadaly's lungs), Edison pretends to be an aggressive theatrical agent who will commission a sculpture of her to be mass-produced and erected in theaters. His performance is utterly convincing to Alicia. Hadaly, therefore, begins her new life as a kind of mock advertisement,[36] as well as a reference to popular female stars—the kind whose likenesses were being reproduced everywhere.[37] At the same time, Edison begins what is meant to be a private, dandyist project in the role of mass-cultural huckster.[38]

In his role as theatrical agent, Edison, of course, does not tell Alicia the truth; he has no desire to use Hadaly as a mass-marketing device. On the contrary, he attempts to regulate unstable values with his mechanized Hadaly, paying back an individual debt in a private economy of two. The android, however, turns out to be an unexpected quantity that escapes the control of her creator. At the end of the novel, we learn that Hadaly may after all possess consciousness.

A SOUL OF GOLD

Sowana, the somnambulist I mentioned earlier, is a character who appears only briefly at the beginning and end of the novel. Without explanation, Villiers shows her engaging in telepathic communication with Edison, "seeing" events that are happening miles away and narrating them through mysterious gadgets (in one case, she and Edison speak to each other through special telephonic rings). Finally, we learn that Sowana is none other than the widow of Edward Anderson, the man whose suicide spurred the creation of Hadaly. After losing her husband, Mrs. Anderson lapses into a trancelike state (Villiers was fascinated by the new practice of hypnosis), acquires a new, mystical identity as seer, and takes the Cambodian name "Sowana" (meaning "mountain of gold").

The climax of *L'Eve future* occurs when Edison sends Ewald out to have a chat with "Alicia," who is, in fact, the newly created Hadaly. So perfect is the simulation that Ewald has not the slightest idea that he is not with the original Alicia. The only difference between the two women is that this new Alicia speaks with surprising philosophical profundity, appearing to understand the very depths of Ewald's soul. Moved by his beloved as never before, Ewald regrets having accepted Edison's offer of a replacement woman and rhapsodizes about his real, human love:

> "Ah!" he murmured, "did I lose my mind? I was dreaming of a sacrilege, of a plaything (the sight of which, alone, would have made me laugh) . . . of an absurd, unthinking doll! . . . Oh my beloved! I now can see you! You are of flesh and blood, like me! I can feel your heart beat! Your eyes have wept! Oh Alicia dear! I love you!"[39] (*Future Eden* 220)

"My friend," interrupts Alicia/Hadaly, "do you not recognize me? I am Hadaly." In the conversation that ensues, Hadaly tells Ewald that, without Edison's knowledge, Sowana has mysteriously infused her own soul into the android's body, turning a perfect but soulless simulacrum into a being animated by spirit. (Later, Edison comes upon the collapsed body of Mrs. Anderson, lifeless, since its spirit has now been transferred to Hadaly.) We can see here Villiers's simplistic version of the Hegelian dialectic to which he was fond of referring. The duality formed by Alicia and Hadaly becomes whole when "une belle âme" is added to it, hinting at a divine redemption of Edison's sacrilegious rivalry with God or a reinsertion of aura into this mechanically reproduced woman.

The novel ends, however, with uncertainty, since the narrator, until now omniscient, does not tell us if Edison is unaware of this last-minute addition to his creation or if he is, in fact, responsible for it—a possibility that would negate much of the mysticism. (Earlier in the novel he does announce that he can improve upon Alicia's soul: "In place of this soul . . . I will infuse a new sort of soul.") Hadaly pleads with Ewald not to discuss this with Edison: "Do not speak to him of what I have just told you, it is for you alone"; and Ewald complies (L'Eve future 1000). In other words, not only does the novel hint that Edison's product is ultimately estranged from him, it leaves us with a plot that has run away from its narrator. Like Hadaly, the novel itself may have a life of its own, independent of what the narrator will tell us.[40]

ALIENATION AND PERFORMANCE

In attempting to recuperate the alienated "other" of the deadly dancer Evelyn (and the potentially deadly Alicia), Edison has created something equally alienating. Though Hadaly does not reproduce the essential, estranging component of female performance (Evelyn's dance or Alicia's singing), her soul and the mysterious nature of its origin offer an equivalent figure for the alienation inherent in any commodity. Indeed, Hadaly strongly recalls Marx's figure for the fetishized commodity, the "dancing table":

> The table . . . [is made of] . . . wood, an ordinary, sensuous thing. But as soon as it emerges as a commodity, it changes into a thing that transcends sensuousness. It not only stands with its feet on the ground, but, in relation to all other commodities, it stands on its head, and evolves out of its wooden brain grotesque ideas, far more wonderful than if it were to begin dancing of its own free will. (K. Marx 164)

Once she becomes a commodity and is exchanged by Edison and Ewald, Hadaly—like the wooden table—begins to exhibit uncanny aspects, for she surpasses her creator's capacities. The novel's final mystery stems precisely from that element which "transcends sensuousness," the android's soul; and we recall that Marx suggests "recourse to the mist-enveloped regions of the religious world" (168) as a way of understanding the relationship between persons and commodities. In the end, Hadaly appears to be even more of an alienated commodity than Evelyn, who indeed "dances of her own free will."

If, in fact, Edison loses control over his production in the end, then he is estranged from his own mechanized work. Earlier in the novel, Villiers raises this issue in a passage spoken by the scientist:

> Look at it this way. At the threshold of a steel refinery, you can distinguish iron, men, and fire through the smoke. The anvils ring. The metal workers who make the bars, arms, tools, have no way of knowing the real use made of their products. These forgers can merely call them by name. Well, that's where we are now. None of us can estimate, really, the actual nature of what he forges. . . . Any knife can become a dagger" (*Future Eden* 70–71).[41]

This is the same process examined by Lukács in his essay "Reification and the Consciousness of the Proletariat":

> The personality can do no more than look on helplessly while its own existence is reduced to an isolated particle and fed into an alien system . . . the mechanical disintegration of the process of production . . . also destroys those bonds that had bound individuals to their community in the days when production was still "organic" . . . [individuals become] isolated abstract atoms whose work no longer brings them together directly and organically. (90)

The individual consciousness of the metal worker in Edison's example, then, is subsumed by the process of his labor. The entire structure of *L'Eve future* reproduces this scenario of reification and testifies to the anxiety that results from it.

Unlike such dandyist classics as Gautier's *Mademoiselle de Maupin*, or Huysmans's *A Rebours*, *L'Eve future* has no one central protagonist. There is, rather, a central process—the creation of the android. This creation process at once refers to and dismantles the motif of the reified hero. Instead of a story of a dandy, whose goal is to appropriate the impassivity and invulnerability of the art object, we have a story of the creation of an "object-person," the literalization of the dandy's goal. Not only does this dismantle the single-sex dandy-hero motif, it reinserts the fetishized object into the economy of mass production from which the dandy tries perpetually to escape, through his unalienated self-creation. Des Esseintes revels in having irreproducibly rare furnishings, liqueurs, paintings, and books (and Dorian Gray's portrait is, of course, unique). Edison, too, wishes to keep Hadaly unique—"I will manufacture no more andreides"—even while admitting that a whole factory assembly-line would be possible: "Having once written the general formula, it is now nothing but a . . . question of workers, clearly there will soon be thousands of such specimens made, the first industrialist to happen along will open a factory producing ideals" (*L'Eve future* 930). But even by putting an end to his android business, Edison cannot put the genie back in the bottle. Hadaly/Alicia/Sowana is no longer really a single being or object, no longer firmly under his control. The new creature contains at least four female entities: the original, metallic Hadaly; Alicia; Evelyn Habal; and Sowana. The fact that a collectivity of women is responsible for a potentially mass-produced being further dismantles the decadent-dandyist topos of the isolated, masculine hero.

Nor is Edison really a lone magician-scientist working in secret, like Mary Shelley's Dr. Frankenstein. He is not even a single personality disguised as a fragmented series of selves, in the manner of Mallarmé in *La Dernière Mode*. Edison is more a factory manager directing a team of workers, another collectivity. And although he laments the estrangement of steel workers from their product's final purpose, his own workers are no more enlightened. We are told at the beginning of the novel that Edison, while paying his workers a princely salary, does not permit them knowledge of their final product. Most important, perhaps, the android produced is in no way an invaluable objet d'art. She is integrally bound up with the economy in miniature that exists between the two men, as Edison's payment of his debt to Ewald. But she is also part of the larger, specifically American, economy. Villiers includes a very witty digression—parodying actual press accounts—about the responses of the American stock market during the period of Edison's long withdrawal from the public eye, while he is creating the android. "The Corporation founded on the Intellectual Capital of Edison and the Exploitation of his discoveries" sees its shares fluctuate wildly on the market as speculators try to foresee what new inventions the chairman of the board is creating. Edison refuses to divulge details of his plans, trying to sequester himself from the public economy. This episode makes clear the absurd hopelessness of such an attempt at economic isolation. Edison's creativity is "capital intellectuel," inscribed a priori within the marketplace.

The Mechanical Music Hall and the Crowds

And while the creation of Hadaly certainly responds to and reflects an increasingly mechanized society, it refers to something else as well: the massification of culture. Just as Hadaly represents a transition from unique and rare possession to factory-produced item, she also represents the parallel transition from the rarefied, upper-class milieu of high culture to the mass-produced entertainment of the cabaret. The *danseuse* Evelyn first works her magic on Edward Anderson while performing in the corps of an opera, Gounod's *Faust*; yet the film that Edison shows to Ewald depicts her performing a "danse mexicaine" complete with castanets, obviously a cabaret revue. Evelyn's destructive powers may have begun in the high-cultural space of the opera stage, but once it becomes a question of "reproducing" her in some fashion, Edison removes her from the opera and deposits her onto the dance-hall stage, known for the regional motifs of its revues.[42]

The last two decades of the nineteenth century in France saw an enormous proliferation of such theaters featuring popular entertainment: *café-concerts*, cabarets, and music halls. This expansion of mass entertainment led to the development of a common cultural consciousness among France's different social classes. Mass society and the always-increasing mechanization of the workplace resulted in mass leisure and mechanized forms of entertainment, what Adorno and Horkheimer would come to call the "culture industry" (120–67).[43]

This new form of entertainment dramatically altered the relationship between spectator and performer. "At its optimum," writes Peter Bailey, "the music-hall was a highly charged social space . . . both a public and private place" (xvii). Bailey expressly refers to music-hall spectators as the "crowds," finding this word "a more helpful designation than audience" (xvii). At the music hall, the audience or crowd no longer sat in rapt silence before a single, all-absorbing show. The music-hall or cabaret format involved a series of short, varied tableaux whose performers engaged much more directly with the audience. For its part, the audience was free to enter and leave the theater at any point, and to eat, smoke, or read during the performance.[44] In other words, the audience had a participatory and audible role in the spectacle.

The threat posed by Evelyn and her dance may point toward the discomfort felt by members of the upper classes upon becoming audience members in the new mass-cultural space of the cabaret, that is, upon becoming members of a somewhat untamed or disorderly crowd. Edison expresses this anxiety when he remarks ruefully that tragic downfalls like Anderson's will keep occurring as long as "small theaters spring up in small towns" (*L'Eve future* 886)—as long, that is, as culture continues to debase itself through massification, which brings small-time theaters to the uncultivated provinces. High culture, presumably, could not produce performers as destructive as Evelyn. We might recall that, although he was attending an opera and not a cabaret revue, Anderson first encountered Evelyn by walking *onstage* himself. It is in entering the performance space, and thus blurring the orderly distinction between audience and spectacle, that he begins his downfall.[45]

Hadaly's greatest attraction is that she exists only for Lord Ewald, who is, then, protected from the discomfort of a mass audience. "My being will depend upon nothing but your will . . . like a woman, I will be for you only what you believe me to be" (*L'Eve future* 991). Alicia Clary yearns for fame and fashionability, using photographic *cartes-de-visite*[46] to disseminate her image hundreds of times over. But Hadaly's spectacle exists for an audience of only one, effacing the crowd in which an individual spectator feels estranged or alienated.

But there is no returning to such a restricted and elite form of entertainment. At the end of *L'Eve future*, a storm at sea destroys Hadaly, who is traveling (in her coffin) with Ewald back to his home in England, the remote Château Athelwold.[47] Her death (or rather, electrical failure) comes as no surprise because a creature such as Hadaly could not exist in the Old World as the plaything of a single aristocrat; she contains within her too much of the modern machine age, the era of the crowd.[48]

Indeed, the crowd lurks just outside the main narrative of *L'Eve future*. Although Villiers includes only two references to American history in this novel set in New Jersey, both conjure a world of crowd politics and reinforce nineteenth-century European stereotypes of a violent and "barbaric" United States. The first reference is to the Civil War; Edward Anderson's disastrous decision to go to the theater comes "one evening in New York at the close of a meeting, in the clamor of hurrahs at the outcome of the famous War of Secession, [when] two of his tablemates proposed topping off the festivities at the theater" (*Future Eden* 117). Anderson's downfall comes, then, in the wake of civil unrest. In the novel's second historical reference, Villiers describes the Battle of Little Bighorn and the publicity surrounding it:

> Suddenly about this time, Sitting Bull, Sachem of the last Redskins of the North, had an unexpected, bloody victory over the American troops sent against him. As everyone knows, he decimated and scalped all the elite young men of the Northeast of the Union. Public attention, struck dumb by the news which resounded through the world, was diverted by the threatening Indians and left Edison out of the limelight for several days.[49] (Ibid., 212)

Here, we might suspect Villiers of using American history to evoke an episode of his own country's recent past. The 1876 attack upon an "elite" population by a savage crowd suggests the Paris Commune—as it would have been seen by someone of Villiers's political stripe.

Villiers's personal politics moved consistently to the right throughout his life. Although he briefly supported the Commune in 1871, he soon renounced his democratic affiliations and, in a sudden reversal, became a committed royalist, going so far as to leave Paris in order to confer and join forces with the Versaillais.[50] Something of a social Darwinist, Villiers came to believe in natural, genetic superiority and the total impossibility of democracy.[51] His unwavering faith in the power of aristocracy and personal genius (especially his own) was apparent to all who knew him. "I think seriously that what he wanted," wrote Mallarmé about Villiers, "was to reign as a monarch" (Mallarmé, *Oeuvres complètes*, 489).

A NEW BREED

L'Eve future stages Villiers's battle with the self-estrangement caused by mass production, the hypnotizing effect of mass politics, and ultimately, perhaps, democracy. The android Hadaly is, in part, Villiers's response to the threat posed by crowds and politics, embodying his losing struggle as a royalist against what he feared was the undesirably equalizing effect of mass society. Yet although she represents an attempt to overcome alienation, Hadaly, a commodity despite herself, only advances it. Among the mass-produced androids of the future, it will be senseless to trace a biblical lineage descending from this Eve.[52] Individual history, the ability to position oneself in relation to others, and the dandy's crucial narrative of cultural genealogy will be rewritten forever. The first manifestation of a new hybrid figure with roots in both the dandyism of the early nineteenth century and the mass culture of the century's end, Hadaly is the logical descendant of the dandy, once the dandy has passed through the looking-glass of mechanical culture and commodity fetishism.

Chapter Four

ELECTRIC SALOME: THE MECHANICAL
DANCES OF LOIE FULLER

A REAL "FUTURE EVE"

> Intoxicating art, and, simultaneously,
> an industrial accomplishment.[1]
> *(Mallarmé on Loie Fuller's*
> *performances)*

U P TO THIS POINT we have been looking at female spectacles created by male artists. But those works provide only one voice in the dialogues between literature and early mass culture and between dandyism and the women of popular spectacles. On the other side are the actual contemporary performing artists whose work captivated socially mixed audiences in cabarets while, at the same time, commanding the attention of elitist, often deliberately esoteric men of letters. The list of these stars is long; it includes singers such as Yvette Guilbert, dancers such as "Nini-Patte-en-l'air," La Goulue, and Jane Avril, and actresses such as Sarah Bernhardt, Eleanora Duse, Ellen Terry, and Jenny Lind. But of all the popular women artists of the period, Loie Fuller most provocatively combined the dandy's fin-de-siècle aesthetic with a commodity-based, mechanized spectacle, drawing out and crystallizing all the themes we have been examining here.

If Villiers's Hadaly was the first literary depiction of the iconic media personality, Loie Fuller was the first actual, historical example of the genre. During her thirty-year career in Paris, Fuller achieved a degree of fame comparable only to that of Sarah Bernhardt or, later on, Isadora Duncan.[2] Despite her extreme celebrity, however, Fuller has, unlike these other two women, faded from cultural memory—probably because her appeal depended upon qualities not traditionally associated with female performers. Fuller differed dramatically from other stars of her era in that her popularity owed more to *technè* than to conventional talent, personality, appearance, or grace. Fuller was seen as a wizard of stage illusion, capitalizing on the public's enormous fascination with that other "wizard," "The Wizard of Menlo Park," Thomas Edison. Fuller, in fact, earned her own magical nickname, "the electricity fairy" ("la fée électricité"). And as we shall see, Fuller was also a proto-camp heroine, product of the marriage of European aestheticism and Yankee ingenuity, "born in America . . . but made in Paris," as she liked to say.[3] As such, she marks a transition from the late nineteenth century's ironic, cryptic subject who hermeticizes the urban crowd for an elite audience to the modern media personality who revels in playing out his or her artistry from within that crowd. She marks the transition, that is, from the likes of Mallarmé and Villiers to Oscar Wilde.

Background

Fuller was born in 1862 in the dust bowl of the American Midwest, in a small Illinois town named Fullersburg, probably after one of her ancestors. Throughout the 1880s she pursued, with little success, a career as a dancer and actress in burlesque and vaudeville theaters across the United States.[4] But moving to Paris in 1891, Loie Fuller transformed her career permanently. Days after arriving, Fuller convinced the director of the already world-renowned Folies-Bergère to let her perform her new "danses lumineuses" in his theater.[5] By the next day, all Paris knew about this "modern Salome," the American who had transformed the hackneyed genre of the "Oriental" cabaret veil dance into a technological marvel. Fuller would appear for three hundred consecutive nights at the Folies (de Morinni 210).

For thirty years Fuller lived and worked primarily in France, enjoying unprecedented international fame and influence as a dancer, choreographer, stage-lighting designer, inventor, and, eventually, filmmaker. Her unusual art form made of her a point of convergence of "high" culture and mass entertainment, for although she was always a music-hall performer (appearing, for example, at the Athenée, the Odéon, and the Olympia), Fuller was a constant subject of study for artists of the highest literary and artistic circles. Whistler and Lautrec painted her; Rodin sculpted her; Lalique rendered her in crystal; Jean Lorrain, André Levinson, and Mallarmé reviewed her performances; Debussy and Massenet wrote music for her. Her iconic status never waned during her lifetime, and she came to be regarded, as Frank Kermode has said, "as a living emblem of a new aesthetic" ("Loie" 9).

From the beginning, Loie Fuller set herself apart from other music-hall artists. Unlike her contemporaries in cabaret theater, Fuller was never admired for her body, for her face, or for any particular balletic agility. Certain critics insisted (and there is, frankly, photographic and cinematic evidence of this) that she was overweight, neither "pretty nor young," and not a particularly good dancer.[6] In his *Journal*, Jules Renard writes of finding Fuller "a shapeless figure . . . sausage-fingered . . . [with] vague myopic eyes" (quoted in Kermode, "Loie," 11). Eve Curie (daughter of

Pierre and Marie) describes her as "an odd, badly dressed girl, with a Kalmouk face" (quoted in Grunfeld 444). By the time she was a household name in Paris, Fuller was already twenty-nine years old—an age when most dancers ended careers—and known offstage as a rather plain matron. Onstage, however, this matron dazzled her audiences, but not with the traditional feminine charms of the *danseuse*. Spectators saw her, rather, as a dreamlike vision of illuminated forms. She was "a priestess of pure fire," "a figure like those dreamed of by Rodin,"[7] "a sun standing in the middle of a shower of stars,"[8] a vision "fallen from the Sun's chariot."[9] She was also, just as frequently, seen as a great inventor, "a woman of genius," as Rodin called her,[10] "at once an artist and a scholar."[11] Reading through the thirty years of journalistic accounts of Fuller's performances, one sees that she acquired the combined aura of a fairy-tale vision and a mechanical wizard. But throughout all the high-flown rhetoric that followed her career, it remains clear that, when she was onstage, Fuller never appeared quite human to her audiences; she had turned herself into an illusion-producing machine, devoid of any apparent bodily characteristics.[12] And although Fuller's dances gestured toward much of the conventional orientalism of the era's music-hall *bayadères*,[13] the entertainment she offered was not sexually titillating, or even, exactly, corporeal. "She hides behind her fabrics," wrote one critic. "She leaves nothing in the light save her arm and her hand."[14] Her appeal lay in technological magic, in the careful choreography of veils, lights, stagecraft, and machines, "the traditional art of old Oriental civilizations, extenuated with science," as one critic wrote.[15] And in this, Fuller resembled the classic, nineteenth-century dandy. Just as the dandy's attraction was based on his impeccable orchestration of dress and manner, Fuller depended upon her flawless control of apparatuses. The dandy's goal was to raise his art of *sprezzatura* to such a high level that all traces of effort disappear, along with any overt acknowledgment of his fleshly body. He performs as a completely cultural body, apparently free of any biological encumbrances, "une méchanique réglée." In a similar way, Fuller's performances strove to dematerialize her physical self onstage. Relying on her own literally mechanical version of the dandy's *sprezzatura* (what Mallarmé called her "industrial accomplishment"), Fuller transformed herself into a weightless vision, a mutating series of sculptures in silk and light. However, Fuller was not a dandy; she was, rather, his clear and immediate successor: the modern media celebrity who combined a highly constructed performance of the self with a genius for mass marketing. In Loie Fuller's brand of cabaret theater, the elaborate, mechanistic, and private performance of the dandy explodes into the age of technology. The dandy and the woman onstage merge.

FULLER ONSTAGE

> The exquisite phantom appears, slips away and then
> reappears; it moves in the multi-colored
> waves of electric emanations.
> *(Roger Marx)*

Fuller's stagecraft functioned on several aesthetic levels at once. Her technical repertoire lent her a dreamy, ethereal quality traditionally associated with the Romantic or symbolist vision of the *danseuse*. At the same time, these techniques conveyed a strong orientalist feeling to Fuller's performances, linking her with the far more carnal, seraglio-style entertainments common to the era's cabaret shows. And, finally, Fuller's stage apparatuses "technologized" her body in such a way that she seemed neither a Romantic vision nor a harem temptress. Since so much of her performance depended upon light and mechanics, Loie Fuller the woman ceded to Loie Fuller the cinematic image, a screen meant to receive and reflect light, a purely mediatic phenomenon.

In the 1890s, when Fuller arrived in Paris, cabarets were switching their lighting systems from gas to electricity, and electric light was to become the most crucial element of all for Fuller's performances. She designed all of her own stage lighting, eventually acquiring an entire team of electricians, which she oversaw personally.[16] Fuller also conducted experiments with lighting and color that were reminiscent of certain turn-of-the-century studies being done on human perception.[17] She herself claimed to have nearly synesthetic powers. "I see the colors," she was quoted as saying, "just as you see them in a kaleidoscope."[18] Camille Mauclair envisioned her as "a changing poem of colors created by electricity" (94), and this fusion of art and technology made Fuller popular with scientists as well as poets. She worked with, among others, Pierre and Marie Curie and the astronomer Camille Flammarrion.[19]

Fuller's stage design owed its visually surprising, indeed revolutionary, aspect to its radical discarding of all conventional scenery.[20] Traditionally, late-nineteenth-century cabaret dance reviews had revolved around a theme or motif that depended upon elaborate backdrops, props, jewels, and costumes. Fuller rejected such trappings entirely, replacing them with lighting mechanisms, optical illusions, and draped or sculpted fabrics.

One such invention involved a glass pedestal about four feet long by four feet wide, set into the stage floor, with a lighting device hidden underneath it. When Fuller climbed atop this pedestal—in a theater that was always completely darkened at her request—she would appear suspended mysteriously above the stage, dancing in mid-air. (This repre-

Patent No. 533,167

7. Patent drawing for Fuller's mirror room. Bibliothèque Nationale, Paris.

sented the first time that a cabaret review was performed in a darkened theater.[21]) Fuller designed this technique, known as "underlighting," in 1893 while performing at the Folies-Bergère; it was patented under her name the same year.

Another of Fuller's inventions consisted of an arrangement of mirrors placed contiguously onstage. Rows of electric lights, mounted at the interstices of these mirrors, formed a tiny octagonal room in which she danced, her body reflected all around her. The result was the appearance of a small crowd of identical dancers in a self-enclosed, mirrored room—a vitrine of infinite images (Fig. 7).

Perhaps Fuller's most dramatic electrical illusion involved a wall of transparent glass that she placed in front of the stage and then brightly illuminated. With the auditorium once again kept as dark as possible, the glass wall became invisible to the audience, but turned into a mirror for Fuller dancing behind it. The audience was aware that she could see only herself reflected back in it, and so watched Fuller watching herself. She danced before them, but did not acknowledge the audience, offering herself up as a specimen of narcissism, caught and held in a glass display case. The mirrored wall also smacks of the period's commonplace—seen often in commercial photographs and postcards—of Oriental women caught gazing at themselves in mirrors.[22]

All three of these inventions recalled the symbolists' vision of the dancer onstage, a weightless apparition, an isolated creature of form and shadow, unhindered by gravity, indistinguishable from a shimmering reflection. At the same time, these apparatuses—particularly the mirrored room and the mirror wall—fit neatly into a much more prosaic and unglamorous aesthetic of commodity fetishism. Philippe Hamon, in *Expositions*, lists the various "glass houses" he sees as emblematic of late-nineteenth-century France's consumer culture of display. He writes of those "creatures of appearance and spectacle on perpetual exhibition, the traveling salesman, the actor, the artist, the society woman . . . who are . . . permanently 'on display'" (171). He goes on to note the frequency with which novels of the era contain characters who, like so much merchandise, appear in actual glass or mirrored cases (similar to Fuller's mirror room).[23]

Regardless of the onstage apparatus being used, Fuller's performance usually depended upon a central lighting device that lent her dances both a cinematic and an orientalist quality, thereby combining American know-how with decadent sensibility in a manner similar to Villiers's in *L'Eve future*. The device, an overhead lantern projector, consisted of rotating pasteboard wheels placed in front of searchlights. Each round piece of pasteboard (from twelve to sixteen inches in diameter) had a border of gelatin disks of different colors. Some of the disks were solid; others were a combination of colors. In some cases, panels of patterned glass were slipped in front of the disks. Fuller created these panels by cutting and then coloring slides of molded glass, using pigment dissolved in a special gelatin concoction, also of her own invention. She would paint her own abstract designs on the glass and then, by shining the colored lights through them, project these designs upon her body as she danced.[24] The intricately patterned light coloring her face, hands, and veils amounted to an electrical version of the *tatouage* that so frequently adorned North African women performers, "technologizing" a conventional trope of orientalism.[25]

The revolving projector also allowed Fuller to replace background scenery with evocative paintings of light. In her 1895 production of "Salomé" (Fig. 8), for example, Fuller used her projector and slides to create successive illusions of a storm, a moonlit seascape, a sea of blood, and passing clouds (Sommer 64).[26] Later in her career, Fuller's colored slides would become more complex, projecting images that resembled "fantastic landscapes . . . [in] riots of luminous splotches or luminous bars."[27] (One special effect could require up to ten thousand amperes of electricity, enough to light a town of 30,000 inhabitants [de Morinni 216].) And by 1921 Fuller had begun to incorporate shadow play into her scenery, using a silk scrim with a light shining behind it to cast giant shadows on the stage, shadows that then "danced" in the performance, dwarfing the human figures onstage. In the 1923 piece entitled "Ombres gigantesques" (Fig. 9), for example, Fuller used this technique to produce

L A LOIE FULLER reparaît brillamment au théâtre
des Arts, dans Salomé, de M. R. d'Humières.

8. Loie Fuller in costume for "Salomé." Bibliothèque Nationale, Paris.

the illusion of a demonic, giant witch whose enormous hand "chases" the dancers across the stage, threatening to scoop them up. Later in her career, when she was making films, Fuller would develop this technique into "negative imaging," a process (still used today) by which film negatives are incorporated into footage to give the appearance of ghostly or translucent figures mingling with the "positive" or opaque images.[28]

But innovations in stage lighting accounted for only part of Loie Fuller's revolution in dance. Much of her onstage magic lay in the manipulation of fabric and costumes. In place of all the conventional

9. Scene from Fuller's "Ombres gigantesques." Bibliothèque Nationale, Paris.

scenery she had discarded, Fuller normally draped her stage and its floor entirely in black velvet or black chenille curtains in order to focus the spectators' attention more closely on the lights and costumes.[29] Early in her career, Fuller used silk costumes upon which she painted her own designs, combining costume and scenery (Fig. 10). But by 1895 she had dispensed with the painted fabrics as well, choosing instead to form the hundreds of yards of silk that she wore into the very designs she had once painted upon them. And so, for example, instead of wearing a costume painted with lilies for her 1895 "Lys du Nil" dance, Fuller transformed her entire body into the lily (Fig. 11).[30]

In order to shape the silk into gigantic patterns, in 1893 Fuller patented a device that allowed her to manipulate the material more easily.[31] She sewed into the material large batons, which acted as extensions of her arms. By manipulating these batons, she could sculpt the silk into countless images and patterns over her head. In the "Lys du Nil," for example, Fuller's costume consisted of five hundred yards of white, gossamer-thin silk, which, thanks to the batons, extended ten feet out from her body in all directions, and, according to Fuller, twenty feet in the air, over her head. An 1896 review of this performance recounts the effect of this dramatic drapery on the audience, and the toll it took on Fuller:

> There is so much of [the costume] that Miss Fuller has to run all the while just as fast as she possibly can, and also to keep her arms in swift motion at the same time, to keep the voluminous gown under control. The wands used in this dress are very long and at the very end of the dance she forms a figure of a colossal white lily, such as could have lived and flourished only in the land of Munchausen. When the big lily wilts out of sight in the last dance she returns to her dressing room and sinks panting into a big chair. . . . "Do you know," she said, "I make that lily by sheer will force? . . . Le Lys du Nil is the hardest thing that I do." (*New York Blade*, April 11, 1896)

In thus eliding her bodily contours in favor of these silken emblems, Fuller came very close to embodying the symbolists' notion of the dancer as pure poetic potential, a cryptic living metaphor to be transcribed and translated by the spectator. This is the dancer as depicted by Mallarmé in his essay "Ballets." The relevant lines are among the most quoted of all the poet's prose texts:

> The dancer is not a woman who dances, for these juxtaposed reasons that she *is not a woman*, but a metaphor resuming one of the elementary aspects of our form, sword, goblet, flower, etc. . . and that *she does not dance*, suggesting . . . with a bodily writing . . . a poem liberated from any scribe's instrument.[32]

As living metaphor, the dancer must appear to be unaware of her own art, devoid of consciousness; and this is frequently how Fuller was perceived by the artists who lionized her. Anatole France, in his preface to

10. Fuller in handpainted butterfly skirt. Bibliothèque Nationale, Paris.

Fuller's autobiography, allows that Fuller is "marvelously intelligent," but finds that she is "even more marvelously instinctive . . . [and that] it is the unconscious in her that counts" (France in Fuller ix). "Her dance" wrote Camille Mauclair, "is the flight of poetry itself" (104). Mallarmé himself referred to Fuller as a source of "unconscious or involuntary inspiration" ("ma très peu consciente ou volontairement inspiratrice,"

11. Fuller in costume for "Lys du Nil." Bibliothèque Nationale, Paris.

Oeuvres complètes 308). And even Fuller contributed to this myth of un-consciousness by publicly insisting upon the "accidental" discovery of her robe-shaping technique, attributing it to audience response instead of her own agency.[33] Fuller, her natural body suppressed ("Elle n'est pas une femme"), certainly seemed to embody Mallarmé's description of the ideal dancer. She *figured* images rather than dancing them ("Elle ne danse pas"), literalizing the idea of dancer *as* flower, for example, in her "Lys du Nil." In this piece she effaced her body to sculpt her silk robes into a gigantic lily onstage. In "La Danse du feu," her body became flame itself.

But the reasons for Fuller's appeal to a poet like Mallarmé reach well beyond her suitability as an abstract topic for *Crayonné au théâtre.* The Mallarmé who loved Loie Fuller is also the gossipy, dandyist Mallarmé of *La Dernière Mode,* the Mallarmé who loved department stores, for at her peak Fuller was not just an esoteric marvel, she was also very much the latest fashion. At moments in his essay, Mallarmé acknowledges this popular side of Fuller and defines her very specifically through "la mode" (even while insisting that true aesthetic appreciation must be extracted from the popular): "In my opinion, it was important, no matter where fashion might scatter this contemporary, miraculous blossom, to extract the meaning and the explanation that emanates from it and affects an entire art form."[34]

At the height of her career, Fuller was the very definition of the fashionable, marketing her own likeness everywhere. She sold dolls, posters, lithographs, bronze reliefs, vases, and lamps depicting her own image, the first female performing artist to mass market herself this way in France.[35] By 1900, throngs of students would regularly wait outside theaters after her performances to pelt her with flowers; and women all over Paris were wearing the "Loie Fuller skirt" (Kermode, "Loie," 11). She socialized and was photographed with celebrities, socialites, and royalty, frequenting the Vanderbilt estate, lunching with Rodin, traveling through Europe with Queen Marie of Romania. At the World's Fair of 1900, Fuller was the only artist to perform in her own pavilion, designed and built especially for her by the celebrated architect Henri Sauvage. She embodied progress, chic, and the latest technology, and became something of a symbol for this World's Fair. To investigate her position at the juncture of symbolist aesthetics, mass culture, and politics, it is worth looking more closely at Fuller's art in the context of the exhibition, which showcased the marvels of electricity alongside the wonders of the increasingly colonized Orient.

The Expo of 1900

The Ancient and the Modern

"All that interests the French about the Empire," Prime Minister Jules Ferry had once lamented, "is the belly dance" (quoted in Girardet 75). And this lack of interest, particularly among the bourgeoisie, was of particular concern to the officials with the World's Fair, of which a major purpose was to promote awareness and acceptance of the French empire, and to ally it in the public imagination with the excitement of progress and modern scientific advancement.[36] Toward this end, the fair's organizers stressed two main themes, technological wizardry and colonial expansion, joining them in a carefully planned atmosphere of mass consumption.

The fair's glorification of technology centered on the miracle of electricity, "that fairy who lights up the world like . . . Napoleon's military glory."[37] Crowds marveled at exhibitions bathed in brilliant spotlights, at the electrically propelled walkways, and at the many tricks of lighting and sound that created the magical panorama and stereorama displays. Twenty-one of the thirty-seven major attractions involved some sort of

dynamic illusion of voyage, simulating train, boat, and even hot-air bal-
loon rides. The exposition featured two museums entirely devoted to scientific advancement: Le Palais d'Eléctricité and La Galerie des Machines.

The main site of the fair's colonial promotion was the Parc du Trocadéro. Here, nineteen pavilions represented all the French colonies and
protectorates. Temples, palaces, pyramids, and huts featured scenes of
native life, using live actors as well as some electrical trompe l'oeil effects. Thanks to a "moving stereorama" in the Palace of Algeria, for example, spectators could board a ship that simulated an ocean voyage to
Oran (Fig. 12). The exhibition recreated the changing sights, sounds, and
sensations that one would experience aboard a ship, with rotating panels offering closer and closer vistas of the approaching Algerian coast.
(This exhibition was so realistic that visitors regularly grew seasick and
needed to be escorted off.) At all of the colonial exhibitions one could
purchase a multitude of native-produced items: costumed dolls, musical
instruments, artwork, food. Naturally, the exhibitioners were as familiar
as Jules Ferry with the drawing power of the "danses du ventre," and
young women performed various "Oriental" veil and belly dances
throughout all the colonial displays (Fig. 13).[38]

And so spectators at this fair could board an electrically propelled
sidewalk that would transport them back in time, to performances designed to vaunt the ancient, seductive charms of veiled dancing girls. The
striking nature of such combinations of advanced technology and "ancient" entertainments of the East—the modern West and the antique Orient—was a frequent theme in the journalistic reports of the Exposition
Universelle. Critic Charles Jean Eugène-Melchior de Vogüé, in an article
published in La Revue des deux mondes, referred to the fair's Oriental
dancing women as "those creatures without nationality or age, broken
with fatigue, who do their wiggling in a setting vaguely between the fair
at Tantah and the fair at Neuilly, between the fishmarkets of Cairo and
the boulevard just outside" (quoted in Leprun 75). Journalist Maurice
Talmeyr likened shopping at the exposition to entering "a sort of Louvre
or Bon Marché of Tyre or Baghdad" (quoted in Williams 61). And Jean
Lorrain described the multicolored lights of the exhibition as "jets and
cascades of liquid sapphires and rubies, then topazes," which transformed "the Trocadéro [into] an Orient of the Ramadan and the bazaar
. . . a gateway of Byzantium . . . Paris, city of the Orient" (Jullian, Triumph, 86).

But what was probably the clearest symbol of this peculiar melding of
old East and new West can be found in a project idea entertained but ultimately rejected by the fair's planning commission: the construction of
a giant 150-meter-high statue of a woman that would have covered the
entire upper half of the Eiffel Tower. The statue suggested was to be in

AU MARÉORAMA : LE BATEAU EN ROUTE

12. Maréorama ride at the 1900 World's Fair. Bibliothèque Nationale, Paris.

the style of Flaubert's Salammbô, in chain mail, veils, and jewels, of course, but with the additional attraction of electric projectors shining colored lights through her eyes.[39] This idea was voted down, and Salammbô was never built; but she did not need to be. Loie Fuller provided a living (if less immense) version of it.

Very much in keeping with the exposition's central motif, Fuller's performances linked the contemporary with the ancient world. She was seen as an artist from "the new world . . . in whom the soul of antiquity seems reincarnated" (R. Marx 7–8). By combining veils and flowing robes (which referred at once to the Orient and ancient Greece) with colored electric lights, she seemed to exist in two realms. Her choreography itself was also both radically new and quite ancient. Fuller modernized cabaret dance in her rejection of licentious clichés: "No more contorsions or arching, no more rotating pelvises," wrote Roger Marx. At the same time, she also rejected ballet's restrictive bodily vocabulary ("The same holds true," continued Marx, "for pointe work, *jetés*, and *entre-chats*"),

AU THÉÂTRE ÉGYPTIEN

Le Temple de la danse orientale. Pendant que les femmes fellahs marquent le rythme par des balancements de corps et des battements de mains, et que les noires Soudanaises se trémoussent en des contorsions où les épaules, les seins et la tête ne sont pas moins mis à contribution que le ventre, l'étoile, Zohara, triomphe dans la danse de la gargoulette.

13. Dancers at the Théâtre égyptien at the 1900 World's Fair. Bibliothèque Nationale, Paris.

preferring the more fluid, natural movements that eventually became the hallmark of modern dance (ibid., 12).[40] But in so revolutionizing popular dance, Fuller also returned to ancient rituals of pagan dance. To her audience, she often seemed to have returned to the dawn of the art and was compared to the dancers of "Herculaneum and Pompeii, who in mistlike robes, with ungirdled waists and sandaled feet, . . . entrance . . . the revelers of cities of the past."[41] And Fuller herself writes, "Let us endeavor to forget what is understood by [dance] today. To rediscover the primitive form of the dance, transformed into a thousand shapes that have only a very distant relationship to it, we shall have to go back to the early history of the race" (Fuller 17).

Like her technique, Fuller's repertoire was well suited to the exposition's goal of wedding contemporaneity to ancient practices, technology to colonialism. The titles of her pieces at the expo included "The Dance of the Thousand Veils," "Les Mille et une nuits," "The Serpentine,"

"The Fire of Life," "Ave Marie," and "Radium," a dance based on Pierre and Marie Curie's discoveries.[42] Inside her specially designed pavilion, Fuller danced stories ranging from the pagan to the biblical, and from the Oriental to the front page of the newspaper.

While Fuller was clearly allied with the Oriental *bayadères* who performed on the other side of the exhibition park, her performances did not take place against any specifically Oriental backdrop, since she deliberately suppressed all decor. She did not recreate a colonial site such as those seen in the fair's colonial pavilions.[43] And yet, Fuller did not eradicate the concept of locale; instead, she subsumed it with her body. Mallarmé appears sensitive to this, and at one point actually attributes to Fuller the quality of a geographical place. He describes her as "the dancer [who] acquires a virginity of undreamt-of places" ("la danseuse [qui] acquiert une virginité de site pas songé," *Oeuvres complètes* 309). Camille Mauclair uses comparable rhetoric, writing, "Loie Fuller tears us away from the destructive conflicts of everyday life and leads us to purifying dreamlands" (104). And Paul Adam writes that her performances made one dream of "returning to Eden." This image of a virginal, undreamt-of site or purifying dreamlands partakes quite manifestly of the very kind of paternalist, feminizing, and orientalist vision of the colonies that fueled and justified imperial expansion.[44] Fuller's dances transformed her into place and occupant at the same time, and so it is fully consistent that she performed in a pavilion that bore only her name. While the Ouled-Nayl troupe performed their veil dances in the Palace of Algeria, Loie Fuller performed hers in the Loie Fuller pavilion, a kingdom—or perhaps a colony—unto itself. By transforming her body into the only scenery, Fuller took the theatrical space upon her own person, "instituting a place" ("instituant un lieu"), as Mallarmé writes (*Oeuvres complètes* 309). And in so doing she gestured toward one of the most basic of colonialist motifs: the colonies as purified, prelapsarian spaces, inhabited by (and resembling somehow) female bodies.

When "Ix," columnist for *La Dernière Mode*, writes of the poetry collection entitled *Le Harem* by d'Hervilly, he suggests that the eroticism of the seraglio in this text could provide a suitable diversion for the bourgeois *lectrice*. He recommends it as a potential remedy for "those empty hours . . . those half-absences of the self to which you sometimes succumb in the afternoon" (*Oeuvres complètes* 803). "Ix" adds reassuringly that there need be no concern that this barbaric excitement might spill over from the pages into the lady's salon: "Let no startled fan flutter over this"—so long, that is, as the harem stays fixed within its book-container: "So long as it is imprisoned in its volume, this gyneceum will remain closed upon your bookshelf" (ibid.).

This recognizable scenario contains an implicit analogy between the woman and the advertised commodity. The female reader falls prey to a languorous malady that suppresses her identity; she has quasi-absences of self in the afternoon. The absent consciousness of this bourgeois woman then becomes a kind of tabula rasa upon which the poet may project his orientalizing, slightly lubricious vision. As Jennifer Wicke has observed, successful advertising requires two stages that resemble this process very closely: first, the commodity's history of production is suppressed or absented; then, a new, glamorizing narrative is offered in its place (Wicke 100).

The women considered the most readily "commodifiable" in late-nineteenth-century France were, of course, Oriental women. Malek Alloula has analyzed the prurient scrutiny and commodification of North African women in *The Colonial Harem*, his study of the thousands of French photographs of costumed (often dancing) women. He compares the women, as they appear in the photographs, to "butterflies and insects that museums of natural history and taxidermists exhibit in their glass display cases" (Alloula 92). Such display cases undoubtedly fall into the category of the nineteenth-century "glass houses" studied by Philippe Hamon. Spectators gaze into these vitrines to find some kind of affirmation or reassurance that their own identities are unfettered, that their gaze can penetrate unilaterally. In much the same way, the decorum of the bourgeois Frenchwoman is thrown into relief and reinforced when she contemplates the supposedly untamed sexuality of the Oriental woman in d'Hervilly's poetry. And of course, at the same time, this Parisian lady acquires some sense of her identity precisely by gazing into this glass case (or by discerning her own features in Baudry's painting of Salome). Loie Fuller's art takes as its starting point these orientalist mythologies and commodified images. Her performances begin with the "glass-case" scenario of which Alloula writes, but then add her interpretative twist to the familiar scene.

Like Villiers's Hadaly, or Mallarmé's *femme à la mode*, Fuller had no "natural" body when she was onstage. She suppressed her physical outline, recreating her shape through coverings of various kinds. Fuller would then mechanically reproduce likenesses of her recreated, reshaped exterior, through her mirrored images on stage and in the many likenesses marketed offstage.[45] And the narrative of the production of her commodities was certainly suppressed: her ingenious stage inventions were celebrated, carefully guarded secrets. In place of their narrative, Fuller substituted the exotic fictions of her veiled personae. In this way, the phenomenon of her art strongly resembles Mallarmé's scenarios of the matrons facing Baudry's paintings or d'Hervilly's orientalist poetry.

Seemingly afloat above the stage, reflected a hundred times in a mirror, or reproduced in countless doll faces and lamp bases, Fuller closely approaches the situation of the floating, decontextualized commodity, whose own history is suppressed.[46]

And Fuller even constructed her own technological version of Alloula's glass-museum case, for, as noted above, she danced often inside a tiny room of one-way mirrors, a vitrine of sorts. Within the glass display room, Fuller, her body obscured by yards of fabric, would transform herself into butterflies and lilies. In this, she re-enacts the process described by Alloula: she is the butterfly in the taxidermist's case—offered up for our scrutiny.

But Fuller is no mounted butterfly with pinned wings. She worked alone, and needed no d'Hervilly, no Thomas Edison, and no taxidermist for that matter. She masterminded her own orientalized commodification, draped herself in her own veils, and built her own glass box. In this, her performances dismantled and ironized the commodification process recounted by Alloula. But it is too simple to say that all this independence makes Fuller a radical or undermines the considerable commercialism of her self-presentation. Fuller was a savvy businesswoman, and even the feminist undertones of her art—its self-directed quality, its rejection of sexist cliché, its unusual mastery of science—do not necessarily permit us to read her as a progressive political figure, either in general or at the Paris Exposition of 1900.[47] Indeed, in some respects she served a highly conservative purpose, acting as patriotic emblem of an imperial government and as icon of tamed female sexuality in an era feeling menaced by a new feminist movement. At the same time, though, as we shall see later, Fuller's aesthetic does look forward to an artistic movement—camp—that would contain within it a definite sexual radicalness.

Nationalism and Yankee Ingenuity at the Fair

Fuller, it should be recalled, never took her clothes off, never gyrated, and never shocked respectable people. And although her classicized choreography marked her as a dance pioneer, it also made her something of a cabaret dancer for salon society. Her provocative otherness was blunted by her being white, by her removal of her dances from any explicit Oriental sites, and by her substitution of technology for eros. True, she was foreign in France, but hailed only from unsensual America, a country that had (and still has) a reputation for sexlessness and a kind of sanitized heartiness very removed from either Oriental or European passion.[48] Hers was the dazzle not of the body but of machinery, technology, and Yankee ingenuity. In the French imagination, Fuller's appeal was always closer to Thomas Edison's than to Josephine Baker's.[49]

"After all, the glory goes to the electrician," wrote Huysmans of Fuller's performances; "it's American" (quoted in "Loie Fuller's Glory Laid to Light," *Chicago Tribune*, January 8, 1928).

Fuller was a veil dancer who never really *un*veiled. She was so unthreatening, in fact, that the Folies-Bergère featured her dances as their very first matinee performances, trying to increase business by attracting an afternoon clientele of women and children. This decision may have had the additional benefit of boosting evening ticket sales, since, their wives' fears calmed, more husbands were free to return in the evening to enjoy raunchier fare (Jullian, *Triumph*).

That Fuller's version of the veil dance was appropriate for mixed audiences explains why she was so dramatically showcased at the exposition of 1900. The Loie Fuller Theatre had been built by the Fair Commission on the "Rue de Paris," a three-hundred-meter-long strip of twenty recreated cabaret theaters, placed at the exhibition's main entrance, on the right bank of the Seine.[50] "The administration," wrote an official with the Fair Commission, "has proposed grouping together those attractions that are most particularly Parisian and that, when placed at the entrance to the expo, before the great gates at the Place de la Concorde, will necessarily become the main route for all visitors."[51] The visitor to the Rue de Paris could choose among the Grand Guignol puppet show, the Palace of Dance, the "Théâtroscope," the "Théâtre Loie Fuller," the "House of Laughter," and the "Tableaux Vivants."[52] Fuller's theater was, therefore, among the very first attractions that most visitors encountered upon entering the imposing gates; she was also the only non-French artist on the strip. The logical path of fairgoers entering through the Porte Binet led from the Rue de Paris through the Champs de Mars, site of such travel-based attractions as the Cinéorama (which offered a filmed aerial view of Europe), onto the Quai d'Orsay, past the displays of European commerce, arts, agriculture, and navigation, and over the Pont d'Iéna to the Trocadéro's huge colonial displays. In other words, the fair was laid out so that the majority of visitors moved from the domestic, light-hearted charms of Parisian cabaret, cinema, and puppetry, through a technological fantasy of global travel, past displays of European artistic and economic accomplishment, and then on to an expansive, festive display of the just extension of these domestic successes: the imperial conquest of Africa and Asia. Virtually at the entrance to this imperial extravaganza, we find Fuller's little theater (Fig. 14).

Fuller's performances provided a whitewashed, apparently de-eroticized version of some of the more lubricious veil dances being performed across the exhibition park at the Trocadéro. She was the unassuming American at the gate, a spritely fairy, "la fée éléctricité," who turned a colonial and capitalist myth into a matinee for children, helping to im-

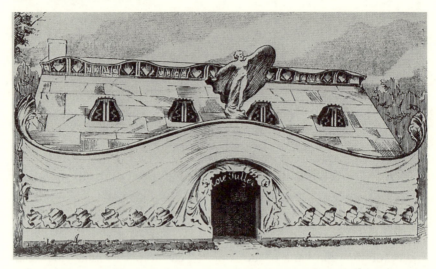

14. Drawing of Fuller's theater at the 1900 World's Fair. From Philippe Jullian, *The Triumph of Art Nouveau.*

plement the process of cultural appropriation that was a main goal of the Exposition Universelle. Fuller also probably helped defuse the menacing image that her native America had been acquiring in 1900. Fresh from a victory in the Spanish-American War of 1898, the United States was emerging as an imperialist power whose success resulted from its superior technological prowess.[53] By so aggressively coding Fuller as the "most Parisian" of entertainers, the French government may have been trying to reappropriate some of the American technological genius that they saw as key in America's imperial successes in Cuba, Guam, and Puerto Rico.[54]

Loie Fuller, Art Nouveau Icon

Fuller's art dovetailed with still another aspect of the exhibition's aestheticized nationalism: its grand-scale promotion of Art Nouveau. By making a pageant of this commercially popular arts-and-crafts-based movement, the French advertised their achievements in commerce and international trade, but they also accomplished other political goals. It has been convincingly argued that Art Nouveau's insistent iconography of the gentle, maternal woman, goddess of the home interior, participated in a conservative backlash against an incipient French feminist movement. Fuller's stylized performances have been consistently described as the one of the World's Fair's clearest displays of Art Nouveau, and in many respects, they indeed embodied the movement's most basic visual qualities.

Art Nouveau originated in the 1890s, partly as an official initiative for design reform, with the goal of finding a distinctively French modern style. Although it spread to many other countries in Europe, Art Nouveau's institutional base remained Paris's Union Centrale des Arts Décoratifs.[55] The Central Union, which included artists, republican politicians, and even some neuropsychiatrists, defined modern style as a combination of rococo craftsmanship and a kind of biologism that reflected science's growing understanding of the interior labyrinth of the human body. Art Nouveau iconography found expression most often in small items of jewelry and home decor, such as pottery in organic forms, jewelry in the shape of insects or reptiles, gilded, curvilinear salon chairs, or lamps molded in the form of women.[56] It relied upon antihistorical decorative motifs, such as "whiplash lines, vegetable curves, female hair, peacocks, sea weeds, lily pads and swans" (Mandell 74). Since the preferred setting for Art Nouveau objects was the domestic interior, part of the World's Fair promotion of this style included a "model home" decorated entirely in Art Nouveau furnishings. The "Maison Bing," as it was called (after wealthy antique dealer and Art Nouveau patron Siegfried Bing), was prominently featured on the fair's Esplanade des Invalides and consisted of six fully decorated rooms, each displaying the work of the most exclusive ateliers in France. The house's furniture, jewelry, tapestries, rugs, and wallpaper were all custom-made by the most prominent artisans of the day according to Siegfried Bing's direction.[57]

The Central Union and Art Nouveau emphasized particularly the feminine nature of the home interior, showcasing women as both the inspiration and the consumers (and sometimes even the artists) of modern style. An example of this feminizing of crafts can be seen in the work of painter and engraver Georges de Feure. De Feure was responsible for the boudoir and the *cabinet de toilette* in the Maison Bing, furnishing these rooms lavishly with silk tapestries and gilded screens. Visitors to the pavilion were struck by the particularly feminine nature de Feure imparted to his designs, visible, for example, in walls adorned with "dream-like rosettes . . . in dawn and twilight shades" (Silverman, *Art Nouveau*, 287). Art historian Debora Silverman describes de Feure as "preoccupied with women and with the theme of the *femme-fleur* that was central to modern organic craftsmen" (ibid., 288).[58]

Obviously, the "femme-fleur" is not a politically neutral image; it suggests, as does so much Art Nouveau imagery, a purely decorative female body, prettified but insubstantial, sexual but only florally so, not corporeally. This aesthetic evacuation of female bodiliness may well have been a reaction to the era's general discomfort with the burgeoning feminist movement. Both the Central Union of Decorative Arts and the related Art Nouveau owed a degree of their growth to French government support; and the government was uneasy with women's struggle for independence. The reactionary subtext of Art Nouveau's alliance of women, the home, and the crafts industry emerges in the following, taken from a statement by Louis de Fourcaud, publicist for the Central Union, and professor of aesthetics at the Ecole des Beaux-Arts:

> A woman excels at small tasks no matter how minute as long as they require nimble hands. She is a born upholsterer, seamstress, refined decorator of intimate space, an inexhaustible orchestrator of worldly elegance. For everything else, her lofty function is to be an inspiration, even when she does not know it. (Quoted in Silverman, "The New Woman," 152)

This passage bespeaks more than one kind of social anxiety. In addition to the obvious wish to confine women to the restrictions of home and distaff, de Fourcaud expresses a desire to preserve not only the human, but also the elite, upper-class touch in industry, and a need to remember the individual artisan, whose work was increasingly rare and expensive. And these were, in fact, two issues on the Central Union's agenda: the repersonalization of French style and exports, and the aesthetic redomestication of the ever more liberated (and therefore less decorative) French woman.

At the 1900 Exposition Universelle, state officials strove to market an image of French products and style as rare, precious, and femininely beautiful. The statue of *La Parisienne* that topped the Porte Binet at the entrance to the exhibition park depicted a calm, smiling woman, wearing a fashionable dress designed by the noted couturier M. Pacquin, and meant to convey immediately this link between industry, the arts, and femininity. Officials at the exhibition sought to portray France's industrial products as the lovingly hand-polished works of noble craftsmen. The dehumanizing reality of mass production and the concerns of the increasing number of factory workers were brushed aside in favor of this romanticizing celebration of the individual craftsman.

Along with this apotheosizing of the (obsolescent) craftsworker, the World's Fair promoted a version of womanhood that was also losing its relevance in France. The 1890s had been, of course, a decade of feminist struggles and successes, the era of *la femme nouvelle*. As an increasing number of "New Women" entered the work force, obtained university degrees, and joined labor unions, the hostility toward them grew. Space does not permit a thorough discussion of this issue here, but a shorthand fashion of evoking this hostility toward Belle Epoque feminism is to recall the frequent satires of the "feminist." The parodied New Woman was routinely depicted dressed in bloomers, riding a bicycle, carrying a gun, or grotesquely chomping on a cigar. In cartoons, she was often seen admonishing a cowering, emasculated husband.[59]

The beatified female icon of Art Nouveau and the World's Fair offered a reassuring alternative to the offensive *femme nouvelle*. Art Nouveau's version of femininity responded to a fear that feminism or gender equality would combine with an industrialized, leveled, and highly technological society "to lead to sensual impoverishment and a de-aestheticized female" (Silverman, "The New Woman," 150). Silverman sees the concentration on the woman as queen and artist of the interior as a version of what was called "familial feminism," a less radical brand of feminism whose adherents included many society women. Familial feminism embraced the notion of "separate but equal" spheres for men and women, reaffirming a sexual division of labor, and glorifying such feminine virtues as motherhood, housekeeping, and interior decorating.[60] *La femme au foyer* was the female counterpart of the old-style artisan; and since they represented corrective images for threatening realities, both figures attracted considerable attention at the World's Fair of 1900.

It is not difficult to see the many Art Nouveau features of Loie Fuller's exhibition at the World's Fair. Even a glance at her theater reveals its affiliation with Art Nouveau principles. Fuller's pavilion was designed to appear covered by a "stage curtain." This concrete curtain dipped and swirled around the building's entrance, and echoed the forms of the draperies that skimmed Fuller's own body. Into this "curtain," architect Henri Sauvage had sculpted curling bunches of gathered material that appeared to ripple at the bottom. The entrance to the building itself was low and cavelike; above it was perched a statue of "La Loie" in all her veils. The pavilion thus proclaimed its alliance with several quintessentially Art Nouveau themes. The standard, squared lines of the main part of the building combined with the femininely curved, undulating exterior curtain to form the recognizable Art Nouveau motif of intermingled inorganic and organic forms. The cavernlike aspect of the entrance partook of the movement's emphasis upon forest or undersea themes. And the female statue above the entrance, with its flowing hair and drapery, is a veritable trademark of Art Nouveau architecture.

Inside the pavilion, Fuller's dances also echoed much of the fair's surrounding Art Nouveau. Her re-enactment of orchids and lilies blowing in the wind, for example, recalled the omnipresent "femme-fleur" motif. Her butterfly, fire, and undersea dances were all versions of Art Nouveau's typical blending of fantasy and the organic. And in general, Fuller's consistent reliance upon the spectacle of the transfigured self allied her unmistakably with the "themes of metamorphosis which characterized the work of . . . Art Nouveau" (Silverman, *Art Nouveau*, 299).

In Debora Silverman's opinion, Fuller's "romantic biologism" makes her "the [embodiment] of the ideals of Art Nouveau" (ibid.).

But though Silverman correctly reads Fuller's close alliance with Art Nouveau, she ignores the ways in which her performances conflicted with or subverted the genre.[61] Art Nouveau celebrated woman as the decorative treasure of the familial, domestic interior; and it is true that onstage, Fuller presented herself as the lone bedraped female occupant of a glass-paned enclosure, an interior space, certainly. But while Fuller's interiors referred clearly to shop windows or display cases, they did not ever partake of Art Nouveau's idealized domesticity.[62]

Fuller could never have been confused with Jules Bois's dream of the *femme familiale* or *femme sociale*.[63] And she staged quite a remarkable rejection of "home" and traditional female skills, for Fuller positioned herself squarely on the side of technology, mass production, and the workplace. Hers was an act based upon the infinite reproducibility of the image, not the rare beauty of a unique original. Spectators at the Loie Fuller Pavilion came to watch the work of a known mechanical genius. Her body was not the calm, maternal, biologic entity of Art Nouveau. It was lit electrically, mirrored in countless whirling reflections around her stage, and reproduced many times over in lamps and other such memorabilia on sale in the lobby of her theater.[64] (It was also well known that Fuller ran her rehearsal studio not like an artisan's studio but like a highly organized factory, demonstrating technical virtuosity that astounded the male technicians who worked under her direction [Harris].)

Another factor that distanced Fuller from the classic conception of an Art Nouveau heroine was her offstage persona. As one of the earliest celebrities in the contemporary sense of the word, Loie Fuller owed her success not only to her onstage artistry but also to the publicly disseminated narrative of her "private" life, since "stardom proper arises when the offstage . . . life of the actor becomes as important as the performed role" (Gledhill 213).[65]

Throughout her career in Europe, even during her early years in Paris, the offstage Loie Fuller seemed somewhat frumpy to the general public. Although a vision of great beauty onstage, offstage she was visibly plump, kept her hair in a matronly bun, and wore dowdy clothes and small round spectacles. She spoke French badly with a strong American accent, and was seen most often in the company of her aged mother. Reviews and interviews stress the "admirable naivete of her heart," and her "magnificent innocence of imagination." Naturally, her American nationality only added to this whitewashed view. One contemporary review described Fuller as a "chaste dancer who lives surrounded by her family; and like a typical American, is of an extremely practical nature" (H.C. 109). Journalists found her demeanor and conversation far less compelling than her glamorous onstage presentation. One reporter sarcastically remarked that "Madame Fuller's conversation would be of extreme interest to an electrician" (De Ménasce 1). In other words, consciously or not, Fuller cultivated an offstage image somewhere between a Disney character and Grandma Moses. And while this slightly plodding image would not necessarily change the audience's perception of Fuller's onstage performances, it might well have influenced their overall view of her. There was simply too great a disjunction between her offstage and onstage personae for Fuller to embody seamlessly the Art Nouveau princess role that critics have assigned her.

A classic piece of Art Nouveau iconography will help put Fuller's relationship to this movement into relief. In 1895, sculptor Louis Ernest Barrias exhibited a work entitled "La Nature se dévoilant devant la science" (Fig. 15). The statue depicts a young woman lifting flowing drapery from her body. Her breasts have already been freed of their veils, and her hands are poised in mid-air, in the act of lifting the rest. Her eyes are lowered demurely.[66] The implications of this figure are clear. "Science" is elsewhere, the unseen, knowledgeable male presence gazing upon this nude spectacle, and causing her to disrobe. The woman, submissive object of this inquiring gaze, is ignorant of the mysterious secrets within her that will be revealed. She represents pure biology, passive unconsciousness.

Unlike Barrias's feminized "Nature," Fuller had no natural, delineated self when onstage; the lines of her body were never part of her act. She never disrobed, either totally or partially, and her veils were not used for titillation. On the contrary, Fuller harnessed science quite spectacularly to stage an endless *re*-robing of her body. While she may have choreographed for herself a position as specimen in a glass case, it was clear to all who watched that Fuller's eyes were never cast downward. She was, at all moments, in control of very impressive scientific machinery. Science was not elsewhere; it was incorporated into her very body.

Fuller's sexuality, furthermore, was far more complex than Nature's in Barrias's sculpture. It was not available for prurient enjoyment. Her breasts promised neither sexual pleasure to men nor the possibility of maternity. In fact, Fuller had an androgynous quality that allied her with the male dandies who were fascinated by her, men like Jean Lorrain, Jules Renard, Huysmans, and even Mallarmé to a certain extent. The dandy stages the appropriation of some attributes considered feminine. Fuller, in her performances, staged the appropriation of qualities that, if not exactly masculine, were clearly not the "feminine" virtues expected of a cabaret dancer. The well-informed, high cultural artists who particularly revered her, furthermore, knew that she lived openly as a lesbian, with a lover—Gabrielle Bloch[67]—who wore only men's suits. It is to this ambiguity of gender and its relation to camp that I now turn.

15. *La nature se dévoilant devant la science*, by Louis Ernest Barrias, 1895. Musée d'Orsay, Paris.

LOIE AS PROTO-CAMP QUEEN

Camp . . . [is] dandyism in the age of mass culture. It makes no distinctions between the unique object and the mass-produced object. Camp taste transcends
the nausea of the replica. . . . Camp is the glorification of 'character.' The statement is of no importance—except of course, to the person (Loie Fuller, Gaudí,
Cecil B. De Mille, Crinelli, de Gaulle, etc.) who makes it. (Sontag 278–80)

The quality shared by all the figures mentioned by Susan Sontag is that
none was considered "campy" during his or her own time. Gaudí did not
understand his architecture to be camp, and de Gaulle did not think of
himself as a campy military leader. What makes these individuals campy
is the great disparity between the seriousness with which they took themselves and their work and the irony with which we can look at them
now.[68] Camp demands this doubleness, this tension between ostensible
intention and perceived effect.[69]

However, the doubleness necessary for camp does not need to come
only from a temporal distance, as in Sontag's examples. Camp occurs
whenever a personality or a work of art exists in two realms simultaneously, and these realms can include the aesthetic and the sexual, as well
as the temporal. If a certain group of spectators, a cognoscenti, can recognize the second realm of significance, then camp is possible. Camp,
furthermore, can be intentional or unintentional. Drag is almost by definition intentional camp; but old John Wayne films are unintentional
camp. John Wayne becomes campy when a particular audience views his
elaborately constructed film persona in relation to ironic gay male re-
constructions of swaggering masculinity.[70] Under this new gaze, Wayne's
performances telegraph both an earnest, heroic, American heterosexuality and an exaggerated, nearly drag machismo.

The study of camp has become something of a political battleground,
with the main issue being whether camp is exclusively queer. Since its beginning—arguably around the turn of the nineteenth century—camp has
been associated with a gay sensibility and countercultural discourse.
With the goal of uncovering culture's constant, insidious process of nat-
uralizing normative desire, camp puts on a grand show of denaturalized
desire and gender. Since 1964, however, when Sontag published her now-
famous "Notes on Camp," the term has expanded to include a broader,
less politicized meaning. Sontag's essay seemed to authorize the use of
"camp" as an adjective for objects, artworks, and styles seen merely as
ironic—to be appreciated for their retro charm, their nostalgia, or their
flamboyance—but not necessarily as political gestures. "Notes on
Camp," it has been argued, allowed camp culture to shade off into pop

culture. In a recent, manifestolike essay, Moe Meyer has lamented what he calls "Sontag's appropriation" of camp, which "banished the queer from discourse, substituting instead an unqueer bourgeois subject under the banner of pop." "It is this changeling," writes Meyer, "that transformed Camp into [an] apolitical badge" (10). Meyer, and others, want to reclaim a politics of camp,[71] to establish it as an agent of "the production of queer social visibility" (ibid., 11).

Camp's doubleness is both social and sexual. It is queer, but not always. It is radical, but sometimes it is commercial.[72] It is for a select few, and it is available to the general public. Loie Fuller's art very much follows this paradigm and is situated within the doubleness of camp. Her androgyny, her revamping of old motifs of femininity, her middle-aged matronliness veiled beneath her "Salome" persona, all these contradictions were yoked together by the sheer, startling force of her personality. Fuller was a famous dancer who did not actually dance all that well. She was weightless "femme-fleur" and plump, eccentric inventor. She was France's beloved "fée élécricité" but came from Illinois. She was a symbolist vision for high cultural artists and a star known to the mass audiences of Europe. She was "chaste," "correct,"[73] and "sans coquetterie érotique,"[74] and an "out" lesbian.

But was Loie Fuller actually camp? A recent article by Emily Apter addresses some of the issues at stake in this question. In "Acting Out Orientalism," Apter makes explicit the important connection between the fin de siècle's lesbian aesthetic and orientalism. "What allowed turn-of-the-century French gay and lesbian sexual identity to perform itself . . . was its mediation by the culturally exotic stereotype" (103). Apter studies fin-de-siècle versions of Oriental heroines such as Cleopatra, Sémiramis, and Scheherazade and looks at the relationship between the extravagance of these characters and the lesbianism of some of the women who played them, such as Colette (in Rêves d'Egypte) or dancer Ida Rubenstein (who appeared in Fokine's Cléopâtre and his Schéhérazade). "Orientalism," Apter writes,

> evolved into feminist and lesbian camp. . . . Not only were women empowered . . . through association with the dominatrix characterologies attached to exemplary princesses, queens, seductresses or women leaders of the East, but more interestingly, their agency was enhanced by "being" these avatars both on stage and off. . . . [These women] expanded the performative parameters of the historic stereotype by moving their larger-than-life thespian personas into the choreography of everyday life. They received their admirers and lovers "at home" dressed à l'Orientale (much like Flaubert's Rosanette, or Proust's Odette), enlivened private theatricals with Egyptiana, and hosted high society versions of fêtes arabes (as in Paul Poirot's 1911 Thousand and Second Night bash, the turn-of-the-century counterpart of Forbes's Morocco party). (109)

There is, of course, an important relationship between the fantastic excesses of orientalist decadence and the "performance" of homosexuality. As such queer-studies critics as Eve Sedgwick, Richard Dyer, and Wayne Koestenbaum have demonstrated, a long history of "passing" for straight, of existing in two roles simultaneously, has given the gay community a particular affinity for theatricality or masquerade.[75] Loie Fuller, however, was not performing queerness "coded" as orientalism. She was lesbian, but this was not overtly incorporated into her art (despite the potentially butch overtones of her mechanical craftsmanship and the sapphic implications of her exclusively female dance troupe, orchestra, staff, and household). Furthermore, the offstage element described by Apter, the enactment of orientalist camp in the performers' personal life, is absent in Fuller's case.

By defining camp as she does, and placing Loie Fuller's name on her list of camp artists, Susan Sontag offers a helpful description of the shift created by the confrontation of the dandy and mass culture. Fuller's dances, her mechanical revolution in stagecraft, and her historical and aesthetic context provide rich ground for an exploration of this shift to a self-conscious indulgence in mass culture. Fuller can be said to *enact* this shift, to perform its process. But in the end, it is only in retrospect that Loie Fuller can be considered camp. One might say that she assembled all the ingredients of the new camp aesthetic without actually cooking them into a final product.

If Fuller enacted the shift from dandyism to camp, it was Oscar Wilde, the quintessential modern dandy, who announced its completion. Wilde, who may have had the occasion to attend a performance by Fuller, appropriated the decadents' much-worked-over motif of Salome and her Dance of the Seven Veils. His Salome is a princess, in some respects, as modern or as "mass cultural" as Loie Fuller's. His play, while unmistakably paying homage to such precursors as Mallarmé and Flaubert, takes fully into account the cultural presence of Fuller, the mediatic Salome, and all that she implies. In writing *Salomé*, Wilde took on, and brilliantly executed, the task of revising a cliché of the nineteenth century, bringing it into the age of the media personality.

Chapter Five

CAMP SALOME: OSCAR WILDE'S
CIRCLES OF DESIRE

CLOUDING DISTINCTIONS

As an "electric salome," Loie Fuller invented a new, iconic celebrity, subverting dandyism and reconfiguring the nineteenth century's hackneyed Salome motif. As we saw, her brand of performance art also heralded the camp aesthetic. (Jean Lorrain proved sensitive to this in his review of Fuller's "Salomé," where he described her as dancing with "the grace of an English boxer and the physique of Oscar Wilde. . . . A Salome for Yankee drunkards" [*Poussières de Paris* 143–44].) Like Fuller, Oscar Wilde borrowed from decadent literary conventions for his version of Salome—but with a different result. Refashioning this biblical legend as drama, Wilde luxuriated in the jeweled, orientalist prose of the French decadents he so admired. Then, using their language, he told the story of the demise of their aesthetic, announcing the emergence of his own modern and unambiguously camp revision of it.

While Loie Fuller's stardom depended upon the public, double narratives of her on- and offstage personae, those narratives always remained distinct and separate. (She was both weightless electricity fairy *and* dowdy matron.) This disparity represents one of the reasons why Fuller's art does not yet exemplify a fully camp aesthetic. Fuller was campy only in retrospect, only unconsciously. For Wilde, on the other hand, the on- and offstage—or literary and extraliterary—narratives were identical. Wilde infused his work at every level with the flavor and texture of his personal life, a life that was already a self-promoting, media-driven camp extravaganza.[1]

Wilde's entire oeuvre is dedicated precisely to collapsing distinctions between private and public, life and work, artist and celebrity. And his only work in a foreign language, *Salomé*, offers a particularly rich opportunity to examine the author's fascination with the blurring of boundaries. Historically, literarily, linguistically, and dramatically, the play enacts and comments upon this phenomenon and the resultant transition to modern spectacles and modern stardom.

Salomé takes the familiar late-nineteenth-century scenario of dangerous performing woman and desirous male spectator and dissolves it from within. Wilde allows the sharp outlines of the roles to melt into the entire text, blurring the individuality of the characters, eventually embracing and implicating the whole audience in a pageant of transgressive desire. In this way, the text turns the spectator dandy into a full-fledged, participatory member of the audience he used to keep at bay, stripping away his self-containment, and dismantling what remains of the distinction between private secrets and public truths.

Salomé is a carefully designed, melodic text whose linguistic and thematic structures recreate and reinforce the play's overarching effect. Repetitive, incantatory dialogue appears and reappears in the mouths of different characters who never seem entirely aware of the shared, enchained nature of their speech.[2] Wilde grants such importance to the floating, unifying language here that he winds up drastically reducing the importance of any individual characters: Herod comes to resemble Salome, who comes to resemble Jokanaan. By extension, the audience comes to resemble the characters onstage.

Earlier decadent works that deal with the Salome story (or the many variations of it) exhibit a series of recognizable elements: lengthy descriptions of precious objects, the prizing of a superior male knowledge, the moribundity and absent consciousness of the performing woman. Wilde takes these well-known elements and uses them to expose what Eve Sedgwick might call "open secrets."[3] He both lays bare the relationship that has always existed between aestheticized commodity fetishism and homosexual desire, and explores the ultimate impossibility of clearly delineating and restricting desire and ownership. Wilde consistently undermines exclusive possession of or dominion over riches, a love object, personality, language, or even one's own gaze. In *Salomé*, all are subsumed by the chorus and the crowd. The rarified is no longer set off from the common. Wilde flings open the door to a highly ornate closet, and the surprise is that we are all inside it.

THE SALOME LEGEND: SOME BACKGROUND

The Bible

It is not difficult to imagine the reasons why the two brief biblical passages devoted to Salome have held such fascination for artists of all centuries:[4]

> But when Herod's birthday was kept, the daughter of Herodias danced before them, and pleased Herod. Whereupon he promised with an oath to give her whatsoever she would ask. And she, being before instructed of her mother, said, Give me here John Baptist's head in a charger. And the king was sorry: nevertheless for the oath's sake, and them which sat with him at meat, he com-

manded it to be given her. And he sent, and beheaded John in the prison. And his head was brought in a charger, and given to the damsel: and she took it to her mother. And his disciples came, and took up the body, and buried it, and went and told Jesus. (Matthew 14:6–12, King James Version)

For John had said unto Herod, It is not lawful for thee to have thy brother's wife. Therefore Herodias had a quarrel against him, and would have killed him; but she could not: For Herod feared John, knowing that he was a just man and holy, and observed him; and when he heard him, he did many things, and heard him gladly. And when a convenient day was come, that Herod on his birthday made a supper to his lords, high captains, and chief estates of Galilee; And when the daughter of the said Herodias came in, and danced, and pleased Herod and them that sat with him, the king said unto the damsel, Ask of me whatsoever thou wilt, and I will give it thee. And he sware unto her, Whatsoever thou shalt ask of me, I will give it thee, unto the half of my kingdom. And she went forth, and said unto her mother, What shall I ask? and she said, The head of John the Baptist. And she came in straightway with haste unto the king, and asked saying, I will that thou give me by and by in a charger the head of John the Baptist. And the king was exceeding sorry; yet for his oath's sake, and for their sakes which sat with him, he would not reject her. And immediately the king sent an executioner, and commanded his head to be brought: and he went and beheaded him in prison. And brought his head in a charger, and gave it to the damsel: and the damsel gave it to her mother. And when his disciples heard to it, they came and took up his corpse, and laid it in a tomb. (Mark 6:18–29, King James Version)

To begin with, the peculiar sketchiness of the story provokes the imagination.[5] Neither Matthew nor Mark mentions the name of the girl whose dance entertains the noblemen gathered to celebrate Herod's birthday; we know only that she is the daughter of Herodias.[6] And neither Matthew nor Mark offers any description of her actual performance. We have, then, a nameless princess who performs an unnarrated dance and brings about the decapitation of John the Baptist, a murder of monumental importance. The text cries out for elaboration. Who is this girl? What kind of dance was this? What was the relationship between the princess and Herod? The story of Salome invites the interpreter to enter the biblical narrative. It beckons enticingly to the artist to insert his own vision of the events.[7]

But not only is the Salome story something of a mystery, it is a striking biblical anomaly as well; and this further contributes to its appeal. The episode is unique for its folktale flavor, and startling in its context. Unlike any other biblical story, it has the feeling of an entertainment, a diversionary episode inserted as a respite between more sober accounts, as a kind of passage from one to the other.[8] Herod's feast adds to the tale's anomalous and ludic quality, for a lavish birthday celebration featuring a dancer is an imitation of a pagan Greek practice. Herod's self-indulgence marks him as worldly and covetous, and distinguishes him sharply from John the Baptist and Christ (*Interpreter's Bible* 426).

Also anomalous in this account is its "flashback" quality; John the Baptist's death has already been announced earlier in both Matthew and Mark. The attribution of guilt to Herod's court represents an uncharacteristic retracing of the biblical narrative. Frank Kermode compares the Marcan account of John the Baptist's death to the "famous flashback in *Odyssey* xix when, into the story of how Euryclea recognized Odysseus, there is interpolated a long narrative of the boar hunt at which many years earlier the hero got his telltale scar" (*Genesis* 127).

The Nineteenth-Century Salome

Since the Salome episode has, therefore, already announced its own partial detachment from its context, for an artist, composer or painter to elaborate upon it seems less of a transgression. It is especially easy to see Salome's particularly fin-de-siècle appeal.[9] In certain respects, she is the embodiment of the symbolist ideal: her suppressed name lends her mystery; she is aristocratic, a princess; she speaks to no one; and she only performs her dance privately, for noblemen. These privileged few, feasting within the palace walls, stand in opposition to the crowds of discontented poor outside who have been following the Baptist's preachings.

And of course, Salome has the makings of the quintessential femme fatale: a seductress whose single performance can bring about monstrous death and destruction. The story offers an originary narrative for countless nineteenth-century scenarios of male ruin at the hands (or feet) of a beautiful performer. The ruminations of Huysmans's Des Esseintes before Moreau's two masterpieces offer the best example of how Salome fits into the decadent aesthetic of the performing woman. Des Esseintes expresses the artist's desire to expatiate on the cryptic suggestions of the Bible, and himself experiences a kind of mimetic desire for the princess, putting himself in the king's position.

> For years Des Esseintes had been obsessed with this type of Salome, who so haunted artists and poets. . . . None of the apostles, not Saint Matthew, Saint Mark, or Saint Luke had written of her delirious appeal, or of the wild depravity of this dancing girl. She remained effaced, lost, mysteriously eclipsed in the far-off haze of past centuries.
>
> Like the old king, Des Esseintes stood crushed, annihilated, close to vertigo, before this dancer. (Huysmans, *A Rebours*, 87–89)

The critics who have written of the nineteenth-century Salome have nearly all agreed that she is a lyrical, idealized figure, and that her mute dance represents the transformative power of literary and aesthetic creation.[10] Françoise Meltzer stresses that the nineteenth-century resurgence of the Salome legend is purely poetic, stripped of any other significance: "The nineteenth-century [Salome] has lost all of her political and historical meaning, symbolizing rather the pure ideal of great beauty without scruples, without restraint, with cruel indifference" (*Salome* 16).

Meltzer refers here to the detachment of Salome from her biblical context. And it is certainly true that the aestheticized retelling of Salome reduces the importance of the power struggle between Herod and John, the history of the marriage of Herod and Herodias,[11] and the mission of Christ's twelve apostles. But this is not to say that the power of these aspects of the biblical story does not come into play at some level, making its presence felt subtly in the many renditions of the tale. In fact, some versions of Salome during this period gesture toward certain nineteenth-century political events that themselves resemble the biblical events that make up the tale's context. Indeed, it is possible that the underplaying of the New Testament history, to which Meltzer refers, results merely from the displacement of that history by some very strong contemporary cultural and historical valences. The nineteenth-century situation, so often depicted in literature, of an encroaching, massified culture that threatens to invade and overturn the privileged enclave of the elite finds an unmistakable analogy in the story surrounding Herod the Tetrarch. Outside of the palace, throngs follow the preachings of Jesus and the apostles. These crowds, who have heard John's announcement of the messiah, are waiting just beyond Herod's walls. Being composed largely of the discontented poor, the crowds are defined in opposition to Herod's royal court. John's promise of an imminent kingdom of God offers them hope, and holds distinctly "revolutionary implications for the zealots as well as for the majority of the lower classes" (A.H.M. Jones 181). And although Salome's dance appears to be a private diversion for noblemen, it brings, in fact, the blood of this leader of crowds right into the palace, and onto a reluctant Herod's hands. In other words, a seemingly harmless entertainment for the privileged few ends by entering into direct and bloody contact with the representative of potentially revolutionary crowds of the lower classes. The inner sanctum begins to dissolve into the outer masses. This is an element of the story that will prove particularly useful to Wilde.

Although he writes exclusively of the biblical text and not of the nineteenth-century refashioning of it, René Girard analyzes Salome in a manner that underscores the story's suitability as an allegory for nineteenth-century political events. Viewing the tale as a study in ritualistic behavior, Girard interprets Salome's performance as a trigger that sets off the irrational behavior of a group: "The guests are on the verge of being possessed by Salome, of a collective trance. . . . The dance does not abolish but exacerbates desire: it accelerates mimetic contagion and substitution" (Girard 321). The dance and what ensues create what Girard calls a "mimetic crisis," in which "cultural institutions dissolve and are returned to the mob" (ibid.). Girard's description of the scene in Herod's palace strongly resembles Gustave Le Bon's explanation of how charismatic performers hypnotize crowds and lead them to bestial actions, mirroring what happens in the political arena when leaders pander to the basest crowd instincts:

> It is in the cabaret, through affirmation, repetition, and contagion that the current beliefs of workers are formed . . . after being spread throughout the popular classes, this contagion moves to the upper levels of society . . . the sentiment provoked is inexplicable . . . but it must be similar to that fascination experienced by hypnotized subjects. (116–18)

In Girard's opinion, Salome's dance does not simply augur the downfall of a privileged world, it actually incites the elite few to behave like the masses. In this reading, Salome resembles John the Baptist; both entrance crowds, both have personalities that magnetize.

Girard's analysis illuminates the connection between the Salome legend and nineteenth-century crowd politics. It brings out the element of the story that allies it most closely with the modern phenomenon described by Le Bon. Girard focuses on and draws out of the legend the implied power of the pressure of the crowds on both sides of the palace walls. He sees in Salome an entertainer whose power over a group resembles the power of a charismatic leader over a revolutionary mob, or that of a compelling performer over her entranced audience. In Girard's reading, Salome might be General Boulanger or Sarah Bernhardt. And the aspects of the biblical story that lead him to such an analysis are some of the very aspects that lured nineteenth-century artists back time and again to this particular interlude in the New Testament.

Of course, it was not only class privileges under siege during the mid- to late nineteenth century. Masculine privilege was being similarly attacked. Taking into account the burgeoning women's movement of the period, many critics have seen the fin-de-siècle Salome as either an emblematic feminist heroine, a strong woman who uses her seductive powers to bring a ruler to his knees, or as a misogynist portrayal of the New Woman, a grotesque, masculinized virago who threatens all around her, and whose appeal only leads to mutilation.[12]

WILDE'S REINTERPRETATION

In writing his own *Salomé*, Oscar Wilde takes all of her cultural reso-
nances into account: symbolist and decadent heroine, allegorical bearer
of the threat of the masses, heroic emblem, and grotesque parody of the
New Woman. But Wilde's Salome differs from her earlier sisters. Rather
than dancing for an elite audience that defines itself against the crowds,
and through the esoteric vision of a male spectator, Wilde's princess
loses herself in the crowd. She becomes a voice in a chorus, rather than
a mute symbol. *Salomé* treats, of course, many of the same issues that
held the attention of Wilde's predecessors; but while he certainly acknowledges his indebtedness to Mallarmé and Flaubert in particular, he
then moves on.[13] When comparing Wilde's *Salomé* to Mallarmé's *Hérodiade*, it is helpful to remember that the latter was also intended for the
stage, although it was never performed. Mallarmé wanted to write a
drama that would be performed publicly, but he abandoned this project. Not even his much later *Noces d'Hérodiade* was ever produced.[14]
Mallarmé may never really have wanted to address directly any audience larger than his regular Tuesday salon. Indeed, when Mallarmé's
close friend Whistler learned of Wilde's plan to write of Salome, he advised Mallarmé against even speaking to Wilde. In an exaggeration of
the elitist clannishness typical of Mallarmé's intellectual circle, Whistler
warned the poet against "fatal familiarity," instructing him to "hold on
to the pearls" ("serrer les perles," quoted in Ellmann, *Oscar Wilde*,
370), by which he presumably meant that Mallarmé should avoid helping a literary rival, and show no work to Wilde. Although Mallarmé
himself never expressed such petty resentment of Wilde, the phrase
"serrer les perles" nonetheless evokes an essential difference between
the two writers. While Mallarmé's Salome would always remain
"under a heavy prison of jewels and iron . . . / . . . dreaming of exile"
("sous la lourde prison de pierres et de fer . . . / . . . rêvant des exils,"
Oeuvres complètes 44), a gemstone locked away, Wilde's was a pearl
meant to be cast, if not before swine, certainly before a crowd.[15] *Salomé* was meant to explode outward, a pageant to be seen and appreciated by many. It would be inconceivable to think of *Salomé* as so
many "perles serrées." Wilde could imagine *Salomé* only as a public
performance, a spectacle that would have a powerful connection to its
audience. He did not separate his conception of the text from his ideas
for its performance. In fact, the play was inspired, in part, by some of
the great female performers of Wilde's day, women who fascinated him,
particularly Sarah Bernhardt,[16] but Eleanora Duse and possibly Loie
Fuller as well.[17]

The Text

Wilde's *Salomé* is unique among his works. A drama, it is nonetheless reminiscent of a symbolist prose poem; and, of course, it is in French.[18] The quintessential mass-culture dandy, Wilde wrote *Salomé* as something of a dialogue with an audience. But to understand and explore any of the extratextual aspects of the play, it will be necessary to look at the text itself. Wilde, in fact, structures the play so that its eventual effect upon and commentary about the audience merely extends effects produced within the text itself.

As I noted earlier, Wilde's major alteration of the Salome legend was his melding into the entire play and all its characters what were hitherto characteristics exclusively of the princess and her dance. A glance back to the decadents' aesthetic of the *femme-artiste*, and of Salome in particular, is in order here. Ross Chambers offers an apt synopsis when he writes of the myth of the actress, whom he calls "a writing to be looked at" ("une écriture qu'on regarde," "L'Ange" 469). In this literature, the dancer and her dance stand for pure mimesis, and the creative process itself. The artist relies on this nonverbal writing for inspiration; he adds his words to the blank, gestural poem provided by the woman. Wilde's *Salomé* shatters this relationship; the dancer and the spectator lose their privileged places. Here, all the play's characters—not just two—act out a single, shared mimetic process, their words echoing with an eerie repetitiveness. It almost ceases to matter who is speaking, since the dialogue seems to live an independent life, detached from speakers' individual motives or psychology.

This peculiar enchained repetitiveness in Wilde's dialogue resonates particularly clearly through the words of Salome, Herod, and his soldiers. As the play opens, a young Syrian soldier—Narraboth—speaks to one of Herodias's pages of his love for Salome:

> *The Young Syrian*: How beautiful is the Princess Salomé to-night!
> *The Page of Herodias*: Look at the moon. How strange the moon seems! She is like a woman rising from a tomb. She is like a dead woman. One might fancy she was looking for dead things.
> *The Young Syrian*: She has a strange look. She is like a little princess who wears a yellow veil, and whose feet are of silver. She is like a princess who has little white doves for feet. One might fancy she was dancing.
> *The Page of Herodias*: She is like a woman who is dead. She moves very slowly.[19] (Wilde, *Salomé*, 1 [Eng.])

This exchange establishes a pattern in which the referent floats indeterminately between Salome and the moon. Both speakers introduce their comparisons with phrases such as "one might fancy," or "she is like" (in French, "on dirait" or "elle ressemble"); and the practice of overtly announcing an impending simile or metaphor will continue throughout the play (as will the use of the moon for many widely divergent comparisons). This announcement of the mimetic process lends it the quality of a communal venture, removing it from the private realm of a lone spectator describing a single spectacle. Salome, too, will rhapsodize about the moon, acknowledging neither the self-referential quality of her words, nor the fact that they repeat the lines of other characters:

> *Salomé*: How good to see the moon! She resembles a little piece of money, [*on dirait*] a little silver flower. She is cold and chaste. I am sure she is a virgin. Yes, she is a virgin.[20] (Ibid., 6 [Eng.])

A bit later, the Page will again speak of the moon:

> *The Page*: Oh! How strange the moon looks. [*On dirait*] Like the hand of a dead woman who is seeking to cover herself with a shroud.[21] (Ibid., 9 [Eng.])

In response this time, the young Syrian soldier also refers to the moon, although he compares it to a young princess:

> *The Young Syrian*: She has a strange aspect! She is like [*on dirait*] a little princess, whose eyes are eyes of amber. Through the clouds of muslin she is smiling like a little princess.[22] (Ibid. [Eng.])

Still later, Herod and Herodias will have a conversation that repeats quite closely the opening scene between the two soldiers. Here again, talk of the forbidden view of Salome leads to talk of the moon:

> *Herod*: Where is Salomé? Where is the princesse. . . . Ah there she is!
> *Herodias*: You must not look at her! You are always looking at her!
> *Herod*: The moon has a very strange look to-night. Has she not a strange look? [*On dirait*] She is like a mad woman seeking everywhere for lovers. . . .
> *Herodias*: No, the moon is like the moon, that is all. Let us go within. . . . We have nothing to do here.[23] (Ibid., 14–15 [Eng.])

Much as the characters here share a single metaphoric practice, so they share the practice of illicit gazing. Throughout the play, characters warn one another continually of the danger of looking at the wrong object. The page cautions Narraboth not to look at Salome; Herodias warns Herod against the same thing. But Salome is not the only forbidden sight here, for another major alteration that Wilde makes in the story of Salome is his addition of the princess's unrequited, sacrilegious, and powerfully erotic love for Jokanaan. Once Salome has seen John the Baptist, she turns her metaphorizing to his beauty; and her language recalls Narraboth's and Herod's when they gazed covetously upon her:

Salomé: It is the eyes above all that are terrible. [*On dirait*] They are like black holes burned by torches into a tapestry of Tyre. [*On dirait*] They are like the black caverns of Egypt in which dragons make their lairs. [*On dirait*] They are like black lakes troubled by fantastic moons.[24] (Ibid., 10 [Eng.])

In this drama, shared language and actions unify the protagonists. Here it is Salome's turn to wield the power of the gaze. And if we see that power as phallic, then the comparison of the Baptist's eyes with black holes or caverns clearly prefigures the eventual symbolic castration, his decapitation. Salome's gaze gouges out his eyes just as her dance will have him beheaded. And just as several protagonists gaze upon forbidden sights, sharing this transgressive activity the way they share linguistic motifs, so are all put at risk by such gazing. No one's gaze remains self-contained or limited to its object. The constant fear surrounding looking implies that the expression of one individual's transgressive desire threatens the entire group; "Something terrible may happen" ("Il peut arriver un malheur"), warns the Page when Narraboth refuses to heed his admonitions (ibid., 4 [Eng.]).

The rhetorical insistence upon the transgressiveness and potential collective danger of the gaze finds a curious material counterpart in the site of John the Baptist's imprisonment, an onstage cistern surrounded by a bronze wall. John remains an unseen presence through much of the play, invisible within this prominently displayed well. Salome's string of metaphors for his eyes—black holes, black caverns, black lakes—evokes the dark hole in which he has been imprisoned, thereby lending the cistern something of the quality of a giant eye gazing out from within the stage. All the characters are profoundly conscious of John's unseen but seeing and disapproving presence. The Baptist knows secrets that threaten the entire structure of Herod's world. He knows of the religious illegality of Herod's marriage to Herodias; and he knows with certainty of the imminent downfall of the tetrarch's world, which will be replaced by Christ's kingdom. The cistern onstage functions symbolically as the knowing eye whose powerful gaze, while shunted aside, makes all uncomfortable. The cistern and the Baptist within are initially just distant observers, a safely contained audience separated from the dramatic action. Eventually, however, the distinction between this audience and the drama it watches will blur, as will the distinction between the actual audience sitting in the theater and the play onstage. Once Jokanaan becomes the object of Salome's desire, he will be implicated in the drama of Herod's palace. There will turn out to be no such thing as an individually contained gaze or a restricted transgressive desire. Indeed, *Salomé* in its entirety will prove to be based upon a model in which the ostensibly discrete realms of spectacle and audience, gazer and gazed upon, merge through the expression of illicit desire. The cistern can be seen as our—the audience's—onstage representative, an overarching eye, a spectator, implying that the melding of gazer and gazed upon will come to include the audience and the drama onstage.

The single scene of conversation between Salome and Jokanaan displays a multilayered complexity that points to still further unifying connections among the protagonists. From the outset, the Baptist establishes himself as an inappropriate object for Salome's gaze, implicating the princess, as I have suggested, in the same brand of trangressiveness of which Herod and Narraboth are both guilty. Jokanaan effectively claims for himself a position analogous to Salome's. Although male, his body is as sacrosanct as hers, and requires equal protection from erotic covetousness: "Who is this woman who is looking at me? I will not have her look at me. . . . Back! . . . daughter of Babylon!" (ibid., 11–12 [Eng.]).[25] Wilde's addition of Salome's desire for Jokanaan not only reverses the usual gender roles,[26] but also contributes to the play's insistence upon the fluid, communal nature of desire. As the princess expresses her increasing erotic fascination with Jokanaan, Narraboth warns her back: "Do not stay here, Princess, I beseech you" (ibid., 10 [Eng.]), thus reconstructing his own earlier scene with Salome and Herodias's page, only this time exchanging the role of entranced gazer for the stance of cautious bystander. But although the characters have changed, a now-familiar tripartite structure emerges, composed of the gazer, the gazed upon, and the moral impediment to the gaze. As always here, individual roles (and sexes) shift, but the words persist in creating parallel, repetitive scenarios among the characters.

Salome praises her beloved in the terms of the Bible's most celebrated erotic language, for much of the text of the only actual conversation between Salome and Jokanaan comes from the Song of Songs.[27] Salome begins by lyrically praising his body for its whiteness; she ends by likening it to the play's universal currency for comparison, the moon:

> *Salomé*: I am amorous of thy body, Jokanaan. Thy body is white like the lilies
> of a field that the mower hath never mowed. Thy body is white like the
> snows that lie on the mountains of Judea, and come down into the valleys.
> The roses in the garden of the Queen of Arabia are not so white as thy body.
> Neither the roses of the garden of the Queen of Arabia, the garden of spices
> of the Queen of Arabia, nor the feet of the dawn when they light on the
> leaves, nor the breast of the moon when she lies on the breast of the sea. . . .
> There is nothing in the world so white as thy body.—Suffer me to touch thy
> body![28] (Wilde, *Salomé*, 11 [Eng.])

When rebuffed by Jokanaan—"Back, daughter of Babylon! By woman came evil into the world"—Salome changes her speech in a curious way, setting the pattern for the rest of the dialogue. She reverses her words, negating all her praise of the preceding line by insulting the same physical attribute that she has just admired. She then redirects her praise to another part of the Baptist's body:

> *Salomé*: Thy body is hideous. It is like the body of a leper. It is like a plastered wall where vipers have crawled; like a plastered wall where the scorpions have made their nest. It is like a whitened sepulcher, full of loathsome things. It is horrible, thy body is horrible. It is thy hair that I am amorous of, Jokanaan. Thy hair is like clusters of grapes, like the clusters of black grapes that hang from the vine-trees of Edom in the land of the Edomites. Thy hair is like the cedars of Lebanon, like the great cedars of Lebanon that give their shade to the lions and to the robbers who would hide them by day. The long black nights, when the moon hides her face, when the stars are afraid, are not so black as thy hair. The silence that dwells in the forest is not so black. There is nothing in the world that is so black as thy hair. . . . Suffer me to touch thy hair.[29] (Ibid., 11–12 [Eng.])

This structure continues, each blazon ending with Salome's plea to be allowed to touch or kiss him, and his horror-struck, condemning refusal. In such fashion, Salome echoes the Song of Songs while recasting it as a repetitive melody that alternates praise and insult, and covers the Baptist's body, part by part.[30] Salome's continual reversal of her words and her displacing of her praise echo the play's ever-circulating repeated motifs. Just as no particular referent needs to be attached to the constant metaphors, so does Salome need no particular body part of Jokanaan's. It is the play of metaphor that matters here; referent is immaterial. The physical body is fragmented and dissolved, ceding its place to the body of metaphor.

This effect suffuses the text's language as well. Individual words or fragments of sentences appear two or more times, each successive appearance embroidering new and different detail into the description, as here in the next verses of Salome's love song to Jokanaan:

> [*Ta bouche est plus rouge que les pieds de ceux qui foulent le vin dans les pressoirs.*[31]] Thy mouth is redder than the feet of the doves who inhabit the temples and are fed by the priests. It is redder than the feet of him who cometh from a forest where he hath slain a lion, and seen gilded tigers.[32] (Ibid., 12 [Eng.])

In this passage, the vehicle of the simile—*les pieds*—attaches and reattaches itself to different phrases, much as Salome's praise attaches and reattaches itself to Jokanaan's different body parts. No new use of this vehicle, however, ever completely erases the lingering resonance of the preceding one. The redness of wine-pressers' feet remains to nuance the redness of the feet of temple doves. The result is an intricate tapestry of description whose weave extends continually outward, repeating on a small scale the play's overarching structure of incantatory, enchained repetition that blurs distinction and unifies the characters.

Wilde seems determined to prevent any one character's exclusive ownership of or claim to any particular piece of language. And yet, paradoxically, at the heart of the Salome legend lies the question of "keeping one's word" ("tenir sa parole"), of holding one's promise valid. The horror of the decapitation of the Baptist stems from Herod's obligation to keep his promise to Salome, to honor his word. But the insistent, repetitive musicality of Wilde's *Salomé* suggests that retaining individual control over words requires that an unnatural violence be done. Left to themselves, however, words, like desire, seep beyond bounds of character, enveloping all, including the audience.

Although Salome, in her scene with Jokanaan, veers from praise to insult and from body part to body part, she never veers from her final statements of intention, all of which begin with "Suffer me" ("Laisse-moi," as in "Suffer me to touch thy body"); in the end, however, she abandons the request in favor of a declarative statement: "I will kiss thy mouth" ("Je baiserai ta bouche"). Like Herod, Salome will keep her promise, even while the rest of her speech testifies to her inability to "keep" her other words, since they belong so clearly to the play's communal, free-floating lexicon of desire.

Salome must have Jokanaan murdered in order to keep her promise of kissing his mouth. In order to keep *his* promise to Salome, Herod must involve himself in the same violent crime. Although language floats freely here, when it must be anchored, when a promise is uttered, the reattachment of words to intention requires death. Both Herod and Salome look upon the forbidden, both make promises to the forbidden objects of their gaze, and the two promises are fulfilled by a single murder.

Herod and Salome do not resemble each other merely in their gazing upon and making promises to a love object. They both murder their love objects as well, for another Wildean addition to the story is Herod's murder of the princess, whom he has his soldiers crush under their shields. Both Herod and Salome kill the object of their impermissible gazes. But of course, in having both Salome and Jokanaan die, Wilde reinforces the similarity between them, as well as the parallel relationship between Herod and Salome. Both Salome and Jokanaan were forbidden, fetishized sights to someone else, and both die as the result of these transgressive, desirous gazes. At this point, René Girard's understanding of Salome's and Jokanaan's analogous positions proves very apt.

Yet there are not two, but three deaths in this play. Upon hearing Salome's declaration of desire for Jokanaan, the enamored young Syrian, Narraboth, kills himself; and his body falls between Salome and the Baptist. Although Narraboth commits suicide out of jealousy and frustrated love for Salome, his falling body actually proclaims still another love, a kind of love that remains unavowed in the text. Upon seeing his companion die, Herodias's page reveals that the friendship between the two men was actually a love affair:

> *The Page*: The young Syrian has slain himself! . . . I gave him a little box of perfumes and ear-rings wrought in silver, and now he has killed himself! . . . I gave him a little box . . . and a ring of agate that he always wore on his hand. . . . Also he had much joy to gaze at himself in the river. I used to reproach him for that.[33] (Wilde, *Salomé*, 13–14 [Eng.])

Both the homosexual love affair and the Page's grief pass entirely unnoticed by the other characters, an "open secret," seen but not acknowledged.[34] The Page's lament plays beneath the main story of the text, a countermelody in the background. And yet, this homosexual union reveals itself through violence at a moment when Salome's tentativeness turns to a defiant announcement of desire, at the moment when she ceases to request the Baptist's permission to touch him and declares instead that she will kiss his mouth despite his repugnance. Just at the moment when her "Suffer me to kiss thy mouth" turns to "I will kiss thy mouth," Narraboth cries out once and dies. He dies, that is, just as Salome announces that she will keep her word at any price. Once again, the effort of restricting the free-floating nature of language, of holding onto the meaning of a promise, is allied with a violent death—Narraboth's.

Narraboth's suicide illustrates how *Salomé*'s thematic structure repeats the play's lyrical, linguistic patterns: each successive motif repeats parts of the preceding one, enlarging and expanding its meaning. A graphic representation of *Salomé* would resemble widening concentric circles, indicating ever more encompassing levels of desire. No circle touches another, yet each new one is dependent on the one that precedes it. The juxtaposition of two kinds of love in this scene demands that they be considered together. From the moment when Narraboth's lifeless body falls between Salome and Jokanaan, the drama of these two main characters begins to take on the weight of expressing an unacknowledged homoerotic desire. Henceforth, the story of Salome's love for Jokanaan and its violent aftermath will be colored by the unavowed love of the two soldiers and the violence attendant upon it. A new circle begins to widen.

The Page's grief over his friend's suicide might not be interpreted as a lover's bereavement were it not for the list of gifts he recalls having given Narraboth. The perfumes, the rings, the earrings, these offerings made to a young Narcissus ("He had much joy to gaze at himself in the river"), announce the specifically erotic connection between the two men. We also learn from the Page's words that sometimes the impermissible, transgressive object of a gaze is oneself: "I used to reproach him for that." This alliance of homosexual love, the object world, and narcissistic gazing emerges for the first time in Wilde's work, of course, in his *Picture of Dorian Gray* (1891). In that text, Dorian's aging portrait and the jeweled breviary of Decadence given him by Basil Hallward herald Dorian's downfall. But Dorian's greatest sin is never named; it is the love that dares not speak its name. Basil's book and the portrait remain tied to the shadowy world of homosexual encounters. The powerful homoerotic desire felt by both Basil and Lord Henry for Dorian is never explicitly mentioned, but is "displaced onto the aesthetic realm" (Cohen, *Talk*, 87), the world of beautiful objects. Dorian's own relationship to his portrait represents an "aesthetic translation" of an erotic, narcissistic relation between two men. "Dorian Gray is what happens when the analogy between homosexual desire and commodity fetishism is driven to the point of identity" (Nunokawa 1). In *Salomé*, Dorian's secret world of precious objects and dangerous love becomes a communal world, opening outward to include all the characters. The entire plot is generated by the characters' fetishistic delectation of one anothers' bodies. Just as they share dialogue, actions, and stolen gazes, so are they all implicated in the alliance of transgressive desire with lists of fetishized treasures. The two male lovers are bound by objects and parted by death. But the erotic attachments of other couples also find expression through lists of treasures of various sorts. Let us recall that Narraboth's death coincides with Salome's lengthy blazon of Jokanaan. The Syrian's death occurs, that is, while erotic desire is taking the form of fetishistic appreciation. In her revision of the Song of Songs, Salome likens Jokanaan's body parts to a long list of riches: a branch of coral, an ivory statue, a pomegranate, vermilion, the arch of the King of Persia. Herod's desire for Salome will also find expression in a list of fetishized body parts. He asks her to drink from his wine goblet, for he loves her "little red lips" ("petites lèvres rouges"); he asks her to bite into a fruit so that he can delight in "the mark of [her] little teeth" ("la morsure de [ses] petites dents"); and he will ask her to dance in order to admire her feet: "Thy little feet will be like white doves. They will be like little white flowers that dance upon a tree" (Wilde, *Salomé*, 28 [Eng.]).[35] With these tributes to individual parts of Salome's body, Wilde again insists upon the symmetrical relationship between Salome's desire for Jokanaan and Herod's for Salome.[36]

Once Salome has danced, and demanded Jokanaan's head, Herod will again speak a list of fetishized treasures, only this time they are the material offerings with which he attempts to bribe her to relinquish her request. (Such a movement from fetishized body parts to fetishized material objects is, of course, a common trope in decadent literature.) In his attempt to dissuade her from her request for Jokanaan's head—"Thou must loose me from my oath," he tells her ("Il faut me délier de ma parole")—Herod will offer Salome a long list of gifts, including "a great emerald" ("une grande émeraude ronde"), "white peacocks that walk in the garden between the myrtles and the tall cypress trees" ("[de] beaux paons blancs, qui se promènent dans le jardin entre les myrthes et les grands cyprès"), and "a collar of pearls set in four rows" ("un collier de perles à quatre rangs," *Salomé* 30–32 [Eng.], 70–73 [Fr.]).

In response to each offer, Salome only makes her own unyielding demand for the Baptist's head: "Give me the head of Jokanaan" ("Donne-moi la tête d'Iokanaan," ibid., 30–31 [Eng.], 71 [Fr.]). She repeats this line to Herod eight separate times, just as she repeated to Jokanaan her intention of kissing him. Salome's firmly repeated words void these treasures of their value just as her dance voids Herod's promise of its intended value.

Although this scene between Herod and Salome replays in certain respects that earlier scene between Salome and Jokanaan, it also alters it significantly. When Salome offers her rhapsodic, fetishistic praise of his body to the Baptist, she ends her own speech each time with her repeated promise, "Je baiserai ta bouche." But when the scene shifts to the palace, it is Herod who offers a list of fetishized treasures to Salome's firm, repeated word. Salome's desirous speech to Jokanaan now divides into two parts, with Herod taking one and Salome the other. This underlines strikingly some of the play's larger issues, while partaking of the play's musical structure: a motif is repeated and rendered more complex.

As I have already suggested, Herod's desire for Salome echoes and recalls the Syrian's for Salome as well as Salome's for Jokanaan. But the effect is more complicated still. Because Herod appropriates half of Salome's role in her dialogue with Jokanaan, his desire for the princess is actually colored faintly by some of his own homoerotic desire for the young Syrian. This should not be a surprise, since Wilde has already given us one opportunity to espy Herod's aesthetic and erotic appreciation of the male body. When the tetrarch learns of Narraboth's death, he responds: "I am sorry he has slain himself. I am very sorry; for he was fair to look upon. He was even very fair. He had very languorous eyes. I remember that I saw that he looked languorously at Salome" (ibid., 16 [Eng.]).[37] Recalling this, one can read in Herod's and Salome's later conversation a splitting and sharing of desire for the male body. And so, although the love between the two soldiers goes entirely unnoticed on the level of dialogue, its "open secret" makes itself felt later in the text, transported via the recitative quality of the play, and inscribed into Wilde's use of the Salome legend of forbidden desire, and the aesthetic reification of the body. Even Herod's words reflect this structure in their enchained repetition, in which sentences pick up words from the previous ones—"sorry," "fair," "languorous" ("regrette," "beau," and "langoureux" in French)—and elaborate upon them. In this fashion, Wilde's play well illustrates the Girardian concept of the "mimetic contagion" of the Salome story. Desire appears again and again, blatant, melodic, yet unavowed.

GREEN FLOWERS AND THE ROLE OF THE AUDIENCE

But Wilde was not content merely to let musical repetition float ever more inclusive circles of desire through the interior of his play. He allowed those widening circles to reach the audience as well. When the young Syrian agrees to bring Jokanaan to her, Salome promises him a token of gratitude: "Thou wilt do this thing for me, Narraboth, and tomorrow when I pass in my litter beneath the gateway of the idol-sellers, I will let fall for thee a little flower, a little green flower" (Wilde, *Salomé*, 8 [Eng.]).[38] This gift bears considerable symbolic weight beyond the confines of *Salomé*. The green carnation was an emblem of the aesthetic movement, of decadent dandyism and "of the triumph of the artificial over Nature and things called 'natural'" (Gagnier 163). It was also the emblem worn by homosexuals in Paris at the time. In having Salome promise the carnation, Wilde allies her with his own public personality as dandy and gay man.[39] Salome here steps out of her ornate, symbolist, orientalist backdrop and refers to her connection to Wilde's oeuvre and to his life, reinforcing the obvious a priori connection between orientalism and gay performance.[40] As Emily Apter has written, "Campy Orientalist scenarios have always been and continue to be good value within gay drama; their over-acted quality points to the way in which nonconformist sexual identity must perform its way into existence, more often than not through the transformation of originally conservative models" ("Acting out Orientalism" 109).[41]

By the time Wilde wrote *Salomé*, he was what Jennifer Wicke has called "a literary totem, capable of conjuring up a fervent world of celebrity and aesthetic rapture" (82). And the flower symbol followed him everywhere, sometimes a sunflower, sometimes a green carnation. Wilde's image was caricatured and reproduced both in the United States (after his 1882 lecture tour) and in Britain, used to sell everything from soap to the circus.[42] Wilde was always depicted in an exaggeratedly fey stance, "wearing a velvet suit and lace collar, carrying a sunflower" (ibid., 83). When Salome promised the green flower to Narraboth, she would instantly have reminded audience members of the playwright himself. Salome, princess of Judea, femme fatale, would have become a version of Wilde, who, in camp fashion, infused his dramatic character with an extrascenic identity that exceeds the fictional boundaries of her character.

Salome's green flower is Wilde's gesture toward his public image; and it is intended to blur the distinction between himself, his work, and the audience. This intention is made particularly clear by a staging idea that he had for another one of his plays: *Lady Windermere's Fan*, written just one year later. For the premiere of this play, Wilde had a plan that "would turn the audience itself into an object of artifice" (Gagnier 165). Wilde asked his friend W. Graham Robertson[43] to wear a green flower to the opening and to persuade as many male audience members as possible to do likewise. Onstage, one young male cast member would also be wearing a green flower. When Robertson asked him the reason for this idea, Wilde replied:

> [The public] likes to be annoyed. A young man on the stage will wear a green carnation; people will stare at it and wonder. Then they will look round the house and see every here and there more and more little specks of mystic green. "This must be some secret symbol" they will say. "What on earth can it mean?" (Quoted in Gagnier 163)

When Robertson asked what, in fact, it did mean, Wilde replied, "Nothing whatever, but that is just what nobody will guess."

As Regenia Gagnier points out, though, Wilde is being disingenuous here, since by having spectators wear a green carnation he was co-opting them into an unwitting performance as a group of gay men. Wilde actually pulled off this theatrical ruse, and at the end of the premiere he came onstage himself and congratulated a perplexed audience on their wonderful performance.[44] The spectators had become the spectacle.

The green carnation episode illustrates how Wilde worked with the crowd rather than over their heads. While it is true that the audience in this case is unaware of its role, this audience differs sharply from the readership, say, of Mallarmé's campy fashion magazine *La Dernière Mode*. In the latter case, Mallarmé used what was supposed to be a mass publication to correspond with a few enlightened compatriots, those poet-friends of his who read the magazine as a cryptic, symbolist message. *La Dernière Mode*'s female readership was supposedly unaware of its high literary status. In the case of Wilde's green carnation, however, we can expect a certain vague level of awareness on the part of the audience. Wilde employs his own aesthetic to make visible an "open secret," to betray the repressed underside of Victorian bourgeois respectability.[45] Here, the inside of the play onstage and the outside of the audience are one. The elite, those with a secret, *are* the crowds, even if they are not entirely aware of this. Wilde's trademark personality was to be used to shape the crowd, emanating from the center of it in true camp fashion. Camp style, as we have seen, often depends upon just such a blending of the author's biographical self with the fictive scenario, forcing the latter to incorporate the former.

This brings us back to *Salomé*, a story that is itself about the collapse of an inner sanctum. Herod watches Salome's dance thinking he is in control of it, thinking he knows its worth, but instead the dance brings back to him his worst fears: that Iokanaan is powerful, and that his own system of currency has become useless. In similar fashion, the crowds at a performance of *Salomé* might have imagined they understood their position in relation to the spectacle before them. Yet Wilde's intention with this drama was to subvert such complacent expectations, to dismantle the boundaries between audience and stage, much as Salome's dance eventually collapsed the distinction between Herod's inner sanctum of privilege and Christ's outer, encroaching world of the underprivileged.

But before going on to examine Wilde's staging concepts for *Salomé*, we must be careful not to draw a facile parallel between his solidly bourgeois audiences and John the Baptist's throngs of disadvantaged poor. There is, certainly, an unmistakable analogy between the story of Salome, with its implied tale of the end of a privileged era and the beginning of the Kingdom of God, and the social and sexual politics of Wilde's theatrical conceptions for *Salomé*. But this analogy is complex, and related to Wilde's political and religious beliefs.

As Regenia Gagnier points out, Wilde consistently depicted the extreme ends of the social spectrum: aristocrats and the unemployed, those normally considered to comprise the inner and outer sanctums. It was the bourgeoisie he chose never to represent. "[Wilde's works] exhibited a [complete] lack of conformity to middle-class norms," writes Gagnier (165). It turns out that for Wilde, the "outer sanctum" encompasses not the disenfranchised masses, but the bourgeoisie. And when I say that he worked his artistry from within the crowd, I mean that he strove to meld his inner sanctum—in which art and free expression of desire were paramount—with the audience's outer sanctum of bourgeois constraints and respectability. In *Salomé*, as we have seen, Wilde insists particularly strongly on the free-floating nature of desire and language. The play consistently suggests that desire and its expression must be shared and unfettered. Every attempt to pin down or constrain meaning with law or with promises ends in violence and death.

The religious implications of the Salome story lend themselves particularly well to Wilde's project of critiquing middle-class inhibitions, and exposing what lies hidden beneath them. *Salomé* is a story that heralds the transition from the unseeable Jewish god to the visible Christian deity. "In these days," says one of the Jews in the play, "God doth not show Himself. God hideth Himself. Therefore great evils have come upon the land" ("En ce temps-ci, Dieu ne se montre pas. Il se cache. Et par conséquent il y a de grands malheurs dans le pays," *Salomé* 18 [Eng.], 42 [Fr.]). John the Baptist announces the coming end of these *malheurs*, misfortunes that plague the followers of a hidden god.

Wilde's own interest in Christianity focuses precisely on the visibility of Christ, and on Christ's power to render visible that which was hidden. The beauty and personal relevance Wilde found in Christ's mission appear most clearly and solemnly in his later work *De Profundis*, a text composed of several long letters written to Alfred Douglas from Reading Gaol. *De Profundis* explores Christ as a force that awoke sleeping senses, and lent expression to the unexpressed. "Christ strove," writes Wilde, "to be the eyes of the blind, the ears of the deaf, and to give voice to the lips of those whose tongues were tied . . . to be a trumpet through which the myriads, who had not the power of speech might raise their cry up to heaven" (*De Profundis* 59). Wilde clearly saw a personal model in Jesus; and in his dramatic rendition of *Salomé*, he was certainly trying to give voice to the unspoken transgressive desires present in his public, to be, that is, their trumpet crying up to heaven (even if they were unaware of needing such a trumpet). *Salomé*'s structure is composed of outward-reaching, ever more inclusive circles of expressed desire that float toward the audience in an attempt to lead them to self-recognition. Wilde appropriated, in a sense, the task of lending shape and form to his audience's unconscious, taking profound pleasure in rendering visible the repressed underside of the Victorian public.

Wilde's appreciation of Christianity emerged partially from his understanding of Christ as social leveler, as a symbol of the ultimately shared nature of all lives: "Though Christ did not teach men the lesson 'Live for one another' He showed them that there was no difference between the lives of others and our own" (*De Profundis* 57). With *Salomé* in particular, Wilde's theatrical vision endeavored to break down the distinction between inner and outer sanctum, spectacle and spectator (and "native" and "foreign" language), in order to loosen, if only for a moment, distinctions he felt were rigid and dishonest, to illustrate the absence of difference among all lives.

Wilde's ideas about the performance of this play were more elaborate than those for *Lady Windermere's Fan*, and were meant to blur even more thoroughly the traditional theatrical boundaries. As Gagnier points out, Wilde's concepts for the staging of *Salomé* could have been constructed on the models articulated by Artaud in the *Premier Manifeste du Théâtre de la cruauté* (Gagnier 166): "Every spectacle will contain a physical and objective element, perceived by everyone . . . the magical beauty of costumes borrowed from certain model rituals, resplendent in the light, the incantatory beauty of voices, the charm of harmony, the rare notes of the music, the colors of objects."[46] Wilde intended to abolish the distinction between the stage and the audience by creating a synesthetic spectacle of startling effects. Instead of an orchestra, he wanted giant braziers of perfume to be placed throughout the theater, burning a new scent for each new emotion expressed.[47] Wilde was disappointed to discover that fire regulations would prohibit this fragrant practice. In his imagination, however, the wafting clouds of perfume would replace the stage curtain, creating partial, diaphanous veils for the drama. His conception of the theatrical space as both perfumed and veiled recalls, in these respects, the classically decadent conception of the Oriental dancing girl. Flaubert's Salammbô, for example, wore earrings made from perforated vials of scented oils, which slowly dripped their perfume over her body throughout the day.[48] Wilde's braziers would treat as a dancing princess not only the entire stage, which would be drenched in perfume, but the audience as well, for its members would be equally scented, even after leaving the theater.

Wilde envisioned masses of color that would distinguish characters in groups: all the Jews in yellow, Herod and Herodias in blood red, and Salome "in green, like a curious, poisonous lizard" (quoted in Worth 66). The stage floor would be painted black to offset Salome's white feet, which would "move like doves," according to Wilde. The sky was to be designed in a particularly Art Nouveau fashion: "A rich turquoise blue cut by the perpendicular fall of gilded strips of Japanese matting forming an aerial tent" (quoted in Jullian, *Oscar Wilde*, 253). Such decadent concepts for the staging of the play reach out to the audience and pull it into the rarefied world of the decadent dandy. Inhaling the different perfumes, watching a stage veiled in fragrant clouds, fetishistically enjoying dancing feet, the audience would play Herod to the Salome that is the entire stage production. But of course, the audience would not merely inhale the perfumes; they would themselves be scented as well, and would leave the theater with perfume lingering in their clothes and hair. And when those clouds of perfume floated through the theater, they would veil not only the stage, but parts of the audience as well. In Wilde's imagined staging of the play, spectators would look about the audience to find their brethren partially veiled by the vaporous clouds. Such a scenario returns us to the premiere of *Lady Windermere's Fan*, in which Wilde's distribution of green carnations deliberately led the audience to examine itself, and to find that they were aesthetically and erotically tied both to the action onstage and to the offstage life of the playwright. By effectively veiling and perfuming the audience, Wilde would maneuver them into Salome's position as well as Herod's; they are at once the gazed upon and the gazers, both objects and purveyors of illicit desire, partaking in the same dismantling of distinctions we have seen within the play's structure itself.

The difference between nineteenth-century decadent dandyism and Wilde's modern, camp revision of it is that Wilde wished to co-opt his entire audience into entering a world of fetishized treasures and illicit desire. With his insistence upon exquisitely colored costumes, jeweled backdrops, and rare perfumes, Wilde would have effectively transformed the theater into an oversized decadent interior. And let us not forget the particular performing artist Wilde envisioned in the title role of Salome: his close friend Sarah Bernhardt, that "serpent of old Nile." Bernhardt was forty-eight when Wilde finished his play, a curious casting choice for the part of a barely pubescent girl. But she was up to the challenge, and scoffed at suggestions that she have a younger stand-in perform the Dance of the Seven Veils for her (Jullian, *Oscar Wilde*, 256). The gifted Bernhardt understood the particular camp appeal of a middle-aged woman portraying (or trying to "pass" as) a nubile princess. She understood that "La Bernhardt" would be as crucial a performed character in the play as "Salome." And with a matron playing Salome, the erotic focus of Wilde's play would have been redirected to the character established as Salome's male counterpart: Jokanaan. The subplot of Salome's desire for the Baptist transforms Jokanaan into the object of erotic covetousness, whose body is as praised and desired as a woman's. The most youthful, tempting body of the play would be male.

Returning to the notion that one can find no trace of the bourgeoisie on Wilde's stage, we can now see that it is too simple. The traces exist in the very completeness of the absence. An audience attending *Salomé* might seek itself narcissistically onstage, and be initially thwarted. But as Robert Brantlinger points out, "Sadistic, antique splendors . . . are as inimical to bourgeois industrial values as the cliches . . . that are ironically expressive of them" (119).[49] The choice of biblical antiquity and ancient treasures as a backdrop for *Salomé* does not in the end so much remove it from the realm of the British middle-class public, as render it sufficiently exotic to be noticed and absorbed by that public. In *The Soul of Man under Socialism*, Wilde writes:

> In Art, the public accept what has been, because they cannot alter it, not because they appreciate it. They swallow their classics whole, and never taste them . . . this acceptance of classics does a great deal of harm. The uncritical admiration of the Bible and Shakespeare in England is an instance of what I mean. (Wilde, *Artist as Critic*, 272–73)

Wilde considered it his task to make his public taste (and smell and feel) his version of the Bible in *Salomé*, to awaken their dormant senses by gathering them into the performance. Using decadent trappings, he wanted to lead the audience into the drama and force them to contemplate their own relationship to the desires expressed onstage. In place of the middle-class household, Wilde's *Salomé* offered a lush, exotic pageant in which subtly, slowly, and perhaps with some alarm, the bourgeoisie would come to distinguish its own image.

THE AFTERMATH

Unfortunately, Wilde was somewhat too successful in alarming the bourgeoisie; *Salomé* was banned by the London Lord Chamberlain's office, which invoked the archaic Pingott law against representing biblical characters on a public stage. Wilde never saw the play performed.[50] By the time *Salomé* was actually produced (in Paris, in 1896), Wilde was in prison. But the moral outrage that the play provoked testifies to its political power, and to its capacity to hold a discomfiting mirror up to society.

Salomé was not officially produced in England until 1931, and even Strauss's operatic version of it was kept off the British stage until 1907 (Showalter 150). When Russian dancer Ida Rubenstein tried to perform a version of the Dance of the Seven Veils based on Wilde's play, the Holy Synod of the Russian Orthodox Church banned her performance on the grounds of sacrilege (ibid., 160).

But the most famous brouhaha connected with *Salomé* involved Canadian dancer Maud Allan, who, in 1907, toured music halls in Europe with a daring rendition of Salome's dance, based on Wilde's play. Almost naked, Allan performed a particularly erotic solo, with the head of John the Baptist on a plate before her, ending her dance with Wilde's famous scene of the princess kissing John's lifeless lips. Allan so scandalized one conservative member of the British parliament, Noel Pemberton-Billing, that he published an essay in his private newspaper, *The Vigilante*, describing Allan as "a lesbian sadist." The title of the article was "The Cult of the Clitoris."[51]

In 1918, Maud Allan responded to this article by bringing a libel suit against Pemberton-Billing. As witness for the defense, the M.P. enlisted a physician, Dr. Serrell Cooke, who offered his professional medical opinion that Allan's Salome "was quite likely to light up dormant perversion in men who did not even know they possessed it, and in women." Allan lost her suit (Showalter 162).

Dr. Cooke's words, however, indicate that Wilde had won his case against bourgeois complacency. Cooke's interpretation of Salome's dance as an alarm that awakens sleeping desires jibes very well with Wilde's expressed interest in preventing the classics from being "swallowed whole," or, one might say, "sleepily." Even after Wilde's death, *Salomé* continued to rouse the public, to wake audiences up by touching something within them that was frightening but recognizable. After all, a "dormant perversion" would not be new or alien, simply a perversion of which one had been unaware. Curiously, although Pemberton-Billing accused Allan of being a lesbian sadist, it is mostly men's dangerous desires to which Dr. Cooke addressed himself at the trial. It might be appropriate here to add that another deep concern of Pemberton-Billing's was what he believed to be the dangerous infiltration of England by German homosexuals (Showalter 162).

The essay in *The Vigilante* and Maud Allan's suit against the paper's editor illustrate well how Wilde's interpretation of Salome impressed upon audiences, even years after the playwright's death, a sense of their own participation in its display of transgressive desire. In London, both Wilde's *Salomé* and the many subsequent performances of the Dance of the Seven Veils based upon the play were considered to contribute to public immorality.[52] It was a question not, therefore, simply of *Salomé*'s depiction of vice or perversion, but of the play's invasive power, which could incite the spectator himself to indulge in transgressive behavior. Once again, Girard's reading of Salome as a tale of "mimetic contagion" seems especially apt.

That *Salomé* created such a long-lived period of public indignation is actually testament to the beauty and force inherent in the play's structure. As we have seen, the play swirls its effect continually outward, embracing ever-larger circles of participants, whose roles become unclear. Wilde's ideas for the staging of *Salomé* clearly implicate the audience in his story of communal transgression; but it turned out that the play's effect went beyond even the walls of the theater, seeping into the general public's cultural consciousness for many years.

WILDE'S CHRISTIANITY

In *De Profundis*, Wilde writes of an earlier period in his life when he "amused [himself] with being a *flâneur*, a dandy, a leader of fashion" (20). He then goes on to describe the revelation that came to him in prison, the "starting-point of a new life . . . a *Vita Nuova*" (23). This second life is based upon Wilde's newfound understanding of Christ, whom he saw as a figure of liberation whose life was a sublime work of art. He wrote, "This is primarily . . . the charm which emanates from Christ: He completely resembles a perfect work of art" (75). In this respect, it is neither sacrilegious nor disrespectful to say that for Wilde, Christ was the ultimate decadent dandy, one whose life affects others through his very existence, rather than through any efforts at persuasion: "[Christ] really does not teach us anything at all; but by coming into his presence by associating with Him, we become something" (ibid.).[53]

And of course, Christ, like the dandy, is a male figure of profound corporeality. He must be looked at and admired, even by other men. As Eve Sedgwick observes: "[Images of Jesus] have indeed a unique position in modern culture as images of the unclothed or unclothable male body, often in extremis and/or in ecstasy, prescriptively meant to be gazed at and adored" (*Epistemology* 140). *Salomé* draws out of the biblical story its subtext of the announcement of Christ's arrival. Wilde then makes use of this aspect of the tale, normally ignored in other renditions, to inject the element of homoerotic desire. The most immediate illustration of this is Wilde's use of Jokanaan as an erotically desirable, tempting male body. But studying the play's structure, we can find that *Salomé*'s more subtle appeal depends, in part, on a model resembling Wilde's understanding of the persuasive power of Christ's personality. The staging ideas, Wilde's insistence on the shared, free-floating nature of language, his introduction of sexual desire that transcends gender, all these elements are consonant with Wilde's aestheticized and socialistic view of Christ.

In *Salomé*, dandyism, camp, and Wilde's personal, aestheticized religion begin to interact. The play functions, on one level, as a quintessential decadent-dandyist mechanism, creating a stir through the force of personality and example alone. And yet, this personality is no longer the private, elitist dandy of the nineteenth century. This is a commercially known personality no longer bounded by social convention, gender, or even a single body. Wilde's celebrated self seeps into all of *Salomé*'s characters, into the stage decor, into the audience, and even, eventually, into the British legal system. It employs a classically camp device in that it explodes the privatist interior of the dandy, to include everyone—onstage characters, offstage spectators, and even, eventually, government officials—in a communal expression of transgressive desire formerly relegated to the enclosed salons of fin-de-siècle literature. In the end, the play's structure actually functions very much as Wilde later imagined Christ's personality to work. *Salomé* owes some of its striking, incantatory power to Wilde's harnessing of decadence and camp to his understanding of Christ (or to an earlier conception, perhaps, of what an ideal, personal magnetism could accomplish), for the play works its magic precisely not by teaching or narrating, but by hypnotically gathering up its audience into its folds.

As we have seen, *Salomé* tells the story of individual desire merging into a chorus of shared longings. Wilde later wrote that since the time

Christ appeared on earth, "the history of every single individual is, or, at least, may become, the history of humanity" (*De Profundis* 57). It was perhaps inspired by such an example that Wilde was able to take the decadents' overworked story of one girl's dance and a stepfather's promise and transform it into the strangely lyrical and politically unsettling text whose influence extends continually outward, in ever-larger circles.

AFTERWORD

THESE CHAPTERS necessarily leave us with several overarching questions. What became of the dandy? Did he disappear completely into the hybrid creature of the media cult personality? And what is the relationship between the camp icon and the media star? The answers require a leap over one hundred years and an ocean. Of course, the advent of mass culture makes it impossible for the contemporary dandy to retreat to the social sequestration of his early nineteenth-century counterpart; and the influence of the so-often feminized or actually female mass-cultural "star" is inexorable. At play among these figures is the camp aesthetic, which, though not always overtly present in media stardom, exists as a subset of the category that works to infuse it with a particular gender ambiguity and sexual charge. Even media personalities who appear completely "straight" are available for a camp appreciation.[1]

It was inevitable that dandyism should merge with the culture industry, an apparatus designed to disseminate the charismatic personality. Equally inevitable was the shift of dandyism's culture of spectacle from Europe to America, corporate headquarters of the mass media. When Loie Fuller and Oscar Wilde combined French dandyism with typically American or Americanized skill in merchandising and promotion, they were forging the first link in a chain that stretches across a century.[2] Links in this chain include such figures as Madonna, (the artist formerly known as) Prince, and Michael Jackson, iconic media stars whose appeal allows easily for both heterosexual and homosexual appreciation.

Much has already been written about the resemblance between our present-day fin de siècle and the previous one.[3] I do not intend to make a case here for this similarity of eras, which clearly exists but seems to become a trite and useless point when argued too diligently.[4] What interests me more is to look briefly at how the lingering trace of part of Europe's late-nineteenth-century culture affects American daily life. From among many possible examples of this vestigial dandyism, I will choose just three: the career of Prince Rogers Nelson, the phenomenon of Jacqueline Kennedy Onassis—thrown sharply into relief by her death in 1994—and, finally, the role of certain Continental literary intellectuals in American universities during the past two decades.

PRINCE

Now known as an unpronounceable symbol (⚥), Prince Rogers Nelson demonstrates how the dandy fused with the woman onstage to create contemporary media stars. Unlike the classic nineteenth-century dandy,

♀ (I'm afraid I shall defy his injunction and henceforth call him Prince) does, of course, produce something: his music. But the persona that creates this music borrows unmistakably from the likes of Beau Brummell, Baudelaire, and Jean Lorrain. A self-styled mass-cultural royal (although his prescient parents really did choose "Prince" as his given name), Prince suppressed his actual family history first by omitting his surname and then by eliminating all linguistic names altogether. His persona is aloof, contemptuous, and as carefully stylized as any nineteenth-century dandy's. Even outside of his presence, staff members closest to him refer to him as "The Artist Formerly Known as Prince" (Baumgold 102), displaying what could only be described as a courtier's obedience in the face of absurd linguistic inconvenience. And, of course, Prince's current unnameability only further allies him with the classic dandy, whose very existence, as Barbey d'Aurevilly teaches us, transcends language and reference, never fully to be captured by words: "His entire life was an influence, that is to say, that which can hardly be recounted" (Barbey d'Aurevilly, *Du Dandysme*, 676). That Prince's name is now a visual symbol proves that his identity has become purely iconic: unconnected to history or family, visual, and instantly recognizable.

Prince appears keenly aware of his debt to nineteenth-century dandyism. In 1995 he paid homage to his predecessors by appearing on the cover of *Esquire* magazine posed as a latter-day Beau Brummell or Disraeli (Fig. 16). Dressed in an all-red suit and high-collared shirt designed by Gianni Versace, Prince leans on a crystal, bejeweled walking stick, his fingers covered with heavy rings.[5] From the zippers on his red high-heeled boots dangle gold replicas of his new name, the symbol ♀ (which is now more a fashion adornment than a name in any traditional sense). The colored drawings and photographs that illustrate the accompanying interview depict Prince in a variety of Versace outfits, including a white bouclé jacket with beaded trim and a pair of snakeskin-patterned trousers. His hair has been dusted with silver glitter. *Esquire*'s clever mixing of drawings and photographs of Prince in different costumes reinforces the star's limbic quality. The photographs convey Prince's physical, human presence; they are large, full-page shots focused on his upper torso. But the drawings are very small renderings of Prince's entire body (Fig. 17). They appear, with no background, right in the middle of the article, next to paragraphs of text, and resemble fashion illustrations or paper-doll cutouts. In choosing to represent Prince in this way, the editors at *Esquire* played with his liminal quality: Prince is both imposing rock star and diminutive dress-up doll, a living human being and a mere template for the ephemera of *la mode*, an artist and a plaything. *Esquire* understands dandyism.

Prince's performance, like the dandy's, must be continuous and apparently seamless; there can be no "backstage Prince" and no photographs

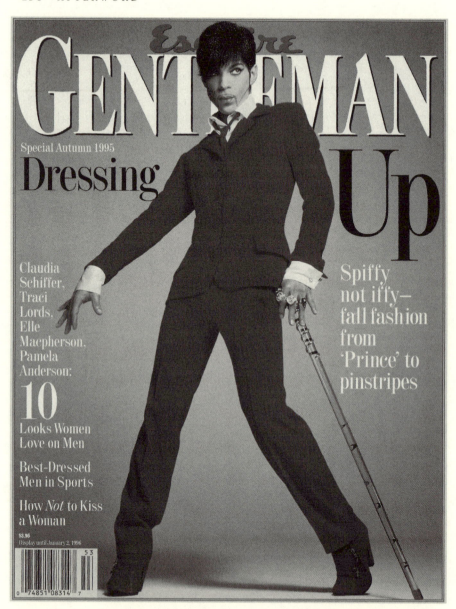

16. The artist formerly known as Prince on the cover of *Esquire*.

calm. He tells me his heart and perhaps his best work are in *Emancipation*. This album is a big surprise to people at Warner. No one seems to know about it.

"He's been here since the '70s," says Baker. "He was very young. Sometimes you love your parents but want to leave home. None of us wants to see it happen."

♀ is a businessman. He has a $10 million studio, Paisley Park, where he produces other recording artists; he has these clubs throbbing until dawn, ♀ stores in London and Minneapolis, where the symbol and the face take on iconic dimensions, his own love scent, and so forth. In 1992–93, *Forbes* ranked him the fifth most highly paid entertainer in the world. But a part of the Warner deal was a restructuring. Right now he is a businessman who made a bad deal. He doesn't want it to happen to others. He says he wants to take care of other artists. His ambition is nothing less than to form an alternative recording industry where artists own their own work and have creative freedom. The NPG, the New Power Generation, the people of the sun, are part of this new quasi-hippie world. When he performs with them he is "Tora Tora," his head and face wrapped in a chiffon scarf, yet another self. He is hidden, as he was in the "My Name is Prince" video when he wore a curtain of chains over his face.

♀ IS IN AN ARTISTIC CONUNDRUM— art versus what is "commercial." When he hears that word, he almost leaps from his seat in the balcony. When they let him handle his single "The Most Beautiful Girl in the World," he says he had his most commercial hit of the decade. ("It would have been spooky if it was the whole album," he says later.) It is every artist's devil—his vision and the world's may not always mesh. His best stuff may be beyond them, but he knows how good or bad it is. Though sometimes he can fool himself, inside the artist always knows. The record company sometimes knows. The dilemma was there as early as his movie *Purple Rain*. People kept warning The Kid (♀'s role): "Nobody digs your music but yourself." Of course, central to artistic freedom is the freedom to fail on your own terms.

He talks about people who don't own their parent's work—Nona Gaye doesn't own Marvin. Does Lisa Marie Presley own Elvis's masters?

He talks of the creative accounting of the record business, how black stores don't always have the digital scanners and miscount, so say, for instance, a big rap artist, who is said to have sold four million copies, might really have sold twenty million. He totally sympathized with George Michael, whom he considers a great talent, in his fight with Sony, which he says is an "even worse" company than Warner. Warner goes ahead and promotes what they want from the NPG album, which isn't always the right song, though the one he likes is nine-and-a-half minutes long. "Everyone gets to play on it. I have the best drummer in the world," he says.

According to his people, his deal is this: He gets an advance that might cover his living expenses while making the album. Once the work is delivered, Warner can decide how or if to promote and market it. The final decisions are not his. Thus, he is a "slave" to the system. Warner, I'm sure, has a different interpretation. I do not say to him that perhaps it trivializes the

The name change was both a spiritual conversion and a business move. Just when he had been around long enough to have generations of fans, he became someone else and was reborn.

African-American experience for a millionaire rock star—who travels with aides, bodyguards, a chef, a hairdresser, valet, backup security, wardrobe, band, technical people, a pyrotechnics expert, a personal dancing muse, and a man who sits behind him on the Concorde handing him freshly sharpened pencils—to write "Slave" on his face. This—glittery chains on the face versus chains on the ankles—is his version of slavery. Though he is half white, he identifies completely as a black man and talks about the lack of images for black children in movies and television.

"And who is at the head of these companies?" he says.

Mayte wafts into the balcony. She is his current inspiration after a long line of protégés including Apollonia and Vanity. ♀ tells her what to wear for the video. Mayte has been with him for four years, since she was a famously virginal seventeen. Mayte, who is also of

17. Fashion illustration of Prince Rogers Nelson wearing costume designed by Gianni Versace, from *Esquire*.

taken when he is not in full costume and makeup. These trappings normally include silk shirts with Byronic ruffles, chiffon scarves, skin-tight leather pants that expose derriere cleavage, heavy black eyeliner, and, most recently, the pencilled word "slave" on one cheek (in protest of his contract with Warner Brothers Records, which Prince considers artistically constraining). These accoutrements lend him an aura of snarling virility commingled with doe-eyed femininity. Even Prince's voice occupies two registers: he can produce both a delicate, reedy falsetto and a growling, funky baritone. (*Rolling Stone* referred to it as Prince's "Jekyll and Hyde" voice [Moon 75].)

To complement his androgyny, Prince normally performs with one central female counterpart who both sings and dances. Although several women have played this role of onstage muse, all have been fashioned into female versions of the star. All have been—like Prince himself—of mixed race (black and white) parents; all have been given one-word stagenames (Apollonia, Vanity, Mayte); all have been dressed in costumes matching Prince's; and all have been known publicly as his lovers. The onstage proximity of women who resemble Prince reinforces the sexual ambiguity of his appeal, accentuating both his feminine beauty and his role as conqueror of women.[6] When Prince performs onstage alongside these women, the tableau created recalls Aubrey Beardsley's *Salomé* drawings of androgynous, erotic, and nearly twin creatures.

But of course, Prince and his various female doppelgängers can never really perform as twins, since that would suggest parity between them. Instead, the women who stand next to Prince function more as visual reminders of elements that he is absorbing or has already absorbed into his stage persona. In particular, the women named "Apollonia" and "Vanity" suggest exterior, allegorized aspects of Prince's persona: his Apollo-like role as a god of music and poetry, and, of course, his much-emphasized narcissism. The interchangeable one-named women onstage are the shadowy remains of the merging of dandy and *danseuse*.

JACKIE

Although she was not technically a performing artist, Jacqueline Onassis was, indisputably, a major star. And her particular appeal owes much to the ultimate merging of decadent dandy and performing woman of the mass-cultural space. It is not possible to discuss "Jackie O" without also discussing Wayne Koestenbaum's lyrical tribute to her: *Jackie Under My Skin* (1995). In fact, in certain respects, Koestenbaum has done my work for me, entitling one of the chapters in his book "Jackie as Dandy." Reminding us that the dandy "produces nothing but himself, his airs, his effects, his bons mots," Koestenbaum recalls that Jackie, too, produced "ephemeral atmospheres," creating the effect of a "momentary oda-lisque that disintegrates as soon as she turns her back" (180–81). For Koestenbaum, Jacqueline Onassis's eerily calm, blank eyes and breathy, babyish voice (which Maria Callas described as "Marilyn Monroe play-ing Ophelia" [Koestenbaum 42]) were part of a studiously created per-sona of dandyist detachment, "self-parody under the guise of seeming 'natural'" (183). He cites Onassis's own avowed interest in such dandies as Baudelaire, Oscar Wilde, and Diaghilev as further evidence of her proximity to this nineteenth-century character-type.[7] And I would add that Jackie's famous love for France and the French language only rein-forces the comparison.

Like a true dandy, Jacqueline Onassis did not owe her fame to any par-ticular action on her part; "but," as Koestenbaum says, "her inactivity was glamorous" (182). Known primarily through her association with "artifice" of all kinds—interior design, haute couture, the fine arts, her famous hairdo—Jackie could not be expected to produce any particular *thing*; her persona could never have allowed her to espouse worthy causes in the manner of Eleanor Roosevelt, for example.

Although she came from a bourgeois family with both French and Irish Catholic roots, Jacqueline Bouvier refashioned her identity accord-ing to her own taste. Despite having been born and raised in America, from girlhood she used the French pronunciation of her first name: "Jac-leen." Later, as First Lady, Jackie began writing an autobiography in an attempt to forestall any other potential biographies that might reveal her unglorious origins. In her own version of her life, Jackie perpetuated the fiction that her family was descended of a different, aristocratic Bouvier clan in France. The autobiography—which was never completed—sup-pressed entirely any mention of the Irish side of the family. Like the great nineteenth-century dandies, Jacqueline Bouvier Kennedy Onassis strove to repackage herself as nobility.

Koestenbaum raises another crucial aspect of Jackie's dandyism: her androgyny. Despite her extremely girlish voice and vast collection of clothes, Jackie's body did not suggest womanliness. "What one knew of Jackie's body: she had a difficult time bearing children . . . flat-chested-ness, collarbone, long neck, muscled arms, big feet (size 10A), large hands, broad shoulders" (119). But Jackie's ambiguous gender does not just ally her with the often effeminate dandy; it coexists with her movie-star femininity, allowing her to exercise the double appeal that comes of the merging of dandy with woman onstage.[8]

Despite Jackie's mass-cultural fame, she remained intent upon limiting any reproductions of her image or persona. These struggles to control publicity illustrate just how much Jackie O embodied the integration of the original dandyist aesthetic and machine-age stardom. While First Lady, she refused to allow photographs of herself while pregnant or smoking, as well as photographs of her children, or even the family dog. She issued an stern edict forbidding reporters to refer to her by the "undignified" "Jackie." And she instructed her official fashion designer Oleg Cassini not to make more than one copy of any outfit she wore: "I want all mine to be originals," she wrote to him, "and no fat little women hopping around in the same dress" (quoted in Kelley 103).

Over two decades later, in 1984, Jackie's strong desire for complete originality led her to litigation: she sued Christian Dior for using her likeness without her permission in a fashion advertising campaign. This court case, which she won, demonstrates particularly well how much the "Jackie" persona had become an independent construction.[9] The advertisement in question, photographed by Richard Avedon, was one of a series featuring "The Diors," a fictional high-society couple who cavorted in lavish surroundings designed to show off Dior clothes and objects of decor. In the fall of 1983, the company published advertisements in *Harper's Bazaar*, *Esquire*, *Time*, *The New Yorker*, and *New York Magazine* depicting "The Diors" getting married. The photograph included the two models portraying the Diors and a wedding party of celebrities. The caption read: "The wedding of the Diors was everything a wedding should be: no tears, no rice, no in-laws, no smarmy toasts, for once no Mendelssohn. Just a legendary private affair" (quoted in Gaines 465). The members of the wedding party included actress Ruth Gordon, television film critic Gene Shalit, model Shari Belafonte, and "Jackie Onassis"—or rather, an actress named Barbara Reynolds whose physical resemblance to Jackie was remarkable. The other celebrities in the ad portrayed themselves, but "Jackie" had been hired from the Ron Smith Celebrity Look-Alike Agency.

The Onassis v. Dior action turned on the right of privacy. In his decision for the plaintiff, Judge Edward J. Greenfield wrote: "If we truly value the right of privacy in a world of exploitation, where every mark of distinctiveness becomes grist for the mills of publicity, then we must give it more than lip service and grudging recognition" (quoted in Gaines 472). The defense argued that Barbara Reynolds's striking resemblance to Jacqueline Onassis was "natural" and that the Dior company had not, therefore, invaded anyone's privacy or stolen any "mark of distinctiveness." The court's decision, however, proved that, by 1983, to be "Jackie O" meant much more than having been born Jacqueline Bouvier. As Jane Gaines writes, "This law [privacy law] is finally not interested in what is commonly thought to be a natural bond between the body and the self" (475). Jackie's self could now exist apart from her body. The decades of careful image-making had worked: Jackie Onassis's face was an indisputable sign of "high society." But, at the same time, the exclusivity of high society had vanished; in its place stood a simulacrum: the "legendary private affair" that was not private, a campy wedding as imagined by Madison Avenue. A recognizable face was now detachable from its original owner.

Although the court enjoined the Dior company from using Barbara Reynolds in their advertising, Jackie could never recapture her persona; the dandyist self she had created metamorphosed into a mass-cultural icon. "Jackie" had become an instantly recognizable persona, seamless and infinitely reproducible, regardless of whether Jackie herself was producing it. In much the same way that John Wayne or Humphrey Bogart could play only "themselves" onscreen (and then be impersonated by countless comedians), Jacqueline Kennedy Onassis became a performance to be endless repeated. No "offscreen" self ever intruded to debunk that performance (and toward that end, friends were sworn to secrecy about her most private life).[10]

Oddly, an undergraduate performance of a classical play illustrates effectively the iconicity of Jackie-ness. In the winter of 1994, students at Mt. Holyoke College staged Euripides' *The Trojan Women*, with "Jackie Kennedy" starring as Helen of Troy. The actress playing Helen/Jackie provoked stunned and thunderous applause when she walked onstage "dressed in a Chanel suit, wrap-around sunglasses, and a pillbox hat" (Monahan 15).

The young director of this play had understood very well the usefulness of the camp icon. Inserting the "Jackie" persona into the role of Helen, she distorted that character's fictional boundaries and added a second layer of performance to the play. Underneath the actor's onstage identity of Helen lay the equally constructed and theatrical persona of Jackie Kennedy. This version of *The Trojan Women* takes the scenario of Mallarmé's *Le Phénomène futur* and reverses it. Instead of a regal and ancient *Femme d'autrefois* returning to inspire a modern audience, here a regal *Femme d'autrefois*—Helen of Troy—conjures a modern media heroine. And, of course, the fact that Jacqueline Kennedy Onassis would, in some sense, represent a "woman of yore" for college students born in the mid-1970s adds a further dramatic twist and another layer of masquerade to the performance.

In my first chapter I wrote of dandyism's contagion of style, its habit of seeping into the lives and prose styles of those who write of it, blurring any line of separation between the performance of dandyism and its literature. *Jackie Under My Skin* proves that a similar contagion of style takes hold when the subject is a media icon instead of a dandy. As a gay man's tribute to a diva, Koestenbaum's book is itself something of a camp performance (although its beauty and subtlety make it, like Wilde's

18. Writer Wayne Koestenbaum photographed for *New York* magazine in full dandy regalia. © Barron Claiborne/OUTLINE.

Salomé, much more than that as well). A commercial press, Farrar, Straus and Giroux, published the book; and the subsequent media attention transformed Koestenbaum, an associate professor of literature at Yale, into a celebrity in his own right. Excerpts of *Jackie Under My Skin* surfaced in popular magazines and newspapers, including *The New York Times Magazine*; and it grew difficult to distinguish Koestenbaum from his subject matter: he was a media star writing about media stars. *New York* magazine, which renamed him "The Philosopher of Fabulousness," seated Koestenbaum upon a salmon-colored brocade divan and photographed him in a blue silk ascot and maroon smoking jacket (Fig. 18). Somehow, Jackie's celebrity had gotten under his skin in the same way it had gotten under Helen of Troy's up in South Hadley, Massachusetts. The power of her performance had combined with Koestenbaum's own talent for performatively arch and lyrical writing. As we have seen, Jackie herself connoted a certain doubleness, embodying both the dandy and the woman onstage. As a result of his elegiacal contemplation of her, Koestenbaum, a dandyist intellectual, melded his own identity with Jackie's. Jackie in turn infused Koestenbaum with her double nature, adding new layers to his own literary performance and shining upon it the light of popular culture. This new performance, made up of Koestenbaum and Onassis, created a modern, reworked version of the duos we saw in earlier chapters, such as Mallarmé and Loie Fuller, when the poet devoted his famous essay to her cabaret art, or again, Mallarmé and his ephemeral "femme à la mode" in *La Dernière Mode*.

Dandyism in the American University

Finally, at the risk of indulging in what is now often called "moi" criticism, I would like to add a word about what I believe initially sparked my interest in dandyist performance and its relationship to women: the experience of doing graduate-level literature studies in America in the 1980s. The intensely performative nature of this world has not received a lot of attention, partly perhaps because the "public" that witnesses the spectacle in this case always belongs to the spectacle; there is, therefore, no "outside" world to receive and critique the show. But there was indeed a show, featuring a few very charismatic, usually male personalities whose force and magnetism generated much of the excitement that surrounded literary criticism in the 1970s and 1980s in America.

I had wondered for several years why the topic of dandyism had so fascinated me. It certainly had not been discussed in any seminars or lectures I can remember. And very little American criticism has actually taken dandyism as a serious topic (books by Ellen Moers, Domna Stanton, and Jessica Feldman, published over a thirty-three-year period, appear to be the only ones). I realized only after writing this book that though dandyism had not provided the content for many individual literary critical works, it had, in fact, been the main mode of *transmission* for much of the theory and criticism that comprised my graduate education.

What I mean by this is that the "golden age" of literary theory in America—the years when a series of major universities on both coasts showcased a Continental cast of visiting intellectuals—depended upon communication accomplished through rapture, through enthrallment. The effect of which I am speaking originated with Jacques Derrida and Paul de Man, whose (albeit very different) personalities elicited more than usual devotion and emulation. I must add here that I am not suggesting that deconstruction is itself a dandyist mode of reading. A version of such an argument has been made by Jessica Feldman and indirectly suggested by Jonathan Loesberg.[11] Instead, I am interested in something that neither Feldman nor Loesberg has examined: the relationship between the cult of personality and the practice of literary scholarship, specifically deconstruction (as it began at Yale University) and its immediate successors.

Dandyism reproduces itself through the charismatic and textual power of its avatars. Brummell rose by dint of sheer social magnetism and inspired others to dandyism through his example, and through the narratives that he engendered. And while dandyist charisma appears to flout social institutions, it is, nevertheless, entirely bound up with them. Brummell's success, for example, depended greatly upon his unlikely proximity, as a commoner, to the prince of Wales. While dandies may turn away from actual class hierarchies, they do so only to recreate them again in their own parallel social universe. A certain bad faith, therefore, lurks at the heart of this movement, which, while mocking society and advocating an overturning of social convention, depends entirely upon that society for its success. Dandyism embodies the contradiction of the self-proclaimed, independent social genius and his need to exist within (and reproduce) the very institutions he critiques. At its height, deconstruction in America embodied the same contradiction.

Like dandyism, the deconstructive movement saw itself as a socially disruptive force, transgressing traditional interpretive practices, taking apart hierarchical binary oppositions, and dismantling Western metaphysics. In the social realm, however, deconstruction recreated some of the very binary oppositions it condemned. Despite its theoretical tenets, the movement constructed a dandyist cult of personality headed by charismatic master professors who dazzled disciples—an inner sanctum, essentially, defined by and against the unenlightened outer world.

The most charismatic of the deconstructive dandies was, of course, Jacques Derrida. While maintaining a persona of serene and benign detachment, Derrida sent powerful waves of desire, anecdote, and anxiety through several generations of graduate students and junior faculty in America.[12] To have traveled to Paris to study with him, to have visited his home, to have met his family or been given his personal telephone number—these were all tokens of exchange, a form of private currency among an entire community of young scholars (much the way a nodded greeting from Beau Brummell was reputed to be more valuable than money in gaining social status). One young man, a well-known American disciple, liked to remind classmates of his close telephonic connection with Derrida by asking them repeatedly (over many years): "Do you have a message for Jacques?"

19. Jacques Derrida as photographed for *The New York Times Sunday Magazine*.
© Richard Melloul/SYGMA.

Derrida's charisma depended (and still depends) upon his powerful force of intellect, certainly, but also upon his hushed voice, which requires that one lean in closely to hear, his famous mane of silver hair, his Parisian charm and urbanity, his exquisite taste in clothes, and his movie-star handsomeness (Fig. 19).[13] (In 1994, a writer for *The New York Times* magazine opined that "Derrida is usually the most elegant man in the room" [Stephens 24].) Since Derrida remains a visitor in America, unlike the late de Man (who lived permanently in this country), his presence in classrooms and lecture halls always carries the excitement of the "foreign," a necessary component of dandyism. ("It [the word 'dandy'] will remain foreign like the thing it represents" ["Il (le mot 'dandy') restera étranger comme la chose qu'il exprime"], wrote Barbey d'Aurevilly [*Du Dandysme* 670].) Mid-nineteenth-century French dandies yearned to achieve Englishness; and the late-Victorian British dandies strove for Gallic elegance. A similar nostalgia and idealization of foreignness pervaded American deconstructive circles as well, where love of French culture extended far beyond intellectual interest. And as is always the case in America, familiarity with France connoted a certain social refinement, an advantageous association with the upper classes.

It is easy to see Jacques Derrida's dandyism; his presence created aesthetic as well as intellectual and social commotion every time he visited the States. Less apparent, but equally powerful, was the dandyism of

Paul de Man. This slightly rumpled Belgian displayed none of the cash-mere-clad panache of his French colleague. Instead, de Man held court with a different, more American version of dandyism, what might be called a "technologized" dandyism.

In *Cultural Capital*, John Guillory has written compellingly of the po-litical ramifications of de Manian deconstruction, its relationship to charisma, and its dependence upon the "technical." Guillory raises the issue of whether deconstruction was, in fact, the "subversive" (the word is de Man's) force that many claimed. To examine that question, he looks to deconstruction's relationship to institutionality. Distinguishing de Man's brand of charisma from the Weberian sort—which, he believes, is anti-institutional in its purest form[14]—Guillory writes: "[Deconstruc-tion] is always and from the first, 'institutionalized' as it has no other locus of practice, dissemination or resistance than university literature departments" (242). Although the powerfully charismatic leadership of someone such as Paul de Man was portrayed as either unimportant (since only the work mattered) or anti-institutional, it was, in fact, as John Guillory has shown, imbricated in the social reality of the university. Despite de Man's insistence that "teaching is not primarily an intersub-jective relationship," and that "the only teaching worthy of the name is scholarly, not personal" (*Resistance* 4), Guillory holds that "the personal talent and charisma of the professor . . . are never entirely distinguishable from the status hierarchy of the institution" (253). He points to de Man-ian deconstruction's denial of its "charismatic network," citing essays by students and colleagues that hold that de Man cared nothing for the cult that formed around him, that he "detached" himself from authority, and that he rejected the adoring fascination of his students. ("To love . . . to desire . . . is always to be dependent," wrote Barbey d'Aurevilly [*Du Dandysme* 686].) It is in this detachment that we begin to find the tech-nological dandyism of de Man. For Guillory, de Man's and his disciples' very denial of their emotional investment in one another "belongs to the official ideology of the bureaucratic organization, to its language of 'im-personal' relations and merely 'technical' standards" (259).

Guillory's reading of American deconstruction uncovers its profound connection to bureaucratic charisma and psychoanalytic transference, its complicated relation to canon formation, and its institutional, and hence unsubversive and unradical, underpinnings. To his brilliant reading of the de Manian movement, I would only wish to add that the *particular* brand of charisma generated by de Man actually belongs to a category that reached its peak in the late nineteenth century. De Manian charisma and the cult of theory staged a grand, dandyist, scientific spectacle. This spectacle drew life from the social stir created around the sublimely calm, apparently disinterested presence of de Man. And like Villiers's Edison, this central dandy protagonist was a technical wizard, a combination of elaborately staged pedagogic performance and a "science" that took theory as its instrument.

"Theory"[15] became a powerful, highly technical tool, "a mimesis of the technobureaucratic itself," as Guillory remarks (262). But de Man did not just disappear anonymously into a routinized, bureaucratized structure: instead, he acquired an individualist, dandyist appeal that stemmed directly from this scientificity. De Man's performance displaced the realm of the aesthetic in dandyism—so evident in Derrida's polished demeanor—onto the realm of the mechanical or scientific (just as in *L'Eve future* Edison's dandyism expresses itself through his catalogue of inventions).[16] Geoffrey Hartman seems aware of this quality in his colleague, writing of de Man: "He did not attract by flamboyance but by rigor and severity" (quoted in Lehman 151). Although defined here as opposites, "flamboyance" and "rigor" are close neighbors in Hartman's remark; both attract, and powerfully.

The stress on the scientific-sounding concept of "rigor" in literary readings (a concept Guillory also dissects) necessarily overflowed into the social. The ideal student of deconstruction needed to display a personal, scientific rigor that matched his intellectual rigor—an aura of self-denial and nearly monastic devotion to a life of literary work. I would argue that the twin realms of science and rigor are coded in our society as male, and that, as a result, despite its many female participants, the deconstructive movement remained predominantly male in character. The most successful, eager graduate-student disciples—those most clearly at ease—were individuals colloquially known as "theory jocks"; and "jocks" (like scientists) are, generally, men. Naturally, I do not imply here that there have been no fine deconstructive critics who were also women (Barbara Johnson, Cynthia Chase). I mean to suggest, rather, that even those women who succeeded in this realm did so only after struggling with a cult of discipleship that reproduced itself through a dandyist structure of charismatic father and chosen sons.[17] And, as in dandyism, that reproduction was accomplished through intense emulation stripped of excess emotion, affect, or adornment. Students and young professors imitated de Man's cryptic, hieratic style,[18] and many of the subsequent, successful deconstructive critics attracted similar, second-tier cult followings.

In recent years, as deconstruction has waned in American universities, the intensity of the dandyist personality cult has waned with it.[19] But moving through an educational system that placed so much emphasis on the male dandy-star personality, I was led inevitably to study what happens when women's performances encounter the dandy's. The answer is complicated. Among those women critics who have achieved a degree of academic stardom, many have done so by engaging in a somewhat auto-biographical form of scholarship, combining their personal lives with their theoretical positions in a way Derrida and de Man never did. Jane Gallop, Alice Kaplan, Eve Sedgwick, and Marianna Torgovnick have all included personal history in their writings.[20] Unlike most male academic celebrities, these women put themselves much more overtly onstage in their work, blurring the distinction between their private and public identities. In so doing, they resemble the female performers of the nine-teenth century, those women who faced the dandies from the other side of the footlights. Personal criticism (including the bit in which I indulge here), made for more overt literary spectacle.

I make no claims for exact parallels between the world of elite American universities of the 1980s and the fin de siècle studied in these pages. Since, however, I have tried in this book to locate the roots of contemporary American culture in European literary culture of the last fin de siècle, I thought it fitting to conclude by finding the origin of my own nineteenth-century interests in the social atmosphere that surrounded my education but has remained, until now, unacknowledged.

NOTES

INTRODUCTION

1. See Richard Halpern's *Shakespeare Among the Moderns* for a discussion of the relationship between foreignness and mechanicity in Schwarzenegger's various film personae.

2. See J. S. Bratton, *Music Hall Performance and Style*, and Peter Bailey, ed., *Music Hall*.

3. See Giovanna Franci's discussion in *Il sistema del dandy*.

4. *Du Dandysme* 672. The original French reads: "En effet, il ne fut qu'un dandy," which, curiously, could also be interpreted as, "Indeed, he was only a dandy"—a possibility that suggests the paradox of the dandy: he is at once unique and endlessly imitable.

5. "On ne citera pas les mots de Brummell . . . il régna encore plus par les airs que par les mots" (ibid., 697).

6. "On touche vite quand on écrit cette histoire d'impressions plutôt que de faits, à la disparition du météore, à la fin de cet incroyable roman . . . dont la société de Londres fut l'héroïne et Brummell le héros" (ibid., 700).

7. Barbey's later *Les Diaboliques* abounds with dandyist characters.

8. About Lorrain's personal, outrageous dandyism, Michel Desbruères writes: "Throughout the chaos of his career, his books were always measured against his own life" (in Lorrain, *Histoire*, 13).

9. See Favardin, especially 68.

10. "Ivres de porto gingembré, ces *blasés*, dévorés de spleen, y venaient chaque nuit cuver le mortel ennui de leur vie et soulever leur sang de Normands. . . . Brummell . . . était l'astre de ce fameux club. . . . Il y avait dans sa gloire et dans sa position un côté aléatoire par lequel l'une et l'autre devaient s'écouler. Comme tous les joueurs, il s'acharna contre le sort et fut vaincu" (*Du Dandysme* 704). (Though the translation of Barbey here is mostly mine, I have borrowed a few phrases from Douglas Ainslie's elegant English version, p. 65.)

11. "Le cerveau enflammé . . . il va de partenaire en partenaire, de corps en corps. . . . Les amours de Lorrain sont comme une partie de cartes: une méchanique qui absorbe l'angoisse profonde dans la palpitante insécurité du hasard et du danger" (Favardin 178).

12. Barbey was fond of writing with colored inks, and appreciated careful, beautiful handwriting. To Trébutien he wrote: "You really have the handwriting of one of those medieval monks who copied manuscripts in such grand style. The vulgar, egalitarian, and plebeian workings of the printing press seem to me so pitiful in comparison" ("Vous avez réellement la main d'un de ces moines du Moyen Age qui copiaient d'une si grande manière les manuscrits. Que les procédés vulgaires, égalitaires, plébassiers de l'imprimerie me semblent misérables en comparaison"; quoted in Kempf, *Dandies*, 64).

CHAPTER ONE
THE TREATISES OF DANDYISM

1. Roland Chollet describes the early political reaction of *La Mode* as "knowingly ambiguous" (305), an adroit attempt to avoid offending either side. An early editorial in the journal went so far as to laud the revolution as "le soleil de juillet 1830" (ibid., 335).

2. French dandyism was sustained and influenced importantly by the rise of journalism during the reign of Louis-Philippe (see Moers). Emile de Girardin, who also published *Le Voleur* and *La Silhouette*, contributed greatly to the spread of dandyist literature by printing articles by dandies such as Balzac and the pre-Socialist Eugène Sue.

3. In a show of aristocratic sympathy (or pretension), the young journalist Honoré Balzac chose, in that same year of 1830, to add the aristocratic particule "de" to his name (Moers 130).

4. "L'homme de goût doit toujours savoir réduire le besoin au simple." "La multiplicité de couleurs sera de mauvais goût" (*Traité* 176).

5. "Un homme devient riche; il naît élégant" (ibid., 162).

6. "Pour être fashionable, il faut jouir du repos sans avoir passé par le travail" (ibid., 155). Rose Fortassier observes that the July Monarchy marked a renaissance of "la vie mondaine," but with a difference. The post-1789 revoking of the "droit d'aînesse," or primogeniture, and the resulting division of fortunes diminished the monumental wealth and power of noble families. A new, compensatory interest in the individual appeared, along with a new emphasis on "l'ornement quotidien" and personal elegance, which were replacing the pre-Revolutionary grandeur (Fortassier 80–85). Christopher Prendergast calls Balzac's text "an attempt to negotiate a deep anxiety with regard to the mapping, the 'legibility,' of the social landscape . . . in which the perception of ranks and occupations, origins and identities, can no longer reliably orientate itself within a fixed structure of differentiation" (*Mimesis* 93).

7. "Il est inutile d'ajouter que nous devons à Brummell les inductions philosophiques par lesquelles nous sommes arrivés à démontrer . . . combien la vie élégante se liait fortement à la perfection de toute société humaine" (*Traité* 165).

8. "Boulogne était son rocher de Sainte-Hélène, tous nos sentiments se confondirent dans un respectueux enthousiasme" (ibid.). It was Lord Byron who first made this comparison, claiming that he would rather have been Brummell than Napoleon (Fortassier 5).

9. "Rien ne ressemble moins à l'homme qu'*un homme*" (*Traité* 167); "les actions . . . ne sont jamais que les conséquences de notre toilette" (ibid., 168). It is most likely that Balzac knew of these remarks through the "fashionable" novels of Bulwer-Lytton or Lister-Normanby (Chollet 321).

10. "Les idées de l'homme barbifié n'étaient pas celles de l'homme barbu" (*Traité* 168).

11. See Habermas's *Structural Transformation* for a discussion of Sterne's redefinition of the role of the narrator and the importance of these novelistic

definition of the role of the narrator and the importance of these novelistic changes in the rise of the bourgeois concept of the public space.

12. In the interview, Brummell advises his interlocutor to devote the second section to general principles—"les lois générales"—of elegant living, the third to "la toilette," and the fourth section to accessories. While claiming some disagreement with this advice, Balzac carries it out, except for the fourth section, which would not be completed until 1833 and was to become his *Théorie de la démarche*. By having this character give advice and staging a conversation with him, Balzac inscribes himself in an eighteenth-century tradition of novelistic free play. That the character in question was a historical personage and a celebrity moves the text toward camp.

13. Playing curiously with the issues of reproduction and originality, Balzac's *Traité* repeats, nearly verbatim, an earlier article—written by someone else—that had appeared in *La Mode* on April 3, 1830. Here, for example, is Balzac on the distinction between elegance and vanity: "Therefore, reduced to the toilette, elegance consists of extreme care in the details of dress: it is less the simplicity of luxury than the luxury of simplicity. There is certainly another elegance; but it is merely vanity in toilette." ("Alors, réduite à la toilette, l'élégance consiste en une extrême recherche dans les détails de l'habillement: c'est moins la simplicité du luxe qu'un luxe de simplicité. Il y a bien une autre élégance; mais elle n'est que la vanité dans la toilette," *Traité* 182.) And here is the relevant portion of the earlier article (which is never acknowledged or footnoted by Balzac): "Reduced simply to toilette, elegance is extreme care in the details of dress, down to those that are the least perceived and perfect harmony in the ensemble.—The other elegance, which is merely external and should be called *false elegance*, can be characterized thus: vanity reduced to toilette." ("Réduite seulement à la toilette, l'élégance est une recherche extrême dans les détails d'habillement, jusqu'à ceux qui y sont le moins aperçus et un accord parfait dans l'ensemble.—L'autre élégance, celle qui n'est qu'extérieure, celle que l'on devrait appeler *la fausse élégance*, peut ainsi se caractériser: la vanité réduite à la toilette"; quoted in Chollet 323.) It would be farfetched to claim that this "borrowing" of another journalist's dandified article represented a conscious, dandyist performance on the part of Balzac. It is more likely that he was in need of extra text and felt free to lift some passages from another writer. Nonetheless, the result is that this article on the importance of originality winds up being, in part, a lifeless copy, a reproduction.

14. Roger Kempf recounts an anecdote in which that other great dandy, Barbey d'Aurevilly, claimed a spiritual, nearly mystical connection with the Beau. In 1855, Barbey was imprisoned for three days for refusing to serve in the National Guard. Having requested writing tools, he was offered grocers' wrapping paper, which he refused as a great indignity, claiming that the specter of Brummell himself had risen up to protect him from such vulgarities: "Old Brummell's soul rose up in my soul and forbade me to touch those bourgeois horrors" ("L'âme du vieux *Brummell* s'est levée dans mon âme et m'a défendu de toucher à ces bourgeoises horreurs"; quoted in Kempf 29).

15. "Camp is the glorification of 'character'," writes Susan Sontag in her famous essay on the topic (285).

16. "Paved Paradise: The Songs of Joni Mitchell" was performed at the West-beth Theatre Center in September 1996. In the first act, Kelly dressed as the 1970s Mitchell, in a long flowered dress. In the second act, he wore a more 1980s-style black lamé gown. His gestures, his laugh, and his between-song patter were all lifted directly from Mitchell's concerts. He never once broke character; the result was at once disturbing, brilliant parody and deeply respectful homage.

17. Dollimore 310–11. Matias Veineger sums up the phenomenon pithily: "If camp treats life as theater, is in part because identity is treated as a role" (251). He goes on to explain this as a consequence of the dissimulation forced upon gays and lesbians, "especially for gays and lesbians who can only survive by *passing*, pretending to be heterosexual."

18. "Semblables aux machines à vapeur, les hommes enrégimentés par le travail se produisent tous sous la même forme et n'ont rien d'individuel. L'homme-instrument est une sorte de zéro social" (*Traité* 153).

19. "En se faisant dandy, un homme devient un meuble de boudoir, un mannequin extrêmement ingénieux, qui peut se poser sur un cheval ou sur un canapé . . . mais un être pensant . . . jamais" (ibid., 177).

20. See Chapter Five for a discussion of this in Wilde.

21. Stoker, though not a dandyist novelist, was very much a fin-de-siècle artist; and the gothic melodrama of *Dracula* shares with decadence its fascination with occult eroticism. The use, in *Dracula*, of the phonograph as a dictation machine is tied to the main plot issues of homoeroticism and nonbiological reproduction of a species (of vampires). Works by Lorrain and Villiers will be discussed in this chapter and in Chapter Three.

22. Emilien Carassus has discussed the purely social dandyism of Balzac's writings: "Balzac's dandies, Maxime de Trailles or Henri de Marsay, are irreproachable in their dress, refined in their manners, but their dandyism is, above all, a means for social climbing" (Carassus 28).

23. Despite the differences in their dandyism, Barbey was a great admirer of Balzac's *Traité*. He writes: "[He] inaugurates in the nineteenth century a particular literary genre that has been known for a long time in England ('fashionable' literature or literature of the 'high life'), and which, not existing in France, is now emerging here, thanks to Balzac's masterpiece. Before him no one had ever thought of writing an *Esprit des Lois* for the elegant life . . . in France and in England—the only two countries where this life is possible—, until Balzac, no one had ever thought of legislating this life or of deriving its philosophy." ("[Il] inaugure dans la littérature française du xixè siècle un genre particulier de littérature qui a son nom depuis longtemps en Angleterre [la littérature fashionable ou de high life] et qui, n'existant pas en France, y débute grâce à Balzac par un chef d'oeuvre. Personne avant lui n'avait eu l'idée d'un *Esprit des Lois* de la vie élégante . . . cette vie avait eu, en France et en Angleterre—les deux seuls pays où elle soit possible—jusqu'à Balzac, personne dans ces pays n'avait pensé à en faire la législation et à en dégager la philosophie," quoted in Fortassier 57.)

24. "Qu'ils prennent l'air dégoûté, s'ils veulents, et se gantent de blanc jusqu'au coude, le pays de Richelieu ne produira pas de Brummell" (*Du Dandysme* 671).

25. "[Le mot *dandysme*] restera étranger comme la chose qu'il exprime" (ibid., 670).

26. Barbey does devote several pages at the beginning to a history of English mores and pre-Brummell, protodandyist figures, such as the "bucks" and the "macaronis."

27. "L'admiration ne se justifiant point par des faits qui ont péri tout entiers, parce que, de leur nature, ils étaient éphémères . . . ce sont les manières, les intransmissibles manières, par lesquelles Brummell fut un prince de son temps" (*Du Dandysme* 677).

28. This struggle between real and acquired royalty mirrors Barbey's own personal conflict with his aristocratic roots. Although his family had been genuinely noble, the Norman d'Aurevillys had been financially ruined by the Revolution. "Democracy is the sovereignty of the ignoble," he wrote. "Believe me. . . . It levels individuals and threatens the original. I may well search for truth among the masses, I will only encounter it in individuals." ("La démocratie est la souveraineté de l'ignoble. On peut m'en croire. . . . Elle nivelle les individus et ménace les êtres originaux. J'ai beau chercher la vérité dans les masses, je ne la renontre que dans les individus"; quoted in Favardin 105).

29. "A dater de ce moment, il se trouva classé très haut dans l'opinion. On le vit de préférence aux plus nobles noms de l'Angleterre, lui le fils d'un simple esquire. . . . Tant de distinction groupa immédiatement autour de lui, sur le pied de la familiarité la plus flatteuse, l'aristocratie des salons" (*Du Dandysme* 685).

30. "Le Régent commençait à vieillir. L'embonpoint, ce polype qui saisit la beauté et la tue lentement dans ses molles entreintes, l'embonpoint l'avait pris, et Brummell, avec son implacable plaisanterie et cet orgeuil de tigre que le succès inspire aux coeurs, s'était quelquefois moqué des efforts de coquette impuissante à réparer les dégâts du temps qui compromettaient le Prince de Galles. Comme il y avait à Carlton House un concierge d'une monstrueuse corpulence qu'on avait surnommé Big Ben ('Le Gros Ben'), Brummell avait déplacé le surnom du valet au maître. Il appelait aussi Mme Fitz-Herbert *Benina*. . . . Telle fut . . . la cause réelle de la disgrâce qui frappa soudainement le grand Dandy. . . . Le 'Quel est ce gros homme?' dit publiquement par Brummell, à Hyde Park, en désignant Son Altesse Royale, et une foule d'autres mots semblables, expliquent tout" (ibid., 701).

31. "Il resta mis d'une façon irréprochable; mais il éteignit les couleurs de ses vêtements, en simplifia la coupe et les porta sans y penser" (ibid., 692).

32. "Un Dandy peut mettre . . . dix heures à sa toilette, mais une fois faite, il l'oublie. Ce sont les autres qui doivent s'apercevoir qu'il est bien mis" (ibid.).

33. "Dans le monde, tout le temps que vous n'avez pas produit d'effet, restez: si l'effet est produit, allez-vous-en" (ibid., 687).

34. "Pourquoi les raconter? C'est du Dandy qu'il est question, de son influence, de sa vie publique, de son rôle social. Qu'importe le reste? Quand on meurt de faim, on sort des affectations d'une société quelconque, on rentre dans la vie humaine: on cesse d'être Dandy" (ibid., 713).

35. Kantorowicz believes that this particular expression was first used at the interrment of Louis XII in 1515. Discussing the distinction between the material body of the king and his invested powers, Kantorowicz writes: "A continuity of

the king's natural body or of individual king's acting in hereditary succession as 'guardians of the crown'—was vouched for the by the dynastic idea" (383).

36. One could make a comparison here between the overweight prince of Wales of this anecdote and the Henry VIII depicted in Hans Holbein's famous portrait. In Holbein's painting, the king's girth is a guarantor of power; in Barbey's text, however, the prince of Wales is merely fat.

37. Leo Bersani echoes this opinion, writing, "Dandyism is the bizarre modern form of individualism. No longer sanctioned by the social authority of an aristocracy, the individual ... discovers himself to be a purely psychological myth" (Bersani, *Culture*, 79).

38. "Les dandys de leur autorité privée posent une règle au-dessus de celle qui régit les cercles les plus aristocratiques" (*Du Dandysme* 681).

39. "Quoique Alcibiade ait été le plus des bons généraux, George Bryan Brummell n'avait pas l'esprit militaire" (ibid., 688).

40. In deference to his recent dandyist history, Barbey referred to Balzac's Henri de Marsay as "le machiavel Alcibiade" (quoted in Fortassier 79).

41. "Natures doubles et multiples, d'un sexe intellectual indécis, où la grâce est plus grâce encore dans la force, et où la force se retrouve encore dans la grâce, Androgynes de l'Histoire, non plus de la Fable et dont Alcibiades fut le plus beau type chez la plus belle des nations" (*Du Dandysme* 718). Brummell's interest in ancient Greece extended to its sartorial style as well. Late in his life, having moved his place of exile from Calais to Caen, he wrote a book on the history of clothing from the Roman invasion to 1822. For Brummell, clothing had only decreased in beauty and purity since the days of antiquity; and he held the flowing lines of Greek and Roman robes to be the most noble and desirable (Coblence 117).

42. "Elles furent les trompettes de sa gloire, mais elles restèrent trompettes. . . . Il n'était ce que le monde appelle libertin. . . . Aimer . . . désirer, c'est toujours dépendre, c'est être esclave de son désir. Les bras les plus tendrement fermés sur vous sont encore une chaîne. . . . Voilà l'esclavage auquel Brummell échappa. Ses triomphes eurent l'insolence du désintéressement" (*Du Dandysme* 686).

43. "La plus follement amoureuse, en posant une fleur ou en essayant une parure, songeait bien plus au jugement de Brummell qu'au plaisir de son amant" (ibid., 687).

44. "The dandy evokes a fully equipped machine, from which all life is absent, a well-regulated artifact," writes Coblence (148). She goes on to compare Brummell to Dr. Frankenstein: "Brummell competes with the Creator no less [than Frankenstein]" (151).

45. Guys was of French origin but was born in Holland. He traveled extensively, especially to England, settling eventually in Paris, and this internationalism marks a move away from the earlier ideal of purely British dandyism (Gilman 141).

46. "L'artiste imaginaire que nous sommes convenus d'appeler M.G. car je me souviens de temps en temps que je me suis promis, pour mieux rassurer sa modestie, de supposer qu'il n'existait pas" (*Le Peintre* 1169).

47. "L'homme attaché à sa palette comme le serf à sa glèbe" (ibid., 1158).

48. De Man, *Blindness and Insight*, 157. De Man looks to Baudelaire's essay on Guys as an example of modernity's "temporal ambivalence" (156–61), its grappling with the problem of re-presenting the present.

49. "Je le nommerais volontiers un *dandy*, car le mot dandy implique une quintessence de caractère et une intelligence subtile . . . mais d'un autre côté, le dandy aspire à l'insensibilité" (*Le Peintre* 1160).

50. "C'est à la peinture des moeurs du présent que je veux m'attacher aujourd'hui" (ibid., 1152).

51. "Le dandy est blasé, ou il feint de l'être . . . sa passion et sa profession, c'est d'épouser la foule. . . . L'observateur est un prince, qui jouit partout de son incognito . . . [il] entre dans la foule comme dans un immense reservoir d'éléctricité" (ibid., 1160). The text here echoes Baudelaire's 1861 prose poem *Les Foules*: "He who weds the crowd easily knows feverish pleasures unknown to both the egotist, who remains closed like a safe chest, and the lazy man who is confined like a mollusk" ("Celui-là qui épouse facilement la foule connaît des jouissances fiévreuses, dont seront éternellement privés l'égoiste, fermé comme un coffre, et le paresseux, interné comme un mollusque," *Petits poèmes en prose* 16).

52. About the December 2, 1851 coup d'état of Louis Napoleon, and the following plebiscite, Baudelaire wrote in a letter dated March 5, 1852, "The second December has physically depoliticized me (*m'a physiquement dépolitiqué*)"; *Selected Letters* 45. "His statement," writes Ross Chambers, "can stand as a motto for the literature of the midcentury and after, which found itself—to borrow a metaphor from Gilles Deleuze and Félix Guattari—'deterritorialized.' . . . Deterritorialized art entered a period of confused self-interrogation concerning the referential value of artistic signs: what was art to be 'about?' A formalist movement proclaimed the separatist doctrine of 'art for art's sake,' which had tempted Théophile Gautier since his preface to *Mademoiselle de Maupin* (1835), itself a response to the July Monarchy's authoritarian turn. It was to flourish in the parnassian movement" (Chambers, "Literature Deterritorialized," 711). On the other hand, Richard Burton, in *Baudelaire and the Second Republic*, maintains that the poet remained very politically engaged, only in a new way. Burton reads Baudelaire's self-proclaimed "depoliticization" as the destruction of "his faith in electoral politics," a move from "the old-style confrontational model of the Blanquists to the new democ-soc strategy of eschewing head-on clashes"—in other words, to a more Proudhonian politics (353ff.).

53. "Une espèce de nouvelle aristocratie . . . basée sur les dons célestes que le travail et l'argent ne peuvent conférer. Le dandysme est le dernier éclat d'héroisme dans les décadences" (*Le Peintre* 1179).

54. "Ici nous sommes à Schumla . . . hospitalité turque, pipes et café. . . . Le roi Othon et la reine . . . sont revêtus du costume traditionnel. . . . La taille du roi est sanglée comme celle du plus coquet palikare, et sa jupe s'évase avec l'exagération du dandysme national" (ibid., 1170).

55. "Les lourdes voitures massives . . . d'où jaillissent quelquefois des regards curieusement féminins, . . . les danses frenétiques des baladins du *troisième sexe* (jamais l'expression bouffonne de Balzac ne fut plus applicable . . . car . . . sous

cet ardent maquillage des joues, des yeux et des sourcils . . . dans ces longues chevelures flottant sur les reins, il vous serait difficile, pour ne pas dire impossible de deviner la virilité)" (ibid., 1172–73).

56. "De ces femmes, les unes ont conservé le costume national, les vestes brodées . . . l'écharpe tombante, les vastes pantalons . . . les mousselines rayées ou lamées . . . les autres . . . ont adopté le signe principal de la civilisation, qui, pour une femme, est invariablement la crinoline, en gardant toutefois, . . . un léger souvenir caractéristique de l'Orient, si bien qu'elle ont l'air de Parisiennes qui auraient voulu se déguiser" (ibid., 1173). Sima Godfrey has remarked that it was Gautier who first introduced the word "crinoline" into the vocabulary of French literature; here, Baudelaire pays homage to this melding of fashion and high culture (Godfrey, "Haute Couture," 761).

57. Four allusions to Guys appear in Section 6, along with five titles of drawings. In the following section, four references are made to M.G. and one title given. In Section 8, "Le Militaire," there are two overt references to M.G, and no titles given.

58. "L'homme riche, oisif, et qui . . . n'a pas d'autre occupation que de courir à la piste du bonheur . . . jouira toujours . . . d'une physiognomie distincte, tout à fait à part" (Le Peintre 1177).

59. It appears that Baudelaire had planned an extended article on dandyism alone, which he never finished; and it has been suggested that Section 9 on the dandy is actually borrowed from that unfinished piece. This would explain its marked detachment from the rest of Le Peintre (Gilman 158).

60. "Le dandysme est une institution vague, aussi bizarre que le duel; très-ancienne, puisque César, Catilina, Alcibiade nous en fournissent des types éclatants. . . . Le dandysme, qui est une institution en dehors des lois, a des lois rigoureuses. . . . Ces êtres n'ont pas d'autre état que de cultiver l'idée du beau dans leur personne" (Le Peintre 1177).

61. "Les considérations et les reveries morales . . . surgissent des dessins. . . . Ai-je besoin de dire que M.G., quand il crayonne un de ses dandys sur le papier, lui donne toujours son caractère historique, légendaire même?" (ibid., 1180).

62. Baudelaire's essay, begun one year after the publication of Gautier's, takes up where De la Mode leaves off. Gautier addressed his text to painters who rejected contemporary fashion in favor of a "classical" ideal. For Gautier, modern Paris fashion was the perfect subject for modern art. Gautier is also credited with coining the word "modernité" (Godfrey, "Haute Couture," 765).

63. "Le dandysme est le dernier éclat d'héroisme dans les décadences; et le type du dandy retrouvé par le voyageur dans l'Amérique du Nord n'infirme en aucune façon cette idée: car rien n'empêche de supposer que les tribus que nous nommons *sauvages* soient les débris de grandes civilisations disparues. Le dandysme est un soleil couchant. . . . Mais hélas! la marée montante de la démocratie, qui envahit et nivelle tout, noie jour à jour ces derniers représentants de l'orgeuil humain" (Le Peintre 1179).

64. Chateaubriand, in his essay "On America and Americans," warned that "the commercial spirit is beginning to take possession of [Americans]," and that "self-interest is becoming their national vice" (51). The Goncourt brothers called

Americans "the barbarians of civilization who will swallow up the Latin World" (quoted in Blumenthal, *American and French Culture*, 471).

65. Humphries 785. In a curious example of his personal dandyism, Baudelaire had actually misunderstood and rewritten Poe's own background. Far from being an aristocrat, Poe came from a family of sharecroppers. But Baudelaire believed that Poe's characters and stories were autobiographical, that Poe's art was indistinguishable from his life, as would be the case for a true dandy. (See Humphries.)

66. Fin-de-siècle perceptions of America will be discussed in Chapter Three's examination of *L'Eve future*—which takes place in the laboratory of a fictionalized Thomas Edison—and in Chapter Four, devoted to the mechanomorphic art of American Loie Fuller.

67. "La femme est 'naturelle,' c'est à dire abominable, aussi est-elle toujours vulgaire, c'est à dire le contraire du dandy" (*Mon coeur mis à nu* 166).

68. "Gautier's 'preface' to . . . *Mademoiselle de Maupin* (1836) is today widely acknowledged to be the first literary manifesto for the doctrine of *l'art pour l'art*. Though Gautier himself may not have been fully cognizant of the fact, the piece builds on and is permeated by a popularized, bastardized brand of Kantianism. 'Nothing is truly beautiful unless it is useless; everything useful is ugly. . . . The most useful place in a house is the lavatory'" (Bell-Villada 437).

Bell-Villada's theory is that *l'art pour l'art* was a doctrine created by artists whose specific mode of discourse and personal rhythms of production were in conflict with the demands of the newly industrialized literary market.

69. "Quel poète oserait, dans la peinture du plaisir causé par l'apparition d'une beauté, séparer la femme de son costume? Quel est l'homme qui . . . n'a pas joui . . . d'une toilette savamment composée, et n'en a pas emporté une image inséparable de la beauté de celle à qui elle appartenait, faisant ainsi des deux, de la femme et de la robe, une totalité indivisible?" (*Le Peintre* 1182).

70. "Nous voyons [les femmes] se promener nonchallament dans les allées des jardins publics" (ibid., 1186).

71. Christopher Prendergast remarks on the importance of speed as one of the "fundamental conditions of the new commodity culture [which returns] again and again in the developing lexicon of 'modernity'" (*Paris and the Nineteenth Century* 5).

72. Bersani sees Baudelaire's artist figure as "intrinsically an unanchored self" (*Baudelaire* 14). He reads the "shattering" of the self depicted in this essay as an "immense jouissance of sacrificing the moi to the non-moi." He sees the "Baudelairean aesthetic [as] inseparable from Baudelairean erotics . . . in both, jouissance is identical to the masochistic pleasure of self shattering" (*Culture* 72).

73. "In *l'art pour l'art* the poet . . . faces language the way the buyer faces the commodity on the open market" (Benjamin, *Charles Baudelaire*, 105).

74. As Richard Burton observes, "Though Cramer 'possesses' La Fanfarlo physically and is able to enjoy the spectacle of her . . . he cannot penetrate the inner sanctum of her being and appropriate for himself the creative secret she possesses . . . his attitude toward her remains . . . that of the uncreative spectator" (75).

75. La Fanfarlo clearly displays an early version of the kind of femininity Baudelaire ponders in *Le Peintre*, as Barbara Wright has noted: "La Fanfarlo prefigures the section 'La Femme' in *Le Peintre de la vie moderne* in that, amid the magic, glitter and fantasy of the theatre, 'la femme et . . . la robe' constitute 'une toilette indivisible.' . . . [La Fanfarlo's] aesthetic control of movements and form is comparable to the blend of 'volupté' and 'connaissance' so central to artistic achievement in the view of Baudelaire" (Wright and Scott 14).

76. Ross Chambers sees *La Fanfarlo* as a tale opposing two realms, the domestic or bourgeois realm that corresponds to literary realism, and a writerly realm that involves the "forgetting" of realist representation, which is associated with modernism. "Art itself," writes Chambers, "is the repressed other of the bourgeois world; but within its deterritorialized space two mutually exclusive regimes of the sign coexist: a sign subjected to naturalistic referentiality . . . and a sign made available for nonrealistic compositions of desire. And this is so whether those constructions are described in terms of the art-for-art's-sake cult of 'pure beauty,' or in terms of some supernatural—or indeed psychic—'other world,' or, finally, as Baudelaire gets close to hinting in *La Fanfarlo* (where the dancer is described as 'poetry equipped with arms and legs'), in terms of a certain *materialism* of the writerly sign—a materialism that, to us, has a surprisingly modern ring" (Chambers, "Literature Deterritorialized," 716).

That breath of the supernatural in *La Fanfarlo* becomes more internalized by the time Baudelaire writes *Le Peintre*, as the Romantic movement's fascination with the occult becomes a more interior, psychological component of Decadence.

77. "La femme est bien dans son droit . . . en s'appliquant à paraître magique et surnaturel; . . . idole, elle doit se dorer pour être adorée" (*Le Peintre* 1184).

78. The historical, orientalist novels of Jean Lombard are an excellent example of the decadents' fascination with crowds. His 1888 *L'Agonie*, and *Byzance* of 1890, both detail with delectation powerful and menacing crowds.

79. A demagogue with a military background, Boulanger was appointed to the Ministry of War and ultimately became leader of the Radical party. Although he had no political commitments and made contradictory promises to opposing groups, his powerful personal charisma hypnotized large crowds. Boulanger's mini-plebiscite won in 1888, and in 1889 his party, the Ligue des Patriotes, won in a Paris by-election. It was then that the party was prosecuted and Boulanger forced to leave France (Birkett 13). It has been suggested that he nearly brought down the Third Republic with a "new Eighteenth Brumaire" (Merton xxiii).

80. Of course, this was not the first time such an interest in the mechanical simulation of life appeared in literature. The fascination with robots and androids dates back to at least the eighteenth century (see Joseph Roach's *The Player's Passion*). The decadents, however, took this old motif and incorporated the new elements of fin-de-siècle culture, such as the presence of crowds, factories, and new techniques in mechanical reproduction.

81. The essay-portrait of women in journals was not invented by the decadents. As Lorrain's biographer Philippe Jullian observes, this was a genre that could be traced to the Second Empire, when studies of the *mondaines* and *demi-mondaines* appeared in such reviews as *La Vie Parisienne* (Jullian, *Jean Lorrain*, 114).

82. "Les cheveux en soie et les dents en vraie nacre, pour la poitrine, elle est émaillée jusqu'au nombril à cause des robes de bal . . . elle dit 'papa,' 'maman' et 'bonjour excellence' grâce à un ressort caché dans la soie du corsage et que Monsieur sait presser à propos . . . produit d'exportation: elle vient d'Amérique, sait manier l'éventail, jouer de la paupière et semble respirer comme une personne tout à fait naturelle. Et je songeais à la belle Olympia du docteur Coppelius" (*Une Femme* 139).

83. Here is another dandyist writer, Joris-Karl Huysmans, describing the ballerinas in Degas's 1879 painting *The Rehearsal*: "Nervous, gaunt girls, whose muscles bulge beneath their leotards, real dancers, with springs of steel" (*Oeuvres complètes*, 6: 55).

84. In Lorrain's novel *Monsieur de Phocas* (his most ambitious work), for example, the protagonist, Freneuse, visits a café-concert to hear a singer his friends admire. Instead of enjoying the *chanteuse*, however, Freneuse can only see in her a corpse: "A dead woman . . . an automaton with separate parts" (74).

CHAPTER TWO
MALLARMÉ

1. Even the general public at the time confused the two camps. See Wallace Fowlie's discussion of the problem in his *Mallarmé* (252–64). In fact, Arthur Symons's landmark 1908 essay, "The Symbolist Movement in France," was originally entitled "The Decadent Movement in France" (Birkett 49).

2. Philippe Jullian's comprehensive book on the topic, for example, reflects this merging of terms: *Dreamers of Decadence: Symbolist Painters of the 1890s*.

3. See Alan Raitt's critical introduction to Mallarmé's *Villiers de l'Isle-Adam* for a discussion of the relationship between the two writers.

4. Catulle Mendès described Mallarmé as having "un dandysme (un peu cassant et cassé) de geste" (quoted in Sartre, *Mallarmé*, 69). And Georges Rodenbach saw Mallarmé's conversation as "luminous and flowering . . . all crystal and roses! . . . Words inexhaustibly subtle, ennobling every subject, and with rare ornamentation: literature, music, art, life, and even news items" (quoted in Deak 91).

5. Although Mallarmé did devote two essays to female dancers (*Ballets*, about "La Cornalba," and *Les Fonds dans le Ballet*, about Loie Fuller), these are not texts that partake of the popular. Instead, they focus on the symbolist possibilities to be found in dance performance, absorbing them into the poet's usual aesthetic.

6. Mallarmé, *Oeuvres complètes*, 269–70. For parts of this translation, I am indebted to Henry Weinfeld's excellent English version (Mallarmé, *Collected Poems*, 87–88).

Le Phénomène futur

Un ciel pâle, sur le monde qui finit de décrepitude, va peut-être partir avec les nuages: les lambeaux de la pourpre usée des couchants déteignent dans une rivière dormant à l'horizon submergé de rayons et d'eau. Les arbres s'ennuient et, sous leur feuillage blanchi (de la poussière du temps plutôt que celle des chemins), monte la maison en toile du Montreur de choses Passées: maint réverbère attend le crépuscule et ravive les visages d'une malheureuse foule, vaincue par la maladie immortelle et le péché des siècles, d'hommes près de leurs chétives complices enceintes des fruits misérables avec lesquels périra la terre. Dans le silence inquiet de tous les yeux suppliant là-bas le soleil qui, sous l'eau, s'enfonce avec le désespoir d'un cri, voici le simple boniment: "Nulle enseigne ne vous régale du spectacle intérieur, car il n'est pas maintenant un peintre capable d'en donner une ombre triste. J'apporte, vivante (et préservée à travers les ans par la science souveraine) une Femme d'autrefois. Quelque folie, originelle et naïve, une extase d'or, je ne sais quoi! par elle nommé sa chevelure, se ploie avec la grâce des étoffes autour d'un visage qu'éclaire la nudité sanglante de ses lèvres. A la place du vêtement vain, elle a un corps; et les yeux, semblables aux pierre rares, ne valent pas ce regard qui sort de sa chair heureuse: des seins levés comme s'ils étaient pleins d'un lait éternel, la pointe vers le ciel, aux jambes lisses qui gardent le sel de la mer première." Se rappelant leurs pauvres épouses, chauves, morbides, et pleines d'horreur, les maris se pressent: elles aussi par curiosité, mélancoliques, veulent voir.

Quand tous auront contemplé la noble créature, vestige de quelque époque déjà maudite, les uns indifférents, car ils n'auront pas eu la force de comprendre, mais d'autres navrés et la paupière humide de larmes résignées se regarderont; tandis que les poëtes de ces temps, sentant se rallumer leurs yeux éteints, s'achemineront vers leur lampe, le cerveau ivre un instant d'une gloire confuse, hantés du Rythme et dans l'oubli d'exister à une époque qui survit à la beauté.

7. In a letter to Henri Cazalis, Mallarmé writes, "He who makes the Venus is more important than he who saves a people" ("Celui qui fait la Vénus est plus important que celui qui sauve un peuple," quoted in Lidsky 31). In the prose poem *Un Spectacle interrompu*, we see a similar scenario: "I would like, for myself alone," writes the narrator—an audience member at an animal show—"to write of how this reality struck my poet's eye, . . . before the *reporters* divulge it, trained as they are by the crowd to lend each thing its most common character" ("Je veux, en vue de moi seul, écrire comme elle [la réalité] frappa mon regard de poète, . . . avant que la divulguent des *reporters* par la foule dressés à assigner à chaque chose son caractère commun," *Oeuvres complètes* 276).

8. In his paean to Mallarmé's poetic power, "Je disais quelquefois à Stéphane Mallarmé," Valéry imagines a scene corresponding very closely to that of *Le Phénomène futur*. Out from the masses, a single worthy male artist communes privately with a representative of poetic genius: "Do you know, do you feel this: that in each city in France there is a secretive young man who would give his life for your poetry and for you? You are his pride, his mystery, his reality. He isolates himself from all others in this lonely love and in his confidence in your work, so difficult to find, to understand, to defend." ("Savez-vous, sentez-vous ceci: qu'il est dans chaque ville en France un jeune homme secret qui se ferait hâcher pour vos vers et pour vous? Vous êtes son orgueil, son mystère, son réel. Il s'isole de tous dans l'amour sans partage et dans la confidence de votre oeuvre, difficile à trouver, à entendre, à défendre," Valéry 1).

9. As is typical of Mallarmé's work, no political or social references appear; this is a generic crowd, whose unhappiness is an inherent condition of its exis-

tence. Yet the very blankness of this future world, its total lack of names, dates, or places, clearly raises the issue of its referentiality and its relationship to history. As Richard Terdiman has observed: "Mallarmé . . . [seeks] to solve the difficult question of the text's contingency upon or adequacy to some preexisting object by amputating the text's representationality altogether. When the referent is thus pulverized, only unique texts are left. But these strategies of amputation are historical productions which ought not to be dissociated from their own determinations. Their ideological implications are of the profoundest sort" (Terdiman, *Discourse/Counter-Discourse*, 25–26).

10. This essay condemns the increasing spread of literature among "la foule." The "philistine," Mallarmé states here, is better off unaware of poetry; teaching art in the *collèges* will lead only to its abasement: "I would rather see him [the philistine] profaned than profaning" ("J'aime mieux le voir profan que profanateur," *Oeuvres complètes* 258–60).

11. In his 1895 work *Psychologie des foules*, Le Bon condemns all political movements of his time as the results of mindless decisions made by crowds: "It is no longer in the councils of princes, but in crowds that nations prepare their destinies. . . . The crowds' only power is to destroy. Their domination always represents a phase of barbarism" (3–6). Le Bon believed that an individual's critical faculties disappeared entirely in a crowd, which hypnotizes its members with its "powerful mechanism": "In crowds, it is stupidity and not thought that accrues . . . the individual . . . finds himself . . . hypnotized" (14–18).

12. In *L'Art pour tous*, Mallarmé writes of his fear that teaching poetry in the schools will lead to its becoming a science: "Poetry will be lowered to the rank of science" ("La poésie sera abaissée au rang d'une science," *Oeuvres complètes* 258).

13. Not coincidentally, perhaps, at the time this prose poem was written, Marie Mallarmé, the poet's wife, was expecting her first child.

14. This sense of abortive paternity whose only redemption lies in literary fatherhood echoes in one of Mallarmé's letters to Cazalis, dated May 9, 1871: "Children . . . there is in them a world of suffering that overtakes us during family hours; because we are fathers only of the products of our imaginations" ("Les enfants . . . il y a en eux un monde de souffrances qui nous possède aux heures de famille; parce que nous ne sommes les pères que de nos productions imaginatives," Mallarmé, *Correspondance* 1: 354, Letter 193).

15. Domna Stanton observes that this theme of the "preëminence of the artist over the masses who incarnate nature at its worst" belongs typically to dandyist literature (184).

16. The woman onstage is generally thought to represent a poetic ideal—a writing in which form and content are one. She is the fusion of interior and exterior, "an organic metaphor expressing the perfect fusion of creation with creator . . . the distinctions between technique and expression seem to disappear" (Shewan 103). Frank Kermode, referring particularly to the related motif of the *danseuse*, writes: "The beauty of a woman, and particularly of a woman in movement, is the emblem of the work of art or image. . . . Throughout this tradition, the beauty of a work of art, in which there is no division of form and meaning . . . is more or less explicitly compared with such women" (*Romantic*

Image, 57, 60). Barbara Johnson, writing of Mallarmé, comments: "The woman dancing is the necessary but unintentional medium through which something fundamental to the male poetic self can be manifested" (127).

17. These famous words first appeared in a letter to Cazalis, composed when Mallarmé was beginning *Hérodiade*, a work concurrent with *Le Phénomène futur*. "I have at last begun my *Hérodiade*. It is with terror since I am inventing a language that must necessarily spring from a very new poetics, which I could define in these few words: *To paint, not the thing*, but the effect it produces." ("J'ai enfin commencé mon *Hérodiade*. Avec terreur car j'invente une langue qui doit nécessiarement jaillir d'une poétique très nouvelle, que je pourrais définir en ces deux mots: *Peindre, non la chose*, mais l'effet qu'elle produit"; quoted in Shaw, *Performance*, 103).

18. Such fascination with the representation of the present, of the "now," appears elsewhere in Mallarmé's work, in *Igitur*, for example: "I have always lived with my soul fixed upon the clock . . . I did everything so that the hour it chimed would remain present in my room" ("J'ai toujours vécu mon âme fixée sur l'horloge . . . j'ai tout fait pour que le temps qu'elle sonna restât présent dans la chambre," *Oeuvres complètes* 439). Writing of *Igitur*, Georges Poulet explains: "Everything in the narrative takes place in a moment . . . midnight exists by itself, the being who kills himself escapes the spiral of time's duration. Past and future collapse into a single moment" (120).

19. "One of the undeniable ideals of our time is to divide words into two different categories: first for vulgar or immediate, second, for essential purposes. The first is for narrative, instruction, or description (even though an adequate exchange of human thoughts might well be achieved through the silent exchange of money). The elementary use of language involves that universal *journalistic style* which characterizes all kinds of contemporary writing, with the exception of literature" (Mallarmé, *Selected Prose Poems*, 42 [trans. Cook]). ("Un désir indéniable à mon temps est de séparer comme en vue d'attributions différentes le double état de la parole, brut ou immédiat ici, là essentiel. Narrer, enseigner, même décrire, cela va et encore qu'à chacun suffirait peut-être pour échanger la pensée humaine, de prendre ou de mettre dans la main d'autrui en silence une pièce de monnaie, l'emploi élémentaire du discours dessert l'universel reportage dont, la littérature exceptée, participe tout entre les genres décrits contemporains," *Crise de vers*, in *Oeuvres complètes* 368.)

20. See "The Dialectics of the Prose Poem," chapter 7 in Terdiman's *Discourse/Counter-Discourse*.

21. In *Quant au livre*, Mallarmé discusses the inherent poetic possibilities of prose: "Poetry, the dispenser, the director of the performance of pages, master of the book. Let it appear visibly in its totality, in the whiteness of the page and in its margins; or let it hide, call it Prose, nevertheless, it is Poetry if there remains within its discursive reserve, some secret pursuit of music." ("Le Vers, dispensateur, ordonnateur du jeu des pages, maître du livre. Visiblement soit qu'apparaisse son intégralité, parmi les marges et du blanc; ou qu'il se dissimule, nommez-le Prose, néanmoins c'est lui si demeure quelque secrète poursuite de musique, dans la réserve du Discours," *Oeuvres complètes* 375.)

22. Having shelved the project in 1867, Mallarmé announced in 1891 that he

would recommence his *Hérodiade*. For the history of the writing of this dramatic poem and relevant information about the poet's sources in myth, biblical legend, and his contemporaries' works, see Helen Grace Zagona's *The Legend of Salomé and the Principle of Art for Art's Sake*, and Sylviane Huot's *Le Mythe d'Hérodiade chez Mallarmé*.

23. In *Hérodiade*, Mallarmé deliberately merges the two figures of the princess Salome and her mother, Queen Herodias. This generational blurring effects the same kind of genealogical disruption suggested by *la Femme d'autrefois*, who lives in both past and future, as a kind of denaturalized, futuristic ancestor. "The predicament of . . . the decadent writer . . .," writes Barbara Spackman, "[is that] he is (and the theological phrase is inevitable) both the beginning and the end. . . . The decadent rupture is caused by declaring oneself the end of the lineage" (38).

24. It is difficult to categorize the rich story of Herodias and Salome as purely biblical, since not only may its origins predate the New Testament, but centuries of artistic elaboration upon the tale added many facets not present in the original. See Zagona's history of this legend.

25. "J'ai laissé le nom d'Hérodiade pour bien la différencier de la Salomé je dirai moderne ou exhumée avec son fait-divers archaïque" (*Les Noces* 51). Sylviane Huot reads this remark as a reference to Wilde's *Salomé*, although it could easily also be Mallarmé's general acknowledgment of the numerous contemporaries who treated this legend, among them Banville, Heine, Flaubert, and Laforgue.

26. These words are taken from a letter, dated February 1965, to Emile Lefébure (*Correspondance* 1: 154).

27. Rescued also, perhaps from the intellectual oblivion into which Mallarmé felt his infant daughter has chased her. "Her crying made Hérodiade run away" ("Ses cris ont fait fuir Hérodiade"), he wrote in exasperation about Geneviève (quoted in Sartre, *Mallarmé*, 56). Such a text confirms, of course, the role of *la Femme d'autrefois* as an antidote to human reproduction.

28. An 1866 letter from Mallarmé to Henri Cazalis stages a similar scene: *Hérodiade* emerges as a superior artwork by passing through, then triumphing over what the poet appears to see as his own potential for coarseness or commonness. Comparing an earlier draft of the *Ouverture* to a more recent version, Mallarmé writes, "Placed next to these lines, the earlier dramatic scene that you have seen is like a common Epinal drawing compared to a canvas by Leonardo da Vinci" ("La scène dramatique que tu connais n'est auprès de ces vers que ce qu'est une vulgaire image d'Epinal comparée à une toile de Léonard de Vinci," *Correspondance* 1: 1442).

29. Mary Lewis Shaw discusses this decision in her book *Performance in the Texts of Mallarmé*, which reads Mallarmé's texts through their emphasis on the *ritual* of theater. She quotes the poet's remark that "all words disappear before sensation" ("toutes les paroles s'effacent devant la sensation"), explaining it in the context of Mallarmé's suppression of Hérodiade's dance: "The displacement of Hérodiade's dance—its extraction from the self-descriptive narrative representation which constitutes the body of the text, and its transplantation into a supplementary 'hors texte'—illustrates for the reader this point" (124).

30. "The human figures that epitomize modernity," writes Paul de Man, "are defined by experiences such as childhood or convalescence, a freshness of perception that results from a slate wiped clear, from the absence of a past that has not yet had time to tarnish the immediacy of perception (although what is thus freshly discovered prefigures the end of this very freshness), of a past that . . . is so threatening that it has to be forgotten" (*Blindness and Insight* 157).

31. "To inoculate contemporary clothing with a bit of dandyism, via Fashion," writes Barthes, "was fatally to destroy dandyism itself. . . . Fashion was, in a sense, given the task of neutralizing dandyism . . . it is in fact Fashion that killed dandyism." ("Inoculer, à travers la Mode, un peu de dandysme à tout le vêtement contemporain, c'était fatalement tuer le dandysme lui-même. . . . La Mode a été en quelque sorte chargée de . . . neutraliser le dandysme . . . c'est bien la Mode qui a tué le dandysme," "Le Dandysme et la mode" 312–15.)

32. These "phases" are borrowed from Renato Poggioli's description of fashion, in his *Teoria dell'arte d'avanguardia* (98).

33. "L'aujourd'hui de la Mode . . . détruit autour de lui, dément le passé . . . censure l'avenir . . . apprivoise le nouveau avant même de le produire" (*Système* 288–89).

34. Mallarmé did, occasionally, include poems or short texts by guest writers, usually friends.

35. See Jean-Pierre Lecercle's excellent book *Mallarmé et la mode* for a complete, scholarly discussion of the relationship between *La Dernière Mode* and other fashion magazines of the period.

36. Lecercle is one of the few critics who see the problem in reading *La Dernière Mode* as just another bit of poetry. His approach is to read it instead as simply "un journal de mode." I am sympathetic to his method and find his book extremely helpful. My *optique*, however, is a little different, since I choose to read the text within several frameworks at once: decadent dandyism, female performance, mass culture, *and* fashion journalism.

37. Lecercle informs us that the magazine's circulation varied between 600 and 5,000 readers (178). And according to Annemarie Kleinert, the journal started out well, with circulation falling off after the first six months (171).

38. A diatribe against the press and advertising appears in "Le Livre, instrument spirituel," where, referring to the newspaper, Mallarmé writes, "I propose to note how this rag differs from the book, itself supreme" ("[Je]] propose de noter comment ce lambeau diffère du livre, lui suprême," *Oeuvres complètes* 379). The advertising section, "la quatrième page," is "an incoherence of inarticulate cries" ("une incohérence de cris inarticulés," ibid.). A similar sentiment appears in "Sur l'evolution littéraire": "Poetry is everywhere in language where there is rhythm, everywhere except in advertising posters and on the fourth page of the newspapers" ("Le vers est partout dans la langue où il y a rythme, partout, excepté dans les affiches et à la quatrième page des journaux," ibid., 867).

39. In this scenario of a nobleman facing a mock tribal chief, we see a microcosm of dandyist sensibilities confronting mass culture. The aristocratic body of the duke is implicitly textual or literary; the body of the Folies performer literalizes this, becoming an overt work of art: "Who knows whether, in his overcoat closed over his medals and badges, he did not, in his turn, envy the authentic

magnificence of the Tattooed Man, made more handsome than all other men by the distinctive luxury inscribed on his very skin, marked only with indelible engravings suitable for a leader?" ("Qui sait, dans son paletot-sac fermé sur ses plaques et ses ordres, s'il n'enviait pas à son tour la magnificence authentique de l'Homme-Tatoué, plus beau par un luxe distinctif inscrit sur sa peau même que tous les autres hommes, et seul marqué des caractères ineffaçables qui conviennent à un chef?" *Oeuvres complètes* 787.)

40. For a brief time, Oscar Wilde held the editorship of *Woman's World* magazine.

41. A similar modern theatrical phenomenon can be seen in a work such as *Twilight Los Angeles, 1992,* in which playwright and sole performer Anna Deavere Smith moves in and out of dozens of roles, representing both sexes, many nationalities, and all ages as she reenacts the story of the 1992 Los Angeles riots.

42. Writing of Octave Uzanne's fashion texts, Emily Apter sees a similar phenomenon, which she describes as "an almost palpable will-to-be woman, a desire to write himself as women, through the art of sartorial describing . . . a masculine travesty of or cross-dressed impersonation of women in prose" (*Feminizing the Fetish* 83).

43. Judith Kravis remarks: "The writing has a secret (in the rich order of events that the poet and not the 'femme du monde' perceives) when it appears to have none" (114).

44. "Robes de danse en satin . . . voilées de tulle illusion blanc relevé de côté gracieusement par des masses de fleurs, puis d'autre entièrement garnies de plumes véritables et de dentelles . . . beaucoup de blondes blanches perlées de jais blanc. . . . Milles effets ravissants. . . . Fermant les yeux à d'adorables motifs dont me tente la description, je poursuis, stricte et brève. . . . Toutes les teintes, ce sont: mauve tendre, réséda, crépuscule, gris tzarine, bleu scabieuse, émeraude, marron doré . . ., mais je m'arrête" (*Oeuvres complètes* 799–800, last ellipsis Mallarmé's).

45. "Marguerite de Ponty," writes Dragonetti, "secretly guided by the invisible hand of the journal's architect . . . expresses a great sensitivity to words" (96).

46. Words, like diamonds, must be set in perfect arrangement. In "Le Mystère dans les lettres," Mallarmé writes: "Words, on their own, are exalted in many a facet" ("Les mots, d'eux-mêmes, s'exaltent à mainte facette," *Oeuvres complètes* 386).

47. For a wonderful discussion of the fashionplate and its position between the "high" culture realm of fine-arts painting and the "lower" world of "feminine visual culture," see Anne Higonnet's *Berthe Morisot's Images of Women.*

48. "Mme la Marquise M. de L. . . ., à Rennes: Nous regrettons beaucoup que notre Numéro-Spécimen ait été reçu par vous défraîchi et froissé: mais les facteurs portent peu de gants, et pour faire entrer le journal dans leur boîte, ils le plient souvent en quatre. . . . A qui s'en prendre?" (*Oeuvres complètes* 742).

49. "Notre journal est une publication de luxe, et, selon l'usage adopté aujourd'hui par les amateurs, chaque livraison doit, après le semestre ou l'année, se relier avec la couverture . . . nous engageons . . . toutes nos Abonnées à la garder fraîche dès maintenant; quant au pliage des Livraisons expédiées en province et à l'étranger, il disparaît à la reliure" (ibid., 775).

50. "Le Patron d'aujourd'hui . . . déplié . . . représente tout de suite (sans qu'il soit besoin même de lire ceci) une charmante confection d'hiver" (ibid., 812).

51. "Le nouveau cachemire . . . se porte le soir . . . mais parmi cette enveloppe . . . va transparaître la femme, visible . . . elle-même" (ibid., 833).

52. Susan Buck-Morss's remarks on the fashionable woman underline this strange quality: "The modern woman who allies herself with fashion's newness in a struggle against natural decay represses her own productive power, mimics the mannequin and enters history as a dead object, a 'gaily decked-out corpse'" (26).

53. "Tunique plissée en travers et fixée par la jupe; dans le bas de la tunique, frange avec perles blanches. Large ceinture en satin prenant de côté, descendant contre la tunique et se nouant sur la traîne: ce noeud fixé lui-même sur la jupe par une couronne de fleurs d'orangers" (*Oeuvres complètes* 763).

54. "It is 'woman'," writes Marge Garber, "whom fashion creates as this illusion of parts. And 'woman' is what can be known, exhibited, disseminated, replicated—while at the same time remaining 'impossible'" (373).

55. "Seule, une dame, dans son isolement de la Politique et des soins moroses, a le loisir nécessaire pour que s'en dégage, sa toilette achevée, un besoin de se parer aussi l'âme. Que tel volume demeure huit jours entr'ouvert comme un flacon; sur les soieries ornées des chimères, des coussins" (*Oeuvres complètes* 716).

56. Jean-Pierre Lecercle is not insensitive to this aspect of *La Dernière Mode*. Although he does not explicitly address the feminization of the text or its element of performance and spectacle, he describes the experience of reading it thus: "Fundamentally, one should read *La Dernière Mode* as one watches a striptease: does it not leave us still hungry? and when we leave, do we not long terribly to possess the poetry that we had hoped to see, but that we have hardly glimpsed? . . . Reading this magazine is to our need for poetry as a striptease is to our sexual needs" (124).

57. "La mode, entr'ouvrant les rideaux se montre subitement à nous, métamorphosée, neuve future" (*Oeuvres complètes* 830).

58. "*La Dernière Mode* dont les huit ou dix numéros parus servent encore quand je les dévêts de leur poussière à me faire longtemps rêver" (*Correspondance* 2: 303).

59. Rhodes, Richard, Huot, Kravis, and Lecercle all showcase this quotation in their discussions of *La Dernière Mode*.

60. See James Laver's *Taste and Fashion from the French Revolution Until Today*.

61. "Le rythme des danses d'hiver vous ramène . . . devant ce miroir impartial, toutes, vous chercherez la reine de la fête par un regard qui ira droit à votre image; car de fait, quelle femme étant toujours cette reine pour quelqu'un, ne l'est pas un peu pour elle-même?" (*Oeuvres complètes* 718).

62. "Oh mirror!," exclaims Hérodiade, "I appear in you like a distant shadow" ("O miroir! Je m'apparus en toi comme une ombre lointaine," ibid., 45).

63. "De son dais royal formé par les étoffes de tous les siècles (celles que porta la reine Sémiramis et celles que façonnent à leur génie Worth ou Pingat)" (ibid., 830).

64. See Michael Miller's *The Bon Marché: Bourgeois Culture and the Department Store, 1869–1920*, for a history of fashion and the French department store.

65. See Lecercle's discussion of the original layout of *La Dernière Mode*.

66. See Kleinert and Lecercle.

67. See Wicke's *Advertising Fictions*.

68. See also Michael Miller.

69. "Mille lettres en diamant étincellent avec l'éclat captivant d'un secret qui se montre et ne se livre pas: prénoms et noms entrelacés de celle qui porte le collier et de celui qui a fait don. La légende est qu'un seul bijoutier fait ces colliers et varie leur mystère, or donner son adresse serait, même entre femmes, un acte de haute trahison: inutile, car ce n'est d'abord pas à nous de les acheter. . . . J'ajouterai toutefois . . . qu'il se fait de ces parures en pierreries de couleurs et en perles" (*Oeuvres complètes* 746).

70. "Une nouvelle mode, inaugurée à Trouville dans une soirée intime: un collier de chien en velours noir avec le nom de celle qui le porte mêlé au nom de l'heureux mortel qui l'a offert, de telle sorte que les deux noms sont illisibles. Les petits diamants qui les composent étincellent sur le velours noir avec l'éclat irritant d'un mystère qui se montre et ne se pénètre pas. . . . Un seul bijoutier fait ces colliers, les varie à l'infini, contourne les lettres avec un art cabalistique et doit à sa discrétion un succès immense. On a absolument refusé de nous donner son adresse. Il faut être initié. Ces colliers se font aussi en petites pierreries de couleurs et petites perles" (quoted in Lecercle 83).

71. In suggesting a rewritten mythological genealogy for these women, Mallarmé's text recalls Hérodiade's lament as she looks in a mirror, "Oh, it is for myself, for myself, that I blossom, barren!" ("O, c'est pour moi, pour moi, que je fleuris, déserte!" *Oeuvres complètes* 47). In that poem, creation or generational descent is forestalled by the princess's isolation, which substitutes the sterile reproduction of a mirror's reflection for creative or procreative female power. In *La Dernière Mode*, the princess becomes a bourgeois lady.

72. "Cette tête, mais c'est Madame X!" "Chère amie, avez-vous donc posé pour les traits de cette autre?" "Ce front ou ce regard, à qui, dites est-ce donc? Je les connais, nobles, purs" (Mallarmé, *Oeuvres complètes*, 735).

73. Théophile Gautier, in his *De la Mode*, argues for less reverence for past styles and increased attention to contemporary fashion. In *La Dernière Mode*, Mallarmé makes a similar argument, praising Baudry's wisdom in immortalizing the contemporary woman and "the talent of an audacious artist who does not hesitate to apotheosize the contemporary face" ("le talent d'un artiste audacieux jusqu'à ne pas hésiter devant l'apothéose du visage contemporain," *Oeuvres complètes* 735).

74. Writing of Baudry's paintings, Charles Bernheimer notes: "In some cases the identity of the idealized woman was an open secret" (105).

75. "*Le Harem*: titre un peu vif peut-être pour quelques dames françaises, donné par M. d'Hervilly à son dernier livre de poésie. Qu'aucun éventail ne s'agite, effarouché: car ce gynécée tant que le tome qui l'emprisonne en ses stances demeure fermé sur votre étagère. . . . Par une loi supérieure à celle qui, chez les peuples barbares, enferme véritablement la femme entre des murs de

cèdre ou de porcelaine, le Poète (dont l'authorité en matière de vision n'est pas moindre que celle d'un prince absolu) dispose avec la pensée seule de toutes les dames terrestres. Jaune ou blanche ou noire ou cuivrée, leur grâce est soudain requise par lui, quand il se met à l'oeuvre; elle vient former les flottantes figures, animant les livres, et, notamment cet album cosmopolite. . . . Secret ô mes aimables lectrices, maintenant divulgué, de ces heures vides tout à coup et sans cause, et de ces quasi-absences de vous-mêmes, auxquelles vous succombez quelquefois pendant l'après-midi; un rimeur quelque part songe à vous ou à votre genre de beauté" (*Oeuvres complètes* 803).

76. Emphasis added. "[Banville] a ressuscité l'âme et le nom de Sémiramis, d'Ariane, d'Hélène, de Cléopâtre, d'Hérodiade, de la reine de Saba, de Marie Stuart, de la Princesse de Lamballe, et de la Princesse Borghese. . . . *A vous de plonger les yeux Mesdames dans ces tableaux profonds à l'égal de miroirs où vous croirez toujours un peu vous contempler*, car il n'est pas une petite fille . . . qui ne porte pas en elle une goutte de ce sang éternel et royal qui fait les grandes princesses d'autrefois" (ibid., 813).

CHAPTER THREE
ROBOTIC PLEASURES, DANCE, AND THE MEDIA PERSONALITY

1. See Naomi Schor's *Breaking the Chain* for a discussion of the relationship between the "detail" and the feminine in nineteenth-century fiction.

2. For a very complete history of the cultural importance of Edison and electricity, see David Nye's *Electrifying America: Social Meanings of a New Technology, 1880–1940.*

3. Like Columbus appropriating the Americas, Europeans could more easily penetrate and control Africa and Indochina with the aid of technology such as electric lighting and the telegraph. A given country's level of technological development, furthermore, was often conflated with its general levels of culture, as well as with its natives' biological capacity. See Daniel Headrick's *The Tools of Empire: Technology and European Imperialism in the Nineteenth Century.*

4. Sections devoted to Edison's frantic and money-hungry stockholders, for example, are distorted versions of actual accounts in the press about the activities of the Edison Company. The first chapters of *L'Eve future*, in which Edison laments having been born too late to record the biblical history, are taken from press accounts that caricatured Edison's reputed arrogance. These references were, naturally, recognizable to Villiers's readers at the time.

5. Edison himself speculated about the phonograph's use in "the preservation of language by reproduction of our Washingtons, our Lincolns, our Gladstones" (Josephson 172), in the preservation, that is, of iconic personalities.

6. "En Amérique et en Europe, une LEGENDE s'est donc éveillée dans l'imagination de la foule, autour de ce grand citoyen des Etats-Unis. . . . Donc, l'Edison du présent ouvrage, son caractère, son habitation, son langage et ses théories sont—et devaient être—au moins passablement distincts de la réalité" (*L'Eve future* 765).

7. "We can find in the *Future Eve*," writes Raymond Bellour, "all the elements necessary for a consideration of the star as machine" (131).

8. The title "Venus Victrix" was invented by Villiers and was clearly meant to suggest both the Venus de Milo and the Louvre's other famous statue goddess, "Winged Victory."

9. "Himself a work of art," writes Domna Stanton, "the dandy will valorize women only as a mediating agency through which to further his quest for beauty. The female's resemblance to a favorite painting as the source of desire is a topos from Balzac to Barbey: Henri de Marsay pursues Paquita Valdes because she is the reincarnation of *La Femme caressant sa chimère*, while Barbey's Robert de Tressignies [from *Les Diaboliques*] is obsessed by the prostitute who resembles Vernet's *Judith* and a courtesan by Veronese. Conversely, Gautier's D'Albert envisages an ideal woman who is the synthesis of his favorite paintings and sculptures" (167).

10. "Or, entre le corps et l'âme de miss Alicia ce n'était pas une disproportion qui déconcertait et inquiétait [l]'entendement: c'était une disparate . . . les lignes de sa beauté semblaient lui être étrangères, ses paroles paraissaient dépaysées et gênées dans sa voix. Son être intime s'accusait comme en contradiction avec sa forme . . . dans les limbes du Devenir cette femme s'était égarée en ce corps . . . il ne lui appartenait pas" (*L'Eve future* 798). For the English version of this and some of the following passages from *L'Eve future*, I am indebted to the translation of Marilyn Gaddis Rose (entitled *Eve of the Future Eden*). Translations fully or partially borrowing from Gaddis Rose cite her work; all other translations from *L'Eve future*, citing the original French edition, are my own. I will include the original French for only those passages where the language is of particular interest.

11. "Les chants et la parole de l'Andréide seront à jamais ceux que lui aura dictés . . . votre si belle amie . . . l'accent, le timbre et ses intonations . . . seront inscrits sur les feuilles de deux phonographes d'or . . . qui seront les poumons de Hadaly . . . l'or vierge même" (*L'Eve future* 855).

12. "C'est cette ombre que vous aimez. . . . C'est elle seule que vous reconnaissez, absolument, comme *REELLE*! Enfin, c'est cette vision objectivée de votre esprit, que vous appelez, que vous voyez, que vous *CREEZ* en votre vivante, *et qui n'est que votre âme dédoublée en elle*. Oui, voilà votre amour" (ibid., 841).

13. Des Esseintes falls in love with a female ventriloquist mainly for her ability to throw and disguise her voice convincingly. Dorian Gray, who falls in love with actress Sibyl Vane for her beautiful dramatic recitations, abandons her upon discovering her "natural," offstage self to be vulgar and uninteresting. Similarly, Ewald finds Alicia enthralling only when she sings or recites the words of others. Of course, Huysmans's and Wilde's novels share an important subtext of homosexuality, which is not apparent in *L'Eve future*, where heterosexuality is replaced almost entirely by pure commodity fetishism.

14. It is not incorrect to say that Ewald "prefigures" Des Esseintes, although *A Rebours* was published in 1884—two years earlier than Villiers's novel. This is because the basic outline of *L'Eve future*, including all protagonists, was in place several years before it appeared in its final form. In fact, Huysmans includes Villiers as one of the favorite authors of his character, Des Esseintes.

15. I use the name "Hadaly" to describe the new android (actually a combination of Alicia and Hadaly), since this creature never receives another name.

16. Andreas Huyssen's analysis of Fritz Lang's *Metropolis* is relevant here. Huyssen sees the robot Maria as "fulfilling the fantasy of creation without mother," as an attempt to "heal" the nature/culture split (71). See Huyssen for a discussion of the woman as emblem of mass culture.

17. "*L'Eve future*," writes Marie Lathers, "is in many ways a compilation of nineteenth-century technological advances" (50).

18. "Comme sous la caresse d'une brise imaginaire, ondulaient des milliers de lianes et de roses d'Orient . . . un vol d'oiseaux des Florides et des parages du sud de l'Union chatoyait sur toute cette flore artificielle, dont l'arc de cercle versicolore fluait . . . avec des étincellements et des prismes" (*L'Eve future* 870). We see here Villiers's orientalization of America. The tropical setting of the cave recreates flora and fauna of Florida and the southern United States. As Chateaubriand envisioned Native Americans as dandies, Villiers tries to turn a New Jersey town into a lush, Oriental, aristocratic hideaway.

19. In his famous essay "The Dynamo and the Virgin," Henry Adams claimed that Americans experienced electricity as an embodied female power, greater than those offered by myth or religion, "the force of the Virgin was still felt at Lourdes," he writes, ". . . but in America neither Venus nor Virgin ever had value as force—at most as sentiment" (383).

20. In what appears to be ironic deference to Keats and the Romantic tradition, the only bird whose natural song is respected by Edison is a nightingale. Although dead and mechanically reanimated, Hadaly's lone nightingale sings a recorded version of the distinctive song it sang while alive. Villiers tweaks the solemnity of this bird's image as pure poetic voice when Edison invites Ewald to make practical use of the bird's electric generator: "You can light your cigar with the soul of this nightingale" (*L'Eve future* 874). Another such reference to Keats appears in Villiers's repeated mention of a disembodied artificial hand used by Edison as a display sample of his ingenious simulated flesh. The realistic skin and feel of "this nonliving hand" are reinforced by an electrical system that, when stimulated by a human hand, responds by squeezing back. "Is this not, in truth, human flesh that I am touching at this moment?" asks an astonished Ewald (ibid., 831). The voice that sings poetry and the hand that writes it have been made over as slighly ghoulish science experiments. (Although I have been unable to find proof that Villiers had, in fact, read Keats, his general familiarity with English literature suggests it strongly.)

21. Villiers was fascinated with World's Fairs. He had published a journalistic account of the 1867 fair, spent time at the subsequent fair of 1878, and, although on his deathbed at the time, insisted upon being carried in a special chair to the fair of 1889. Alan Raitt remarks: "[Villiers] multiplies allusions to the curiosities of the Exposition; and to the processes of modern industry, such as galvanoplasty, photochromy or photosculpture" (Introduction to *L'Eve future* 1453).

22. The preface to Villiers's *La Révolte* provides an example of his belief in a natural ruling class, an elite of personal genius and achievement: "He who, at birth, does not carry within him his own glory, will never know the real meaning of this word" (*Oeuvres complètes* 383). Ewald echoes these words in *L'Eve future* (see note 51 below).

23. The name "Habal" comes from the Hebrew, meaning "vanity," while "Hadaly" is Persian for "ideal."

24. "[Une] vision, chair transparente . . . dansait, en costume pailleté, une sorte de danse mexicaine populaire. Les mouvements s'accusaient avec le fondu de la vie elle-même, grâce aux procédés de la photographie successive, qui, le long d'un ruban de six coudées put saisir dix minutes des mouvements. . . . Soudain, une voix plate . . . une voix sotte et dure se fit entendre, la danseuse chantait" (*L'Eve future* 897).

25. "Un petit être exsangue, vaguement féminin, aux membres rabourgris, aux joues creuses, à la bouche édentée et presque sans lèvres, au crâne à peu pres chauve.—'Qu'est-ce que cette sorcière?' demanda lord Ewald" (ibid., 898).

26. "Voici l'élancé de la démarche, la cambrure, la sveltesse d'un pied féminin, où rien ne décèle l'intrusion d'une race servile, lâche et intéressée" (ibid., 902; emphasis added).

27. The term is Emily Apter's (see *Feminizing the Fetish*).

28. There is no need here to belabor the obvious psychoanalytic reading of such a scene. Evelyn's "masquerade of femininity," to borrow from the title of Joan Rivière's famous article, only too clearly embodies the void beneath, and the concomitant threat of castration. For a very interesting discussion of nineteenth-century depictions of fetishism and their theoretical implications for feminism, see Emily Apter's *Feminizing the Fetish*.

29. In her discussion of the political dangers of setting science apart from feminist social theory and of overvaluing the purely cultural body politic, Donna Haraway remarks that "we have perversely worshipped science as a reified fetish" (9). Villiers's portrayal of Edison's fetishistic world marks this novel as a step in the process Haraway describes.

30. As Emily Apter writes, "The obviousness of feminine artifice . . . guarantees the failure of an autonomous (nonpatriarchal) definition of femininity" (*Feminizing the Fetish* 74).

31. The titles of the chapters that describe Hadaly in Book 5 form a kind of machine-age *blason*, a Baudelairean list of fetishized female charms, improvements upon Evelyn's (and eventually Alicia's) nontechnological assets: "Balance," "Flesh," "Rosebud mouth and teeth of pearls," "Eyes," "Hair," "Skin," and so on.

32. Philippe Hamon concentrates on just such a figure of pure surface in his *Expositions*, which discusses the display culture of the late nineteenth century and its effect on literature. "It is no longer a matter of some secret backstage in the wings," he writes; "surfaces have killed the wings." This results, for Hamon, in "a world of characters put on display or exhibited, but having lost all depth or fleshly 'volume'" (166). Leo Bersani reminds us that dandyism depends upon this kind of exteriority, in words that seems to replicate Villiers's description of Hadaly's function: "[The dandy] makes no claims whatsoever for his own interiority, but he forces others to infer, more exactly to create, his uniqueness" (*Culture* 79).

33. Interestingly, in the history of automatons, singing and dancing females appear frequently. The most famous makers of androids, Jacques Vaucanson and Pierre Jaquet-Droz, both produced female robots that played music and sang (de

Panafieu 128). For more on the history of automatons, see also Joseph Roach's *Player's Passion*.

34. See Chapter Two, note 16.

35. Mark Seltzer, in his *Bodies and Machines*, makes the point that just such an economic change coincides with the age of mechanization. He describes this shift as a transformation from relations based on status, custom, and traditional authority to relations based on contracts, promises, and legality (72–73).

36. This plot element is reminiscent of Villiers's earlier *Conte cruel* "L'Affichage céleste," an ironic meditation on using the sky and constellations as advertising space. "The sky will wind up being good for something after all, finally acquiring intrinsic value" (*Oeuvres complètes* 580).

37. Referring to the most popular female performers of the day (again using figures from real life), Edison asks Alicia, "Have you never seen, then, the statues of Rachel, of Jenny Lind, of Lola Montès?" (*L'Eve future* 962). When Alicia demurs, Edison continues, "What a great oversight, this is the most indispensable form of advertising for true artists." The pitch works; Alicia acquiesces: "If that is the fashion, I must have one!" (ibid., 965).

38. It was the real, historical Edison who was largely responsible for the "credit" system in the film industry. He understood the importance of the "star" and instituted the practice of listing the actors' names in the films produced by his company (Staiger 11).

39. "Ah! murmura-t-il, étais-je donc insensé? Je rêvais le sacrilège, d'un jouet—dont l'aspect seul m'eût fait sourire . . . d'une absurde poupée insensible! O bien-aimée! Je te reconnais! . . . Tu es de chair et d'os, comme moi! Je sens ton coeur battre! Tes yeux ont pleuré! . . . O chère Alicia! Je t'aime!" (*L'Eve future* 983).

40. Marie-Hélène Huet offers another interpretation of Sowana's role in *L'Eve future*. In her book *Monstrous Imagination*, Huet sees both Hadaly and Edison as creatures of monstrosity. Invoking the Old Testament story of Idumea (to which Mallarmé refers in his *Le Don du poème*), Huet interprets Sowana into that biblical story of denaturalized reproduction. Quoting biblical scholar Denis Saurat, Huet writes, "Saurat explains: 'For the Jewish Kabbalah, God first created a monstrous mankind. He replaced it with our own mankind. Jacob replaced Esau: the kings of Idumea were pre-adamic men; they were sexless beings and reproduced in God's image . . . the poet makes his poem alone without a woman like a king of Idumea, a monstrous birth. The monster will be humanized if woman welcomes him.' This sheds some light on Sowana's mysterious role, the fecundating mother, although we know that neither Sowana nor Hadaly can be saved" (237).

Huet's chapter on *L'Eve future* makes a compelling case for the novel's subtext of monstrosity and places it within the Romantic tradition of monsters and their creators. "The act of artistic creation," she writes, "thus appears as the imitation of a monstrous genetic process; painted models, errant passions, striking resemblances, sterility" (236). The point of connection between my reading of the novel and Huet's would hinge on the etymological connection between "monster"—from "monstrum," or divine portent of misfortune—and "monstrare," to show or demonstrate. A monster is a creature of compulsive visibility, that which must be shown, displayed, and looked at, much like the new celebrities of the late nineteenth century.

41. "Voyez-vous, au seuil d'une usine de forge, on distingue dans la brume, du fer, des hommes et du feu. Les enclumes sonnent, les laboureurs du métal, qui exécutent des barres, des armes, des outils, ignorent l'usage réel qui sera fait de leurs produits. Ces forgeurs ne peuvent les appeler que du nom convenu—Eh! nous en sommes là, tous! Nul ne peut estimer, au juste, la véritable nature de ce qu'il forge . . . tout couteau peut devenir poignard" (*L'Eve future* 834).

42. For intelligent and varied views of these cabaret reviews, see Colette's *L'Envers du music-hall*, Huysmans's *Croquis parisiens*, and Georges Montorgeuil's *Paris dansant*.

43. Maurice Verne, a historian of the music hall, saw the connection between this new, popular form of entertainment and the mechanization of the factory. In *Aux Usines du plaisir*, Verne details the extensively mechanical nature of the typical music-hall revue, including in his book interviews with stage technicians and set designers who provide elaborate descriptions of their crafts. Verne also analyzes the social and economic position of the female music-hall performer, whom he sees as "dispensing of oblivion . . . at a factory pace . . . drowning in baths of electric lights, an industrialized body . . . molded by the factory" (Verne 72).

44. See Charles Rearick's *Pleasures of the Belle Epoque*, especially 150–55.

45. Guy Debord's critique of the society of the spectacle begins with just such a scenario. According to Debord, the spectator's identity dissolves into the ever more powerful spectacle, which mirrors and reinforces the increasingly alienating nature of labor, producing a dangerously contemplative, will-less state: "The alienation of the spectator for the benefit of the contemplated object . . . is expressed thusly: the more he contemplates, the less he sees; the more he agrees to see himself in the dominant images, the less he understands his own existence and his own desire. . . . His gestures are no longer his own . . . the spectator feels at home nowhere, for the spectacle is everywhere" (22–23). When Anderson first steps drunkenly onto that stage, he enters the spectacle—represented by the fetishized, menacing sexuality of the female performer—and begins his surrender to it.

46. The first glimpse Edison has of Alicia comes from one of these photo-portrait calling cards. Abigail Solomon-Godeau discusses the link between female performers (dancers in particular) and photography in her landmark essay "The Legs of the Countess": "The traffic in (dance) photography, like the traffic in dance women is charged in this period with another discursive current: namely an intensified and expanded notion of celebrity" (92). Solomon-Godeau also discusses the albums into which these photo-cards were collected, albums noteworthy for their mixture of mass-culture celebrities, royalty, artists, and political figures.

47. Villiers borrows here from a famous, perhaps apocryphal story about Descartes. According to this story, Descartes himself had fabricated an android, named Francine, which was destroyed onboard a boat by a sea captain who believed her to be a witch (de Panafieu 142).

48. The distasteful or menacing nature of crowds appears elsewhere in Villiers's work, most notably in two of his *Contes cruels*: "La Machine à gloire"

(1874) and "Vox populi" (1880), allegorical short stories in which mindless, hypnotized crowds commit grotesquely foolish or inhuman actions. Villiers's crowds in these stories behave much as Mr. Anderson does in response to the specious but alluring *danseuse*. For Villiers, the "vox populi" is always mechanical and meaningless, clearly not the "vox dei." Like Mallarmé, Villiers anticipates the work of conservative fin-de-siècle sociologists such as Gustave Le Bon, who saw only disaster and moral decay in the ever-increasing presence of crowds.

49. Marilyn Gaddis Rose points out that while Villiers suggests in Book 1, Chapter 7 of *L'Eve future* that the novel takes place in 1884, Sitting Bull's victory occurred in June 1876 (*Future Eden* 212).

50. See Alan Raitt's discussion of Villiers's political career in *The Life of Villiers de l'Isle-Adam*.

51. "In this century," says Lord Ewald early in *L'Eve future*, "one must be— or be born—noble, the hour having long past when one might become noble" (*L'Eve future* 813).

52. "Villiers' Eve," writes Michel Carrouges (who includes Hadaly in his series of "bachelor machines"), "is not a woman . . . any more than she is the mother of a new generation of women" (116).

CHAPTER FOUR
ELECTRIC SALOME

1. "Une ivresse d'art et, simultané un accomplissement industriel" ("Les Fonds dans le ballet," *Oeuvres complètes* 307).

2. This July 18, 1902 review of Fuller's performance at the Théâtre Marigny is typical: "We know the extraordinary appeal of Loie Fuller's performances, which have become the true meeting place of all of Parisian and foreign society; they come from the provinces, they leave the seaside, they abandon the mountains, they'll put off the hunting season, in order to go applaud La Loie Fuller, or risk breaking one of the most basic rules of Parisian life" (review by "Arlequin," Rondel Collection on Loie Fuller, Bibliothèque de l'Arsenal, Paris).

3. Quoted in Sommer 53.

4. See Sommer, Lista, Harris, Brandstetter and Ochaim.

5. In fact, by the time Fuller got to the Folies-Bergère, an imitator of hers was already performing there. This woman, who had heard of Loie Fuller's earliest experiments in "luminous dance" in America, had just begun there. Fuller convinced the manager that hers was, in fact, the original version of the dance (de Morinni 208).

6. See Harris; Jullian, *Triumph*; and Kermode, "Loie."

7. Mauclair 103.

8. From a review of the Folies-Bergère in the *Chronique théâtrale*, August 22, 1892.

9. "She must have fallen from the gods' chariot on the marble of the Acropolis" (review by Pierre Plessis, "Le Dernier Miracle de Mme Loie Fuller," Rondel Collection on Loie Fuller, Bibliothèque de l'Arsenal, Paris).

10. Rodin, quoted in de Morinni 215.

11. From a July 18, 1902 review of Fuller's performance at the Théâtre Marigny (Rondel Collection on Loie Fuller, Bibliothèque de l'Arsenal, Paris).

12. Fuller is reminiscent not only of Villiers's Hadaly, but also of Jules Verne's character La Stilla, the phantom opera singer in *Le Château de Carpathes* whose enchanting song and appearance turn out to be produced without the benefit of a human body; they are the products only of film and sound recording.

13. For discussions of the influence of Middle Eastern and North African music and dance (especially women performers) in the aesthetic imagination of nineteenth-century France, see Malek Alloula's *The Colonial Harem*, Sylviane Leprun's *Le Théâtre des colonies*, and Sarah Graham Brown's *Images of Women in Photography of the Middle East, 1860–1950*.

14. Nozière.

15. Mauclair 93.

16. I would like to thank M. Daniel Garric, who graciously shared with me descriptions of his experiences as a teenaged electrician with Les Ballets Loie Fuller.

17. The symbolists, elaborating on Baudelaire's famous theory of "Correspondances," were writing about "auditions colorées" ("colored sounds"); and in 1891 a group known as the "synesthesiasts" mounted a production of "The Song of Solomon" in which they attempted to create synesthetic images, mingling color, sound, and perfumes in the performance. In 1893, a journalist who called himself "Rastignac" wrote in *L'Illustration* of the proximity of Loie Fuller's dances and popular aesthetic theories of the late nineteenth century: "I perfectly understand that symbolism and occultism . . . are fashionable. At least they take us away from daily life. He who troubles about dreams of eternity could care less about what's happening in Panama. And I understand Loie Fuller's great success to be due to the feeling that she offers the ideal, visions of infinity. . . . Is she pretty, this American woman? I have no idea. She is superior to life itself. She is not a woman with brown hair, in flesh and blood. She is an apparition comparable to the ideal, troubling, seductive, and unearthly creatures one finds in the paintings of Mantegana" (*Courrier de Paris*, January 14, 1893, 26).

18. Quoted in Sommer 62.

19. With help from the Curies and Flammarrion, Fuller invented, for example, a process for treating cloth with phosphorescent salts, which produced a luminescent effect on costumes (de Morinni 203–7). Flammarrion also helped Fuller get inducted into the French Astronomical Society (de Morinni 214).

20. "We are only at the beginning of the theater of pure light," said Fuller in an interview with a French newspaper, ". . . the theater must have no decor, no accessories. The stage must be completely free" (quoted by journalist Legrand-Chabrier [28]).

21. Harris 13.

22. Part of the elaborate merchandising of African women at this time, particularly dancing women, consisted of photographs or paintings depicting them in postures of great self-absorption, in enclosed, private settings. Writing of these popular and widely marketed images, Malek Alloula notes that "the harem,

though opened by the photographer, must remain symbolically closed" (69). Fuller understood the power of this genre of voyeurism and used her mirror tricks to stage the public's intrusion into the private realm of a veiled woman.

23. For Hamon, most notable among the literary "glass houses" is the one appearing in Zola's *Le Ventre de Paris*. In that novel, *la charcutière* Lisa Quenu resembles her merchandise in that she is "exposed" in large plate-glass shop windows, right next to the various arrayed cuts of meat. In one scene, Lisa's reflection is multiplied numerous times by the butcher shop's facing mirrored walls: "In the mirrors around the store, [she] was reflected from behind, from the front, from the side, even on the ceiling . . . there was an entire crowd of Lisas" (quoted in Hamon 168). "The woman here," writes Hamon, "is multiplied and exhibited, as merchandise is" (ibid.). The similarity to Loie Fuller's "mirror-room" device is striking.

24. Of course, the practice of projecting colored lights onto fabrics was not new. As Sally Sommer has pointed out, the technique had been made popular by such early mass-cultural entertainments as the panorama, diorama, phantasmagoria, and the magic lantern shows (Sommer 54). The difference here is that for the first time, the screen (Fuller's costumed body) as well as the lights moved.

25. One can see a similar effect today at Paris's Institut du Monde Arabe, where the windows are fitted with mechanical apertures of varying sizes that spill elaborate patterns of sunlight onto the galleries' floors, creating the look of Middle Eastern carpets.

26. Fuller liked to say that she could fit six thousand different stage settings in a small handbag, since her backgrounds could be infinitely altered by lights (de Morinni 216).

27. See Sommer 64.

28. See Haxell; Silvagni.

29. Mallarmé's words on this subject: "Soon the traditional placement of permanent stage decor in opposition to choreographic movement will disappear, like an imbecility. . . . The liberated stage becomes the pure result, following the whims of its fictions, exhaled in the play of a veil with poses and gestures." ("Tout à l'heure va disparaître comme dans ce cas une imbécilité, la traditionnelle plantation des décors permanents ou stables en opposition avec la mobilité chorégraphique. . . . La scène libre, au gré de fictions, exhalée du jeu d'un voile avec attitudes et gestes, devient le très pur resultat," *Oeuvres complètes* 309.)

30. According to her autobiography, Fuller came upon this idea by chance when she was still an actress in America. She claims that, while performing a scene in which she was costumed in a long, cumbersome robe, she became entangled in the material and attempted to sweep it out of her way. This random motion shaped the robe into patterns that moved the audience to flights of interpretive fancy. In the folds of her costume they saw fantastic shapes and interrupted her performance by calling out, "It's an orchid!" "It's a butterfly!" etc. Fuller says that she decided at that moment to make this a standard part of her act. "This was a moment of intense emotion," she wrote, ". . . I realised that I was in the presence of a great discovery, one which was destined to open the path which I have since followed. Gently, almost religiously, I set the silk in motion,

and I saw that I had obtained undulations of a character heretofore unknown. I had created a new dance. Why had I never thought of it before?" (Fuller 33).

31. In her application for the patent Fuller wrote: "My invention consists of certain improvements . . . which materially assist the dancer in posing, and, in causing, by movements of the body, the folds of the garment to assume variegated and fanciful waves of great beauty and grace. . . . By use of wands (of aluminum or bamboo) connected to the dress a double purpose is afforded. First it facilitates the creating of a waving motion in the folds of the garment, and second, it arrests the dancer in performing statuesque poses, in imitating different styles of wings. By providing at the end of the wand a single or double curve, it will be readily seen that by holding the wands aloft the garment will be spread out to give another form of wing. . . . In hanging the skirt from the head of the wearer it will be readily seen that the curves or spread of the garment will have much more radial latitude" (quoted in Sommer 60).

32. "La danseuse n'est pas une femme qui danse, pour ces motifs juxtaposés qu'elle *n'est pas une femme*, mais une métaphore résumant un des aspects élémentaires de notre forme, glaive, coupe, fleur, etc. . . . et qu'*elle ne danse pas*, suggérant . . . avec une écriture corporelle . . . poème dégagé de tout appareil du scribe" (*Oeuvres complètes* 304).

33. Fuller's account of the origin of this technique changes from one source to another. (See Roger Marx and Hélène Pinet-Cheula on this subject.)

34. "A mon avis importait, où que la mode disperse cette éclosion contemporaine, miraculeuse, d'extraire le sens sommaire et l'explication qui en émane et agit sur l'ensemble d'un art" (*Oeuvres complètes* 309).

35. Private conversation with Giovanni Lista, Paris 1992. See also Philippe Jullian's *Triumph*; Harris; Pinet-Cheula; and Kermode, "Loie."

36. During the last fifteen years of the nineteenth century, France increased its territories from 1 million to 9.5 million square kilometers, mostly in North Africa but in Indochina as well. The colonized population increased from five million to fifty million people (Girardet 80).

37. This is Jacques Duquesne's description of the palace of electricity at the 1900 expo (10).

38. In an account written thirty-one years after his visit to the Exposition Universelle, Paul Morand describes evocatively the atmosphere of the colonial exhibitions, indulging himself in their orientalism: "Under the Eiffel Tower, near a little lake, was hidden the Tonkinese village with its junks and women chewing betel. . . . In the Ceylonese pavilion there were also the 'Dancers of the Devil,' wearing terrifying masks with bulging wooden eyes. The entire hill was nothing but perfumes, incense, vanilla; the aromatic fumes of the seraglio . . . the cries of the Ouled-Nail with their mobile bellies; I followed this opiate mixture, this perfume of Javanese dancing girls, sherbets and vahat-loukoum as far as the Dahomean village. Among the mosques and straw huts, tall negroes walked about barefoot . . . still savages" (quoted in Jullian, *Triumph*, 158). André Hallays wrote: "There were too many belly dancers on all sides of the exhibition, and the *Rue de Paris* was too perfect a monument to a certain kind of Monmartre-style idiocy. With slow, measured gestures, the dancers gyrated their supple torsos and shook their handkerchiefs" (ix).

39. See Philippe Jullian, *Triumph*.

40. Fuller, along with Isadora Duncan and Ruth St. Denis, was a pioneer of the modern dance movement, which also rejected ballet's elaborate decor and narrative structure in favor of an emphasis on the sculptural forms of the human body. For more on the history of modern dance, see Paul Magriel, Randy Martin, Sally Banes, and Susan Foster. Although Fuller is often overlooked in the history of modern dance, it is likely that Duncan based some of her principles on choreography she had learned from Fuller early in her career.

41. *Vanity Fair* 1936, in Fuller Archives, Special Collection of the New York City Public Library, Lincoln Center Library of the Performing Arts. Roger Marx imagined her communing with "the Maenads of Dionysos and the sublime dancers who inspired Paenios to sculpt his Winged Victory" (R. Marx 8–9).

42. Fuller was so fascinated by the discovery of radium that she wrote to the Curies asking them for a sample of the element to use in one of her performances. They wrote back, thanking her for her interest, but explaining that radium was far too dangerous a substance to be handled in such a context. Fuller decided to compose her dance without the actual radium (see Pinet-Cheula).

43. The celebrated Ouled-Nayl troupe, for example, performed their dances against a recreated Algerian landscape.

44. Here, for example, is historian Georges Hardy on the colonial landscape: "We feel the need for a sort of promised land, an edenic place . . . where the light is more gay . . . where animal and human life are embellished with all the grace of childhood. This Old Testament vision . . . is the colonial landscape" (Hardy 37).

45. Fuller was also intrigued by the possibility of simulating herself onstage by using other dancers identically costumed. Toward the end of her career, she took pleasure in fooling her audience by sending her sister-in-law out onstage dressed in complete imitation of herself. With the audience believing this other woman to be authentically "La Loie," Fuller would then stride onstage to perform the last piece of the evening, revealing the hoax to cheers from the audience (Holman-Black).

46. Indeed, even offstage, Fuller constantly varied her account of her personal life, choosing to replace factual biography with more commercially glamorous details. She lied about her age, for example, by as many as ten years. Her memories of her early theatrical experiences varied widely as well.

47. That Fuller was interested in feminism is clear. She loved the writings of Louisa Mae Alcott and Carrie Nation. She spoke often of the importance of education for girls, and decried the discomfort and social tyranny of the corset. Her general demeanor was often recognized as somehow "feminist," too. One critic felt that she had "a rather disturbing air of the suffragette" (Silvagni). Another saw her in the tradition of the "sévriennes," students at Paris's most elite university for women (Vuillermoz 47).

48. "Woman, as interpreted by Fuller," writes dance critic Gilles Dusein, "is no longer inscribed as an object of desire or arousal (as in the can-can or Arab dances . . .) but as a work of art" (86).

49. Indeed, Thomas Edison felt a great kinship with Fuller and longed to film her. He invited her many times to his New Jersey laboratory, but was refused

every time. Eventually, in 1894, Edison contented himself with filming a young imitator of Fuller's—Annabelle Whitford Moore—performing a version of the "Serpentine Dance." Surprisingly, Edison later brought this film to the Paris "kinetoscopes" and presented it under the fraudulent title "Danse de la Loie Fuller" (*Encyclopedio dello spettacolo* 763).

50. *Le Livre d'or de l'exposition de 1900* 101.

51. Program no. 1 for the Palais de la Danse, Rondel Collection on Loie Fuller, Bibliothèque de l'Arsenal, Paris.

52. The entire street consisted of a restaurant, "La Maison du Rire" ("The House of Laughter"), "Le Phono-Cinéma-Théâtre," "Le Théâtroscope," "Les Tableaux Vivants," "Le Jardin de la Chanson" ("The Garden of Song"), "La Roulette," "Une Annexe des Serres avec Kiosque à Musique" ("A Greenhouse Annex with Music Kiosk"), "Le Grand Guignol," "Les Bonhommes Guillaume," "Le Théâtre des Auteurs Gais," "Le Palais de la Danse," "Le Théâtre Loie Fuller," "Le Manoir à L'Envers" ("The Upside-Down House"), and a post office (Picard, *Rapport général administratif et technique*, 9).

53. Victory in war had left the United States with something of a small empire. As a result of President McKinley's imperialist campaign against Spain (justified as an attempt to "liberate" Cuba), the Americans now had influence in Cuba and held control of the Philippines, Puerto Rico, and Guam; they had also recently annexed Hawaii. Looking then like powerful new participants in global imperialism, the United States alarmed the French, who feared that America's new colonial expansionism might lead to competition, and possibly even aggression, in the French-controlled Caribbean. (See Blumenthal; Dementyov; and R. Miller.)

54. For more on this, see Headrick.

55. The Union Centrale was founded in 1882 and was the result of the merging of the Union Centrale des Beaux Arts Appliqués à l'Industrie and a society whose goal was to create a museum of decorative arts (Jullian, *Triumph*, 224).

56. See Mandell; Silverman, *Art Nouveau*; Williams; Jullian, *Triumph*.

57. For an excellent description of Bing and Art Nouveau, see Deborah Silverman's *Art Nouveau in Fin-de-Siècle France*.

58. In 1895, for example, de Feure prepared a series of illustrations entitled Féminiflores, in which female figures were merged with drawings of various flowers (Silverman, *Art Nouveau*, 371).

59. See Rabaut; Moses. In the fin-de-siècle classic *Dracula* (1897), Bram Stoker's peculiarly saintly and maternal heroine Mina Murray mocks the New Woman's threat to gender roles: "Some of the New Woman writers will some day start an idea that men and women should be allowed to see each other asleep before proposing or accepting. But I suppose the New Woman won't condescend in future to accept; she will do the proposing herself. And a nice job she will make of it too!" (Stoker 91).

60. An excellent example of a "familial feminist" treatise is Jules Bois's *L'Eve nouvelle*. In this essay, Bois blames equally the New Woman and the Fashionable Woman (*la femme à la mode*) for the decay of society. He asks women to abandon their makeup, clothes, and seductions for the home and hearth. "It is time to send back to the store all these theatrical props.... Modern thought has

nearly drowned in a sea of lace. . . . Let us have no more of the doll-woman who is anti-family and anti-social" (Bois 24). The most essential of feminine tasks, according to Bois, is the moral direction of the species. He stresses the importance of "monogamods," or monogamous, married couples. See also *Eve réhabilitée* by Claire Galichon.

61. The tension between Fuller's aesthetic and Art Nouveau confirms Benjamin's observation about the tension within Art Nouveau itself. For Benjamin, Art Nouveau "represented the last attempt at a sortie on the part of art imprisoned by technical advance within her ivory tower. It mobilized all the reserve forces of interiority. They found their expression in the mediumistic language of line, in the flower as the symbol of the naked, vegetable Nature that confronted the technologically armed environment. The new elements of construction in iron girder form obsessed Art Nouveau. Through ornament it strove to win back these forms for Art" ("Paris" 168).

62. There is, certainly, a relation between the nineteenth-century vitrine and Art Nouveau's female domestic interior. This era saw the emergence of the consumerized woman and the domesticized shopping space. To encourage women customers to view the commercial arena as an extension of the home, department stores like the Bon Marché and the Louvre created sitting areas and letter-writing salons that imitated bourgeois apartments. They offered refreshments and entertainments to shoppers' children (M. Miller). It is fair to say, however, that Fuller's onstage vitrines separated the two realms, being commercial while staging the rejection, rather than the embracing, of the domestic.

63. See note 60 above.

64. Indeed, Loie Fuller onstage comes close to embodying a version of what Michel Carrouges originally called the "bachelor machine," after Duchamps's "Large Glass: The Bride Stripped Bare by Her Bachelors, Even." "The bachelor machine," writes Constance Penley, "is typically a closed, self-sufficient system. Its common themes include frictionless, sometimes perpetual motion, an ideal time and the magical possibility of its reversal . . . electrification, voyeurism and masturbatory eroticism, the dream of the mechanical reproduction of art, and artificial birth or reanimation" (57–58). Penley cites Michel de Certeau's assertion that the bachelor machine "does not write the woman," and goes on to ask if there could be a way to modify the machine so that it did. I submit that in some respects, Fuller's performing persona sketches out a version of such an apparatus . . . a "bachelorette machine." (See Michel Carrouges, *Les Machines célibataires*.)

Marinetti saw in Loie Fuller an important precursor of his own mecano-morphic forms. In his 1917 manifesto *Futurist Dance*, he lists her along with Nijinsky and Isadora Duncan as artists admirable for being "free of mimicry, and without sexual stimulation," representing "pure geometry" (quoted in Goldberg 18).

65. Much has been written about the increasing importance of performers' private lives in the early part of this century. Typically, critics of "stardom," such as Richard De Cordova, see this phenomenon as dependent upon "a fairly thoroughgoing articulation of the paradigm professional life/private life." "With the emergence of the star," writes De Cordova, "the question of the player's exis-

tence outside his/her work . . . entered discourse. . . . The private life of the star emerged as a new site of knowledge and truth" (26). Although De Cordova is discussing early film stars in particular, Loie Fuller's precinematic celebrity already fits this paradigm.

66. See Elaine Showalter's discussion of this sculpture in *Sexual Anarchy*.

67. Gabrielle Bloch was sometimes known professionally as Gabrielle Sorère, particularly when working as Fuller's business manager and (later on) occasional film co-star.

68. Andrew Ross defines camp effect as occurring "when the products . . . of a much earlier mode of production, which has lost its power to dominate cultural meanings, become available in the present, for redefinition according to contemporary codes of taste" (Ross 5).

69. "Camp sensibility," Sontag writes, "is one that is alive to a double sense in which something can be taken" (281).

70. See Richard Dyer's *Heavenly Bodies*.

71. Two recent anthologies, *The Politics and Poetics of Camp* (1994), edited by Meyer, and *Camp Grounds* (1993), edited by David Bergman, have refocused attention on the connection between gay politics and camp. Of camp, the late director Charles Ludlam wrote, "The worst thing that happened to camp was that the straight world took this cult word and decided they were going to do camp. Then you get something that has nothing to do with camp. There's no vision . . . it has . . . become a meaningless cliché."

72. For more on the coexistence of commercial culture and camp, see my "Outrageous Dieting: The Camp Performance of Richard Simmons."

73. "Her life was . . . as correct as her feeling," wrote Janet Flanner in her obituary of Fuller (Flanner 67).

74. Legrand-Chabrier 28.

75. See Sedgwick's discussion of performativity and orientalism in *Tendencies*, Dyer's discussion of queerness and melodramatic acting in *Heavenly Bodies: Film Stars and Society*, and Wayne Koestenbaum's remarks on the appeal of opera divas for gay men in *The Queen's Throat*.

CHAPTER FIVE
CAMP SALOME

1. Wilde's 1882 tour of the United States had apparently impressed upon him the power of commercial advertising. By the 1890s, his face, body, distinctive dress, and witty aphorisms were being reproduced and caricatured constantly. In the United States, there was even an "Oscar Wilde Forget-Me-Not Waltz." For a complete discussion of Oscar Wilde's campaign of self-promotion, see Regenia Gagnier and Jennifer Wicke.

2. The repetitiveness of the dialogue may owe something to the work of Maeterlinck. See Gail Finney.

3. In her *Epistemology of the Closet*, Sedgwick uses the term "open secret" for the phenomenon of a homosexual identity that all can see but none will acknowledge.

4. As Brad Bucknell observes, "The word 'Salome' calls up a tradition of rep-

resentation in the visual, verbal, and musical arts, and seeing 'Salome' requires looking at this tradition, this series of repetitions which constitutes the word" (Bucknell 503). According to Rita Severi, at least 2,789 poets in France alone have treated the story of Salome in one form or another (458).

5. Although the New Testament version is normally considered to be the original, some evidence suggests that the Salome story finds its roots in much older legend, such as that of a god like Adonis or Attis sacrificed to a goddess. One compelling detail supporting this theory is that John's birthday is June 25, which coincides with the summer solstice; his death on August 29 corresponds with the harvest, with the cutting of the grain suggesting his beheading. John's life therefore mirrors the Earth's cycle. It has been known since the nineteenth century that the diverse European festivals of Saint John, which occur between June 21 and June 24, are Christian reworkings of pagan sun festivals. See Kuryluk for a complete history of the legend.

The Dance of the Seven Veils is also probably prebiblical in origin, especially since the number seven is most commonly associated with the seven wonders of the ancient world. A dance uncovering seven veils may originally have been a spectacle celebrating these cultural achievements. The dance may also have been a ritual celebrating the creation of the universe, since for a long time only seven planets were known to exist. See Severi for a complete discussion of the Dance of the Seven Veils.

Although it remains unclear when the Salome legend became associated with this dance, it was most likely during the late Middle Ages or early Renaissance.

6. In 93 A.D., Flavius Josephus asserts (*Antiquities of the Jews* 17.4) that the princess is Salome, whose father was Herod, son of Herod the Great and the stepdaughter of the tetrarch, Herod Antipas. Josephus, however, also distinguishes between the princess Salome and the young girl who dances for Herod. Although Rémy de Goncourt apparently reproached Oscar Wilde for conflating these two figures, Wilde was unconcerned. See Ellmann, *Oscar Wilde*.

7. The story of Salome has enjoyed several periods of aesthetic popularity. Seneca writes of her in the ninth book of his *Controversiae* (Shewan 104). After biblical times, there was little interest in her until the fourth century, when Roman decadent literature turned its attention to her. The construction in the fourth century of the church in honor of John the Baptist in Alexandria may have also contributed to this period of interest. During the Crusades of the Middle Ages, the cult of the Baptist directed the public's attention once again toward Salome. The most famous example of this era's fascination with the legend is the depiction of a dancing Salome on the bronze door of San Zeno's in Verona, built in the eleventh century. On the door, Salome dances in a particularly contorted, serpentine manner. At the end of the twelfth century, Herrade of Landsberg, the famous prioress of the Sainte-Odile nunnery, illustrated the *Hortus deliciarum* with a painting of Salome. In Herrade's depiction, the princess dances upside down, standing on her hands. The exaggeratedly unnatural pose evokes a world of monstrosity and inverted morality, a theme then taken up by many subsequent artists and writers. The tympanon above one of the entrances to the Cathedral of St. John in Rouen, for example, depicts Salome in a similarly contorted position, dancing upside down, on her hands. See Kuryluk.

8. Directly preceding the story is the account of the missions of the Twelve, in which Christ sends out his apostles in pairs. Directly following the episode is the miracle of the loaves. The Salome story that appears in Matthew 14:6–12 is, in fact, the only one in this book of the Gospel that does not treat the story of Jesus or his disciples.

9. The nearly eighty-year-long Salome craze of the nineteenth century began with Heinrich Heine's 1841 narrative poem *Atta Troll,* and included Flaubert's 1863 *Salammbô,* Henri Regnault's 1868 painting *Salomé,* Gustave Moreau's two 1876 paintings *Salomé dansant* and *L'Apparition,* Jules Laforgue's 1885 story *Salomé,* and Mallarmé's 1864 *Hérodiade* and his 1898 *Noces d'Hérodiade.* See Décaudin.

10. "She possesses an immense power of metamorphosis," writes Starobinski; "at first glance, she is only a marvelous object . . . a thing, a victim. . . . But this victim has muscles of steel. . . . Herod grants her everything in exchange for the spectacle of her dancing body" (56). Rodney Shewan writes that the dancer, particularly Salome, "expressed intuitive truths, . . . reached only through the sophisticated literary evocation of a non-verbal kinetic form, the most primitive discursive form known to mankind" (127). Referring to the constant presence of the *danseuse* in nineteenth-century art and literature, Frank Kermode writes, "Throughout this tradition, the beauty of a work of art, in which there is no division of form and meaning . . . is more or less explicitly compared with the mysterious inexpressive beauty of such women, and particularly with that of Salome. The femme fatale is certainly the pathological aspect of this image" (*Romantic Image* 60).

11. Herod Antipas (known in most of the Gospels simply as "Herod") marries Herodias after luring her away from her politically ineffectual first husband—his own half-brother Herod—with the promise of greater wealth and power. (According to biblical scholars, Mark confuses Herodias's first husband Herod with Philip, the tetrarch's other brother. Philip eventually marries Salome, and would never have married his own daughter.) John the Baptist is eventually imprisoned by Herod Antipas for inveighing against the tetrarch's marriage, which contravened Jewish law in two ways: a wife was not permitted to divorce her husband, and a widow could not marry her husband's brother if children had been born to the first marriage (A.H.M. Jones 181; Smallwood 88).

12. Bram Dijkstra, in his *Idols of Perversity,* develops this theory. Seeing "Salomania" as part of a vicious backlash against feminism, Dijkstra writes, "In an acute, lurid, antifeminine symbolism . . . men everywhere, of every possible political persuasion, declared their emancipation from the viraginous, decapitating sword of woman's regressive, degenerate concern for the real" (305). On the other hand, Jane Marcus, in her famous article "Salome: The Jewish Princess Was a New Woman," interprets the princess as "a Biblical Hedda Gabler . . . [agent] of the revolution and martyr to the cause of freedom" (110–11). See also Elaine Showalter's *Sexual Anarchy,* and Nina Auerbach's *Woman and the Demon.*

13. Wilde wrote *Salomé,* in fact, while keeping in close touch with many of Mallarmé's closest friends—Marcel Schwob, Adolphe Retté, and Pierre Louys—who advised him on matters of French diction and verse style (Ellmann, *Oscar Wilde,* 341).

14. In April 1891 Mallarmé announced that he would recommence work on his long-abandoned *Hérodiade*. He was, perhaps, responding to Wilde's announced intention to write a play about Salome, since later, in December 1891, Wilde would finish his French drama. In February of that same year, the two men, who were already friends, had met in Paris. Mallarmé specified that he would retain the name *Hérodiade* to distinguish his work (*Les Noces d'Hérodiade*) from what he called "la Salomé moderne, ou exhumée," and by this he most probably meant Wilde's (Huot 194). Two years later, in March 1893, Mallarmé wrote in admiration to Wilde: "My dear poet: I so admire that in your *Salomé* everything is expressed in continually dazzling strokes, and that also, from every page floats something of the unsayable, of dreams. In this way the innumerable, precise gems [of language] serve as the accompaniment to Salome's costume and to the young princess's supernatural gestures, which you have definitively evoked." ("Mon cher poète: J'admire que tout étant exprimé par de perpétuels traits éblouissants, en votre *Salomé*, il se dégage aussi à chaque page de l'indicible et le songe. Ainsi les gemmes innombrables et exactes ne peuvent servir que d'accompagnement sur sa robe au geste surnaturel de cette jeune princesse, que définitivement vous évoquâtes," quoted in Ellmann, *Oscar Wilde*, 374).

15. This is hardly to say that Wilde had an unequivocal appreciation for the masses. In a letter to Robert Ross, dated June 1900, Wilde writes of his experience visiting the Exposition Universelle: "The only ugly thing at the Exhibition is the public" (*Letters* 738). In a later letter to Reginald Turner (May 11, 1898), Wilde expresses similar distaste—and a good deal of misogyny—toward a cabaret audience: "A kind friend took me to the Folies-Bergère last night. . . . The acrobats were more wonderful than ever, but the audience was dreadfully mulierastic, and aged women covered with diamonds of the worst water came up and begged for *bocks*. On being refused they left with horrible imprecations" (ibid., 829).

16. Shortly after writing *Salomé*, Wilde saw his friend Sarah Bernhardt at a party; she asked him to write a play for her. "I have already done so," he replied. Evidence that Wilde had always conceived of Bernhardt as the princess Salome is the inscription he offered with a packet of his poems sent to her, "A Sarah Bernhardt, Comme la Princesse Salomé est belle ce soir" (quoted in Ellmann, *Oscar Wilde*, 371). On September 2, 1900, Wilde wrote in a letter: "What has age to do with acting? The only person in the world who could act Salome is Sarah Bernhardt, that 'serpent of old Nile,' older than the Pyramids" (*Letters* 834).

17. Wilde was a close friend of Duse's for many years; and five years after the publication of *Salomé* he asked her to consider playing the title role. In a letter dated December 10, 1897, Wilde wrote to Leonard Smithers: "Eleanora Duse is now reading *Salomé*. There is a chance of her playing it. She is a fascinating artist though nothing to Sarah" (*Letters* 695). As for Loie Fuller, several critics, including Elaine Showalter and Katherine Worth, suggest that Wilde was very familiar with her work. Fuller settled permanently in Paris in 1891, but had already visited the city earlier. Wilde, who was in contact with Mallarmé and his circle from the mid-1880s on, may have heard of Fuller's earliest performances

through them. He may also have seen her perform in America during his 1882 visit. He certainly attended her performances at the 1900 World's Fair in Paris. But it remains unknown whether Wilde had actually seen Fuller's various veil dances before he wrote his own *Salomé*, heard vaguely about Fuller's dances through friends, or only took part in a general artistic climate informed, but not directly influenced, by Fuller.

18. On February 21, 1893, Wilde wrote to Florence Balcombe Stoker, "Will you accept a copy of *Salomé* my strange venture in a tongue that is not my own, but that I love as one loves an instrument of music on which one has not played before?" (*Letters* 330).

19.

Le Jeune Syrien: Comme la princesse Salomé est belle ce soir!

Le Page d'Herodias: Regardez la lune. La lune a l'air très étrange. On dirait une femme qui sort du tombeau. Elle ressemble à une femme morte. . . .

Le Jeune Syrien: Elle a l'air étrange. Elle ressemble à une petite princesse qui porte un voile jaune, et a des pieds d'argent, Elle ressemble à une princesse qui a des pieds comme des petites colombes blanches. . . . On dirait qu'elle danse.

Le Page: Elle est comme une femme morte. Elle va très lentement. (Wilde, *Salomé*, 3–4 [Fr.])

The English translation in the text comes from Oscar Wilde's own translation of his original French. Occasionally, Wilde's translation omits a phrase or locution of his original French that is relevant to my argument, which I here will indicate in brackets in the English text.

20. "Que c'est bon de voir la lune! Elle ressemble à une petite pièce de monnaie. On dirait une toute petite fleur d'argent. Elle est froide et chaste, la lune. . . . Je suis sûre qu'elle est vierge. Elle a la beauté d'une vierge. . . . Oui elle est vierge" (Wilde, *Salomé*, 14 [Fr.]).

21. "Oh! Comme la lune a l'air étrange! On dirait la main d'une morte qui cherche à se couvrir avec un linceul" (ibid., 21 [Fr.]).

22. "Elle a l'air tres étrange. On dirait une petite princesse qui a des yeux d'ambre. A travers les nuages de mousseline elle sourit comme une petite princesse" (ibid., 22 [Fr.]).

23.

Herod: Où est Salomé? Où est la princesse . . . ah la voilà!

Herodias: Il ne faut pas la regarder. Vous la regardez toujours.

Herod: La lune a l'air très étrange ce soir. N'est-ce pas que la lune a l'air très étrange? On dirait une femme hystérique qui cherchait des amants partout. Elle est une aussi.

Herodias: Non, la lune ressemble à la lune c'est tout. Rentrons vous n'avez rien à faire ici. (Ibid., 33 [Fr.])

24. "Ce sont les yeux surtout qui sont terribles. On dirait des trous noirs laissés par des flambeaux sur une tapisserie de Tyr. On dirait des cavernes noires d'Egypte où les dragons trouvent leur asile. On dirait des lacs noirs troublés par des lunes fantastiques" (ibid., 24 [Fr.]).

25. "Qui est cette femme qui me regarde? Je ne veux pas qu'elle me regarde. . . . Arrière! Fille de Babylone!" (ibid., 25 [Fr.]).

26. Salome's desire for Jokanaan is often cited by critics who wish to see the princess as a model of the emancipated New Woman.

27. For example, Song of Songs 1:2 reads: "Let him kiss me with kisses of his mouth." Wilde's Salome says: "Suffer me to kiss thy mouth" (Wilde, *Salomé*, 14 [Eng.]). Song of Songs 4:3 reads: "Your cheek is like a half-pomegranate behind your veil." Salome says: "Thy mouth . . . is like a pomegranate cut in twain with a knife of ivory" (Wilde, *Salomé*, 12 [Eng.]). See Kuryluk's helpful appendix for more examples of Wilde's borrowings from the Song of Songs.

28. "Iokanaan! Je suis amoureuse de ton corps. Ton corps est blanc comme le lis d'un pré que le faucheur n'a jamais fauché. Ton corps est blanc comme les neiges qui couchent sur les montagnes, comme les neiges qui couchent sur les montagnes de Judée, et descendent dans les vallées. Les roses du jardin d'Arabie ne sont pas aussi blanches que ton corps. Ni les roses du jardin de la reine d'Arabie, ni les pieds de l'aurore qui trépignent sur les feuilles, ni le sein de la lune quand elle couche sur le sein de la mer. . . . Il n'y a rien au monde d'aussi blanc que ton corps.—Laisse-moi toucher ton corps!" (Wilde, *Salomé*, 27 [Fr.]).

29. "Ton corps est hideux. Il est comme le corps d'un lépreux. Il est comme un mur de plâtre où les vipères sont passées, comme un mur de plâtre où les scorpions ont fait leur nid. Il est comme un sépulcre blanchi, et qui est plein de choses dégoûtantes. Il est horrible, il est horrible ton corps! C'est de tes cheveux que je suis amoureuse, Iokanaan. Tes cheveux ressemblent à des grappes de raisins, à des grappes de raisins noirs qui pendent des vignes d'Edom dans le pays des Edomites. Tes cheveux sont comme les cèdres du Liban qui donnent de l'ombre aux lions et aux voleurs qui veulent se cacher pendant la journée. Les longues nuits noires, les nuits où la lune ne se montre pas, où les étoiles ont peur, ne sont pas aussi noires. Le silence qui demeure dans les forêts n'est pas aussi noir. Il n'y a rien au monde d'aussi noir que tes cheveux. . . . Laisse-moi toucher tes cheveux" (ibid., 28 [Fr.]).

30. For example, Salome will soon find his hair repugnant: "Thy hair is horrible. It is covered with mire and dust. It is like a knot of serpents coiled round thy neck," and turn her attention to his mouth: "A band of scarlet on a tower of ivory. It is like a pomegranate cut in twain with a knife of ivory . . . redder than the feet of the doves who inhabit the temples and are fed by the priests" (Wilde, *Salomé*, 12 [Eng.]).

31. This line is not translated by Wilde in his English edition.

32. "Elle est plus rouge que les pieds des colombes qui demeurent dans les temples et sont nourries par les prêtres. Elle est plus rouge que les pieds de celui qui revient d'une forêt où il a tué un lion et vu des tigres dorés" (Wilde, *Salomé*, 29 [Fr.]).

33. "Le jeune Syrian s'est tué. . . . Je lui avais donné une petite boîte de parfums, des boucles d'oreille faites en argent, et maintenant il s'est tué. . . . Je lui ai donné une petite boîte . . . et une bague d'agate qu'il portait toujours à la main. . . . Aussi il aimait beaucoup à se regarder dans la rivière. Je lui ai fait des reproches pour cela" (ibid., 33 [Fr.]).

34. The subplot of the love affair between two soldiers is a detail that Wilde owes to Flaubert. In *Salammbô*, a similar relationship is suggested between Matho and his devoted aide Spendius. There are also frequent suggestions throughout the novel that many of the soldiers share erotic bonds.

35. "Vos petits pieds seront comme des colombes blanches. Ils ressembleront à des fleurs blanches qui dansent sur un arbre" (Wilde, *Salomé*, 70, 73).

36. Aubrey Beardsley also saw the symetrical relation between Salome and Iokanaan. In his 1894 illustration "John and Salome," he portrays the two facing each other, their bodies nearly mirror images. Although Salome's breasts are displayed, both figures are of generally indeterminate gender, somewhat masculine of face, but in feminine, curving robes. They are more androgyne twins than anything else (see Wilde, *Salomé*, 13 [Eng.]).

37. "Je le regrette. Oui je le regrette beaucoup. Car il était beau. Il était même très beau. Il avait des yeux très langoureux. Je me rappelle que je l'ai vu regardant Salome d'une façon langoureuse. En effet, j'ai trouvé qu'il l'avait un peu trop regardée. . . . Je regrette qu'il soit mort" (ibid., 37 [Fr.]).

38. "Vous ferez cela pour moi Narraboth, et demain quand je passerai dans ma litière sous la porte des vendeurs d'idoles, je laisserai tomber une petite fleur pour vous, une petite fleur verte" (ibid., 20 [Fr.]).

39. The idea of a "homosexual identity" was of course just being formed around this time; and in a certain sense, Wilde's entire career took part in the forging of the first publicly gay personalities. "The nineteenth-century homosexual became a personage, a past, a case history, and a childhood, in addition to being a type of life, a life form, and a morphology . . . the homosexual was now a species" (Foucault 43). For a discussion of Oscar Wilde's trial and its role as a critical moment in the emergence of "the homosexual," see Ed Cohen's *Talk on the Wilde Side*.

40. Again, a drawing by Beardsley eloquently expresses the connection. His "Woman in the Moon" (1894) shows two androgynous figures, the Page and Narraboth, gazing at a large round moon on the horizon. The face on the moon is unmistakably Oscar Wilde's. Since both Salome and Jokanaan are compared to the moon, Wilde in this illustration is both the Man and the Woman in the Moon, a figure of many desires, transcending gender (see Wilde, *Salomé*, 5 [Eng.]).

41. We also see here to what extent the Orient "was the great 'external reality' of modern Europe—the most common object of exhibition," as Timothy Mitchell has said (303).

42. See Jennifer Wicke's discussion in *Advertising Fictions*.

43. Robertson was an artist and writer who formed an important collection of Blake drawings, designed many stage costumes, and wrote children's plays (*Letters* 213, editor's note).

44. See Gagnier 164ff.

45. Upon its publication, Wilde wrote of *Salomé*: "That tragic daughter of passion appeared on Thursday last and is now dancing for the head of the British public" (quoted in Ellmann, *Oscar Wilde*, 374).

46. "Tout spectacle contiendra un élément physique et objectif, sensible à tous . . . beauté magique des costumes pris à certains modèles rituels, resplendissement de la lumière, beauté incantatoire des voix, charme de l'harmonie, notes rares de la musique, couleurs des objets" (Artaud 90).

47. See Ellmann, *Oscar Wilde*; and Showalter.

48. "My Salome is a mystic, the sister of Salammbô," declared Wilde (quoted in Jullian, *Oscar Wilde*, 257).

49. Although Brantlinger is here discussing the relationship between Flaubert's *Salammbô* and *Boucard et Pecuchet*, his remarks certainly hold true for Wilde's *Salomé* as well.

50. See Showalter; and Jullian, *Oscar Wilde*.

51. The essay's author, commissioned by Pemberton-Billing, was Harold Spencer (Showalter 161).

52. See Showalter 162.

53. In *Du Dandysme et du George Brummell*, Barbey d'Aurevilly sees the essence of the successful dandy as "the magic potion of his influence" ("le philtre magique de son influence," 694). Domna Stanton has also noticed the relationship between dandyism and Christianity: "Dandy writers from Balzac to Huysmans stressed the 'similarity between our doctrines and those of Christianity'" (Stanton 45, quoting Balzac's *Traité de la vie élégante*).

AFTERWORD

1. Richard Dyer makes this point clear: "There is a whole other way of relating to stars, a way that is essentially deconstructive, that refuses the guarantee that appearances are not deceiving. The most widespread form of such deconstructive reading is camp" ("A Star Is Born" 132).

2. America's tremendous influence on early European mass entertainment is well documented. Along with Edison, Clyde Barnum—circus master and professional showman—helped create early mass-cultural "fame" in Europe when he traveled there with his "Greatest Show on Earth" in the 1870s. (In the 1850s Barnum had helped turn singer Jenny Lind into one of the earliest "stars," promoting her concerts and increasing her ticket sales enormously.) In the 1880s, American entertainer Buffalo Bill took his Wild West Show on tour to Europe and was also received with great acclaim. See Braudy; Rearick; Nye; and Wicke.

3. One could cite Showalter and Deak here, both of whom posit the existence of a twentieth-century "decadence" that mirrors the earlier movement. Hollywood has also taken hold of this idea recently, producing movies that reprise nineteenth-century decadent stories while suggesting certain thematic connections to the contemporary world. The most frequently "revamped" fin-de-siècle tale is *Dracula*, which has been made into at least half a dozen films and television movies of the week, either as retellings of the Stoker novel or as "modern" vampire tales touching on contemporary fears of tainted blood exchange. (Examples include *The Hunger*, *The Lost Boys*, *Bram Stoker's Dracula*, *A Vampire in Brooklyn*, or Abel Ferrara's *Addiction*.)

An article by Marshall Blonsky follows these lines. Entitled "Madonna's Wilde 'Sex'," it sees a (debased, vulgarized) Wildean quality in Madonna's 1992 book of erotic photographs.

4. Certain parallels are unavoidable, of course. In the world of the arts, the resemblance between the nineteenth century's antidecadent movement, exemplified by such works as Max Nordau's 1892 *Degeneration*, strangely resembles the brouhaha over NEA grants to artists and what constitutes "obscenity" in art. The hate-filled discourse that surrounded the Robert Mapplethorpe exhibition in

1990 recalled strongly the propaganda that exploded around Oscar Wilde's *Salomé* and his subsequent trial for sodomy.

5. In 1991, Prince entitled his second film *Diamonds and Pearls*.

6. Prince is now married to Mayte.

7. In 1951, Jacqueline Bouvier won *Vogue* magazine's Prix de Paris contest by submitting an essay listing Baudelaire, Wilde, and Diaghilev as the three dead individuals she most wanted to meet. The essay especially praised Diaghilev for creating "transitory performance" (Koestenbaum 179–81).

Another section of the Prix de Paris competition required the contestant to imagine themes on which to base an entire issue of *Vogue*. Jacqueline Bouvier suggested the theme of nostalgia, "You can swish out to lunch," she wrote, "at your new little restaurant in a jacket cut like a Directoire Dandy's; you can wrap yourself in a great Spanish shawl in your own very U.S.A. living room" (reprinted in *Vogue*, August 1994). For her imagined issue of *Vogue*, Jackie also envisioned photographs of celebrities in designer clothes: "Madame Pandit Nehru in a Mainbocher sari standing on an Indian prayer rug . . . Princess Alexandra of Greece in a dress like Grès's calla lily tunic, standing beside a Greek Statue" (quoted in Brenner 300).

8. Koestenbaum acknowledges Jackie's doubleness by devoting much space to her proximity to Elizabeth Taylor, herself an enduring mass-cultural icon and a figure connoting a somehow debased, lower-class sexuality and availability.

9. See Jane Gaines for an extensive discussion of the legal and cultural ramifications of this lawsuit.

10. See Heymann; Brenner; Kelly.

11. For Feldman, dandyism is a precursor not only of de Man and Derrida, but of Barthes and perhaps even Judith Butler. Her argument combines versions of both deconstruction and contemporary gender theory to read dandyism as the dismantling of binary gender oppositions. For Feldman, dandyism is a realm "beyond patriarchal myths" (182). "Dandies," she writes, "reveal the nineteenth-century roots of some twentieth-century semiotic and post-structuralist understandings. For example, dandies flaunt what a culture usually attempts to ignore or hide, that the human body is never 'natural' or 'naked of cultural clothing,' but is instead a system of signification, cultural construct" (270).

The weakness of Feldman's argument stems from her avoidance of issues of social class. While dandyism certainly questions gender roles, this would not be sufficient to move it beyond patriarchy, whose essentially class-based system dandyism did little to question. A self-proclaimed pure meritocracy, dandyism always refused to acknowledge its dependence upon a system of social class. (The primary gauge of Brummell's success, for example, was his proximity to the prince of Wales.) The dandy was never politically subversive, nor was he a feminist. (Feldman's definition of dandies includes women rather more easily than mine would. She sees Willa Cather as a dandy; and she also makes a case for the dandyism of the famous "passante" of Baudelaire's poem, turning the dandy from active spectator to passive spectacle.)

Jonathan Loesberg's book *Aestheticism and Deconstruction* makes a case for deconstruction's proximity to Paterian aestheticism, while defending both movements against accusations of social detachment or nihilism. Aestheticism is, of course, a larger philosophical category than dandyism, but the nineteenth-century aesthete shares many of the dandy's qualities. See also Hillis Miller's impassioned attack on Loesberg's "defense" of deconstruction.

12. Naturally, Derrida had profound influence in his native France as well, but I believe the cult of personality surrounding him was far more an American phenomenon.

13. Indeed, Derrida has appeared in one film, Ken McMullen's 1982 *Ghost Dance*, and a video by artist Gary Hill in 1987 (R. Jones 24). I should mention also that even in France, Professor Derrida, as an Algerian Jew, carries the appeal of foreignness.

14. Guillory disagrees, for example, with Howard Felperin's and Lindsay Waters's interpretation of de Man. In their article "The Anxiety of American Deconstruction," the two authors assert that "deconstruction is . . . amenable to routinization at the hands of the institution to whose authority it once seemed to pose such a challenge of incompatibility. More than that, it has all but become an institution, as its life and activity rapidly become indistinguishable from the life and activity of the institution at large" (Felperin and Waters 157). For Guillory, though, this reliance upon the Weberian concept of the "routinization" of a charisma incompatible with institutions is a mistake. For him, de Man's charismatic authority was specifically un-Weberian, having "never [been] exclusive of, nor incompatible with, his institutional authority" (244).

15. In using "theory" to mean deconstructive theory, I knowingly reproduce what John Guillory sees as a "symptomatic" inaccuracy. I, too, see it as symptomatic. As Guillory points out, de Man himself seemed to conflate all theory with *his* theory—a typically dandyist move (see Guillory 178).

16. De Man himself referred to the unaesthetic nature of his theory in "Sign and Symbol in Hegel's *Aesthetics*," writing, "There is something bleakly abstract and ugly about literary theory that cannot be entirely blamed on the perversity of its practitioners. Most of us feel internally divided between the compulsion to theorize about literature and a much more attractive, spontaneous encounter with literary works" (761).

17. Deconstruction generally frowns upon "biographizing" critical readings that refer too heavily to an author's extratextual life. Though I am certainly no advocate of literal-minded arguments based on intentionality, I find the status of biographical criticism within deconstruction curious. The problem with any form of biographical criticism is that it deflects one's critical gaze from the text, that it can obscure or prevent the work of reading, and that it presumes a transparency of representation—that works of art "reflect" some external reality. Ironically, though, biography—the story of a noteworthy individual's life—propelled the whole social mechanism of the deconstructive movement, just as it did the dandyist movement. Individuals' relationships to the life of the master critic determined their value on the intellectual market.

18. For illustrative examples of the imitation of de Manian prose, see Guillory, particularly his discussion (200ff.) of "the reproduction of the master's style" (201).

19. Examples of the dandyist personality still exist—for example, the Scottish-born, charismatic Andrew Ross of New York University. Ross, however, has not generated an entire generation of emulators, to my knowledge. Interestingly, though, he has increasingly associated himself with "scientific" topics, publishing *Technoculture* (an anthology he edited with Constance Penley) and *Strange Weather*, both in 1991.

20. Jane Gallop is famous for academic performances that include wearing a skirt made entirely out of men's neckties and using a photograph of herself giving birth on the cover of one of her books. Her 1997 book, *Feminist Accused of Sexual Harassment*, takes her recent legal troubles as its subject. Alice Kaplan's memoir, *French Lessons*, chronicles her own graduate education at Yale and its social implications. Eve Kosofsky Sedgwick discusses personal friendships and her battle with breast cancer in *Tendencies*. And Marianna Torgovnick details her adolescent struggles with ethnicity and class in *Crossing Ocean Parkway*.

BIBLIOGRAPHY

Adam, Paul. Review article. *Le Courrier de la Presse*, Feb. 13, 1893. Archives, Musée Rodin.

Adams, Henry. *The Education of Henry Adams*. New York: Modern Library, 1918.

Adorno, Theodor W., and Max Horkheimer. *Dialectic of Enlightenment*. New York: Herder and Herder, 1972.

Alloula, Malek. *The Colonial Harem*. Translated by Myrna Godzich and Wlad Godzich. Minneapolis: University of Minnesota Press, 1986.

Anzalone, John. "Golden Cylinders: Inscription and Intertext in *L'Eve future*." *L'Esprit créateur* 26, no. 4 (Winter 1986): 38–47.

Apter, Emily. "Acting Out Orientalism." *L'Esprit créateur* 24, no. 2 (Summer 1994): 102–16.

———. *Feminizing the Fetish: Psychoanalysis and Narrative Obsession in Turn of the Century France*. Ithaca, N.Y.: Cornell University Press, 1991.

Armstrong, Nancy. Introduction to *Ideology of Conduct: Essays on Literature and the History of Sexuality*. Edited by Nancy Armstrong and Leonard Tennenhouse. New York: Methuen, 1987.

Artaud, Antonin. *Oeuvres complètes*. Vol. 4. Paris: Gallimard, 1978.

Auerbach, Nina. *Woman and the Demon: The Life of a Victorian Myth*. Cambridge, Mass.: Harvard University Press, 1982.

Bailey, Peter, ed. *Music Hall: The Business of Pleasure*. Philadelphia: Open University Press, 1986.

Balzac, Honoré de. *Oeuvres complètes*. Vol. 2, *1830–35*. Paris: Louis Conard, 1938.

———. *Théorie de la démarche* (1830). In *Oeuvres complètes*, 613–43.

———. "Traité de la vie élégante." In *Oeuvres complètes*, 152–85.

Banes, Sally. *Writing Dancing in the Age of Postmodernism*. Hanover, N.H.: University Press of New England, 1994.

Barbey d'Aurevilly, Jules. *Dandyism*. Translated by Douglas Ainslie. New York: PAJ Publications, 1988.

———. *Les Diaboliques*. Paris: Gallimard, 1973.

———. "Du Dandysme et de George Brummell" (1843). In *Oeuvres romanesques complètes*, 2: 667–733. Paris: Gallimard, 1966.

———. "Premiers articles." In *Les Annales de l'université de Besançon*, 85–89. Paris: Belles Lettres, 1973.

Barthes, Roland. "Le Dandysme et la mode." In *Le Mythe du dandy*, edited by Emilien Carassus, 312–15. Paris: Librairie Armand Colin, 1971.

———. *Système de la mode*. Paris: Editions Seuil, 1967.

Baudelaire, Charles. *L'Art romantique*. Paris: Gallimard, 1968.

———. *La Fanfarlo* (1847). In *Les Paradis artificiels*, 237–79. Paris: Louis Conard, 1928.

———. *Mon Coeur mis à nu*. Paris: Editions Gallimard, 1930.

Baudelaire, Charles. *Oeuvres complètes*. Edited by Claude Pichois. Paris: Gallimard, 1961.

——. *Le Peintre de la vie moderne* (1863). In *Oeuvres complètes*, 1152–92.

——. *Petits poèmes en prose*. Edited by Melvin Zimmerman. Manchester: Manchester University Press, 1968.

——. *Selected Letters of Charles Baudelaire*. Translated by Rosemary Lloyd. London: Weidenfeld and Nicolson, 1986.

Baumgold, Julie. "Glitter Slave." *Esquire* 3, no. 2 (Fall 1995): 100–105.

Bell-Villada, Gene H. "The Idea of Art for Art's Sake: Intellectual Origins, Social Conditions, and Poetic Doctrine." *Science and Society* 50, no. 4 (Winter 1986): 415–39.

Bellour, Raymond. "Ideal Hadaly." Translated by Stanley Gray. *Camera Obscura: A Journal of Feminism and Film Theory* 15 (1986): 111–34.

Benjamin, Walter. *Charles Baudelaire: A Lyric Poet in the Era of High Capitalism*. Translated by Harry Zohn. London: Verso, 1983.

——. "Paris, the Capital of the Nineteenth Century." Translated by Quintin Hoare. In *Charles Baudelaire*, 155–76.

——. "The Work of Art in the Age of Mechanical Reproduction." In *Illuminations*, translated by Harry Zohn, 217–52. New York: Schocken Books, 1969.

Bergman, David. Introduction to *Camp Grounds: Style and Homosexuality*. Edited by David Bergman. Amherst: University of Massachusetts Press, 1993.

Bernheimer, Charles. *Figures of Ill Repute: Representing Prostitution in Nineteenth-Century France*. Cambridge, Mass.: Harvard University Press, 1989.

Bersani, Leo. *Baudelaire and Freud*. Berkeley: University of California Press, 1977.

——. *The Culture of Redemption*. Cambridge, Mass.: Harvard University Press, 1990.

Birkett, Jennifer. *The Sins of the Fathers: Decadence in France, 1870–1914*. London: Quartet Books, 1986.

Blonsky, Marshall. "Madonna's Wilde 'Sex.' " *Washington Post*, Oct. 18, 1992, C1, C4.

Blumenthal, Henry. *American and French Culture, 1800–1900*. Baton Rouge: Louisiana State University Press, 1975.

——. *France and the United States: Their Diplomatic Relations, 1789–1917*. Chapel Hill: University of North Carolina Press, 1970.

Bois, Jules. *L'Eve nouvelle*. Paris: Editions, 1901.

Bouvier, Jacqueline. Prix de Paris essay. Reprinted in *Vogue* (Aug. 1994): 250–52.

Bowlby, Rachel. "Modes of Modern Shopping: Mallarmé at the Bon Marché." In *Ideology of Conduct: Essays on Literature and the History of Sexuality*, edited by Nancy Armstrong and Leonard Tennenhouse, 185–205. New York: Methuen, 1987.

Brandstetter, Gabriele, and Brygida Maria Ochaim. *Loie Fuller: Tanz, Licht-Spiel, Art Nouveau*. Freiburg: Verlag Rombach, 1989.

Brantlinger, Patrick. *Bread and Circuses: Theories of Mass Culture as Social Decay*. Ithaca, N.Y.: Cornell University Press, 1983.

Bratton, J. S. *Music Hall Performance and Style*. Pglihhilly, Wales: Open University Press, 1986.

Braudy, Leo. *The Frenzy of Renown*. New York: Oxford University Press, 1986.

Brenner, Marie. "The Unforgettable Jackie." *Vogue* (Aug. 1994): 246–49, 300–302.

Brown, Sarah Graham. *Images of Women in Photography of the Middle East, 1860–1950*. New York: Columbia University Press, 1988.

Buck-Morss, Susan. *The Dialectics of Seeing: Walter Benjamin and the Arcades Project*. Cambridge, Mass.: MIT Press, 1989.

Bucknell, Brad. "On 'Seeing Salome'." *English Literary History* 60 (1993): 503–26.

Burton, Richard. *Baudelaire and the Second Republic*. Oxford: Clarendon, 1991.

Carassus, Emilien. "Dandysme et aristocratie." *Romantisme* 4, no. 70 (1990): 25–37.

Carrouges, Michel. *Les Machines célibataires*. Paris: Editions du Chêne, 1976.

Chambers, Ross. "L'Ange et l'automate: Variations sur le mythe de l'actrice de Nerval à Proust." *Archives de lettres modernes* 9, no. 128 (1971): 467–71.

———. "Le Fade et le pimenté: Modes de séduction dans 'La Fanfarlo' de Baudelaire." In *Littérature et gastronomie*, edited by Ronald W. Tobin, 175–93. Paris: Biblio 17, 1985.

———. "The *Flâneur* as Hero." *Australian Journal of French Studies* 28, no. 2 (1991): 142–53.

———. "Literature Deterritorialized." In *A New History of French Literature*, edited by Denis Hollier, 710–16. Cambridge, Mass.: Harvard University Press, 1989.

Chateaubriand, François René de. "On America and American Literature" (1850). In *Transatlantic Mirrors: Essays in Franco-American Literary Relations*, edited by Sidney Braun and Seymour Lainoff, 47–52. Boston: Twayne, 1978.

Chollet, Roland. *Balzac, Journaliste le tournant de 1830*. Paris: Klincksieck, 1983.

Coblence, Françoise. *Le Dandysme, obligation d'incertitude*. Paris: Presses Universitaires de Paris, 1988.

Cohen, Ed. *Talk on the Wilde Side: Toward a Genealogy of a Discourse on Male Sexualities*. London: Routledge, 1993.

———. "Writing Gone Wilde: Homoerotic Desire in the Closet of Representation." *Publications of the Modern Language Association* 102 (Oct. 1987): 801–13.

Colette. *L'Envers du music-hall*. Paris: Gallimard, 1928.

Deak, Frantisek. *Symbolist Theater: The Foundation of the Avant-Garde*. Baltimore: The Johns Hopkins University Press, 1994.

Debord, Guy. *La Société du spectacle*. Paris: Duchet Chastel, 1967.

Décaudin. Michel. "Un Mythe fin-de-siècle: Salomé." *Comparative Literature Studies* 4, nos. 1–2 (1967): 109–18.

De Cordova, Richard. "The Emergence of the Star System in America." In *Stardom: Industry of Desire*, edited by Christine Gledhill, 17–29. London: Routledge, 1991.

De Lauretis, Theresa. *Technologies of Gender*. Bloomington: Indiana University Press, 1987.

Delbourg-Delphis, Marylène. *Masculin singulier: Le Dandysme et son histoire*. Paris: Hachette, 1985.

de Man, Paul. *Blindness and Insight: Essays in the Rhetoric of Contemporary Criticism*. New York: Oxford University Press, 1971.

———. *Resistance to Theory*. Minneapolis: University of Minnesota Press, 1983.

———. "Sign and Symbol in Hegel's *Aesthetics*." *Critical Inquiry* 8 (Summer 1992): 761–75.

De Ménasce. J. "Loie Fuller." Press clipping. Rondel Collection on Loie Fuller, Bibliothèque de l'Arsenal, Paris.

Dementyov, I. *USA: Imperialists and Anti-Imperialists*. Translated by David Skvirsky. Moscow: Progress Publishers, 1979.

de Morinni, Clare. "Loie Fuller: The Fairy of Light." In *Chronicles of the American Dance: From the Shakers to Martha Graham*, edited by Paul Magriel, 203–20. New York: Da Capo, 1984.

de Panafieu, Christine Woesler. "Automata: A Masculine Utopia." In *Nineteen Eighty-four: Scenes Between Utopia and Dystopia*, edited by Everett Mendelsohn and Helga Nowotny, 127–45. Dordrecht, Holland: D. Reidel, 1984.

Dictionary of the Interpreters Bible. New York: Abingden, 1967.

Dijkstra, Bram. *Idols of Perversity*. New York: Oxford University Press, 1986.

Dollimore, Jonathan. *Sexual Dissidence: Augustine to Wilde, Freud to Foucault*. Oxford: Clarendon, 1991.

Dragonetti, Roger. *Un Fantôme dans le kiosque: Mallarmé et l'esthétique du quotidien*. Paris: Editions du Seuil, 1992.

Duquesne, Jacques. *L'Exposition universelle*. Paris: Editions, 1982.

Dusein, Jacques. "Loie Fuller: Expression choréographique de l'art nouveau." *La Recherche en danse* 1 (1982): 82–86.

Dyer, Richard. *Heavenly Bodies: Film Stars and Society*. New York: St. Martin's Press, 1986.

———. "A Star Is Born and the Construction of Authenticity." In *Stardom: Industry of Desire*, edited by Christine Gledhill, 132–40. New York: Routledge, 1991.

Ellmann, Richard. *Oscar Wilde*. New York: Alfred A. Knopf, 1988.

———. "Overtures to Salome." In *Modern Critical Views: Oscar Wilde*, edited by Harold Bloom, 77–90. New Haven, Conn.: Chelsea House, 1985.

Encyclopedio dello Spettacolo. Vol. 5. Rome: Unedi-Unioni Editoriale, 1954.

Favardin, Patrick. *Le Dandysme*. Lyon: La Manufacture, 1988.

Feldman, Jessica. *Gender on the Divide: The Dandy in Modernist Literature*. Ithaca, N.Y.: Cornell University Press, 1993.

Felperin, Howard, and Lindsay Waters. "The Anxiety of American Deconstruction." In *The Textual Sublime: Deconstruction and Its Differences*, edited by Hugh Silverman and Gary Aylesword, 147–61. Albany: State University of New York Press, 1990.

Figaro: Guide bleu de Figaro à l'Exposition de 1900. Paris: Le Figaro, 1900.

Finney, Gail. *Women in Modern Drama: Freud, Feminism, and European Theater at the Turn of the Century.* Ithaca, N.Y.: Cornell University Press, 1989.

Flanner, Janet. *Paris Was Yesterday, 1925–1939.* New York: Viking, 1972.

Flaubert, Gustave. *Oeuvres complètes.* Paris: Gallimard, 1951.

Fortassier, Rose. *Les Ecrivains français et la mode: De Balzac à nos jours.* Paris: Presses Universitaires de France, 1988.

Foster, Susan Leigh. *Reading Dancing: Bodies and Subjects in Contemporary American Dance.* Berkeley: University of California Press, 1986.

Foucault, Michel. *A History of Sexuality.* Vol. 1. Translated by Robert Hurley. New York: Random House, 1978.

Fowlie, Wallace. *Mallarmé.* Chicago: University of Chicago Press, 1970.

Franci, Giovanna. *Il sistema del dandy.* Bologna: Casa Editrice Patron, 1983.

Frappier-Mazur, Lucienne. "Narcisse travesti: Poétique et idéologie dans *La Dernière mode* de Mallarmé." *French Forum* 7, no. 1 (Jan. 1986): 41–57.

Fuller, Loie. *Fifteen Years of a Dancer's Life.* London: Herbert Kenkins Ltd., 1913.

Fuller Archives. Special Collection of the New York City Public Library, Lincoln Center Library of the Performing Arts.

Gaddis, Marilyn. "Decadence and Modernism." *Modernist Studies* 4 (1980): 195–206.

Gaddis Rose, Marilyn. "The Synchronic Salome." In *The Languages of Theatre: Problems in the Translation and Transposition of Drama,* edited by Ortrun Zuber, 140–53. Elmsfield, N.Y.: Pergamon, 1980.

———. "Two Misogynist Novels: A Feminist Reading of Villiers and Verne." *Nineteenth-Century French Studies* 7, nos. 1–2 (Fall-Winter 1980–81): 117–23.

Gagnier, Regenia. *Idylls of the Marketplace: Oscar Wilde and the Victorian Public.* Stanford, Calif.: Stanford University Press, 1986.

Gaines, Jane. "Jacqueline Onassis and the Look-Alike." *South Atlantic Quarterly* 88, no. 2 (Spring 1989): 461–86.

Galichon, Claire. *Eve réhabilitée.* Paris: Librairie Générale des Sciences Occultes, no date.

Gallop, Jane. *The Daughter's Seduction: Feminism and Psychoanalysis.* Ithaca, N.Y.: Cornell University Press, 1982.

———. *Feminist Accused of Sexual Harassment.* Durham, N.C.: Duke University Press, 1997.

Garber, Marjorie. *Vested Interests: Cross Dressing and Cultural Anxiety.* New York: Routledge, 1992.

Garelick, Rhonda. "Bayadères, Stereorama, and Vahat-Loukoum: Technological Realism in the Age of Empire." In *Spectacles of Realism,* edited by Margaret Cohen and Christopher Prendergast, 294–319. Minneapolis: University of Minnesota Press, 1994.

———. "Outrageous Dieting: The Camp Performance of Richard Simmons." *Postmodern Culture* (cyberjournal) 6, no. 1 (Sept. 1995). http://jefferson.village.virginia.edu/pmc/copyright.1995.html

Gasché, Rodolphe. "The Stelliferous Fold." *Studies in Romanticism* 22, no. 2 (Summer 1983): 293–327.

Gautier, Théophile. *De la mode*. Paris: Gallimard, 1976.

———. *Mademoiselle de Maupin*. Paris: Lettres françaises, 1979.

Gilman, Margaret. *Baudelaire the Critic*. New York: Columbia University Press, 1943.

Girard, René. "Scandal and the Dance: Salome in the Gospel of Mark." *New Literary History* 15, no. 2 (Winter 1984): 311–24.

Girardet, Raoul. *L'Idée coloniale en France de 1871 à 1962*. Paris: La Table Ronde, 1972.

Gledhill, Christine. "Signs of Melodrama." In *Stardom: Industry of Desire*, edited by Christine Gledhill, 207–29. London and New York: Routledge, 1991.

Godfrey, Sima. "Baudelaire, Gautier, and une toilette savamment composée." In *Modernity and Revolution in Late Nineteenth-Century France*, edited by Barbara T. Cooper and Mary Donaldson Evans, 74–87. Newark: University of Delaware Press, 1992.

———. "Haute Couture and Haute Culture." In Hollier, 761–68.

Goldberg, Roselle. *Performance: Live Art, 1909 to the Present*. London: Thames and Hudson, 1979.

Grunfeld, Frederic V. *Rodin, A Biography*. New York: Henry Holt, 1987.

Guillory, John. *Cultural Capital*. Chicago: University of Chicago Press, 1993.

Habermas, Jürgen. *The Philosophical Discourse of Modernity*. Translated by Frederick Lawrence. Cambridge, Mass.: MIT Press, 1990

———. *The Structural Transformation of the Public Sphere*. Translated by Thomas Burger, with the assistance of Frederick Lawrence. Cambridge, Mass.: MIT Press, 1992.

Hallays, André. *En flânant: À travers l'exposition de 1900*. Paris: Perrin, 1901.

Halpern, Richard. *Shakespeare Among the Moderns*. Ithaca, N.Y.: Cornell University Press, 1997.

Hamon, Philippe. *Expositions: Littérature et architecture au XIXème siècle*. Paris: José Corti, 1989.

Haraway, Donna. *Simians, Cyborgs and Women*. New York: Routledge, 1991.

Hardy, Georges. *Les Eléments de l'histoire coloniale*. Paris: Renaissance du livre, 1920.

Harper's Bible Commentary. Edited by James L. Mays. San Francisco: Harper and Row, 1988.

Harris, Margaret Haile. *Loie Fuller, Magician of Light*. In the Virginia Museum Richmond Exhibition catalog, 13–33. 1979.

Haxell, Nichola Anne. "*Le Serpent qui danse*: Woman as Dancer in the Works of Baudelaire, Mallarmé and Colette." *Romance Studies* 19 (Winter 1991): 117–23.

H. C. Review article. *Revue encyclopédique* (Feb. 1893): 107–9.

Headrick, Daniel. *The Tentacles of Progress: Technology Transfer in the Age of Imperialism*. New York and London: Oxford University Press, 1988.

———. *The Tools of Empire: Technology and European Imperialism in the Nineteenth Century*. New York: Oxford University Press, 1981.

Heymann, C. David. *A Woman Named Jackie*. Secaucus, N.J.: Lyle Stuart, 1989.

Higonnet, Anne. *Berthe Morisot's Images of Women*. Cambridge, Mass.: Harvard University Press, 1992.

Hobsbawm, E. J. *The Age of Empire, 1875–1914*. London: Weidenfeld and Nicolson, 1987.

Hollier, Denis, ed. *A New History of French Literature*. Cambridge, Mass.: Harvard University Press, 1989.

Holman-Black, Charles. "Loie Fuller: Artist and Genius." *Paris Telegram*, Jan. 14, 1928.

Hospodar de Kornitz, Blaise. *Salome: Virgin or Prostitute*. New York: Pageant, 1953.

Huet, Marie-Hélène. *Monstrous Imagination*. Cambridge, Mass.: Harvard University Press, 1993.

Humphries, Jefferson. "Decadence." In Hollier, 785–88.

Huot, Sylviane. *Le Mythe d'Hérodiade chez Mallarmé*. Paris: A. G. Nizet, 1977.

Huysmans, Joris-Karl. *A Rebours*. Paris: Fasquelle Editions, 1970.

———. *Croquis parisiens*. Paris: Editions Marcel Valtrat, 1981.

———. *Oeuvres complètes*. Vols. 6, 19. Paris: Gallimard, 1936.

Huyssen, Andreas. *After the Great Divide: Modernism, Mass Culture, Postmodernism*. Bloomington: University of Indiana Press, 1986.

The Interpreter's Bible. Vol. 7. New York: Abingden, 1970.

Jacobus, Mary. *Reading Woman: Essays in Feminist Criticism*. New York: Columbia University Press, 1986.

J. M. "Loie Fuller fait de beaux rêves." Article, July 23, 1924. Rondel Collection on Loie Fuller, Bibliothèque de l'Arsenal, Paris.

Johnson, Barbara. *A World of Difference*. Baltimore: The Johns Hopkins University Press, 1981.

Jones, A.H.M. *The Herods of Judea*. New York: Oxford University Press, 1938.

Jones, Richard. "Sing Doo Wah Diddy with Derrida." *Virginia Quarterly Review* 70, no. 1 (Winter 1994): 1–37.

Josephson, Matthew. *Edison: A Biography* (1959). Reprint. New York: John Wiley and Son, 1992.

Jouhet, Serge. Article. *Danses* (May 1983).

Jullian, Philippe. *Dreamers of Decadence: Symbolist Painters of the 1890s*. Translated by Robert Baldick. New York: Praeger, 1971.

———. *Jean Lorrain ou le satiricon, 1900*. Paris: Fayard, 1974.

———. *Oscar Wilde*. Translated by Violet Wyndham. New York: Viking, 1968.

———. *The Triumph of Art Nouveau*. Translated by Stephen Hardman. New York: Larousse, 1974.

Kantorowicz, Ernst H. *The King's Two Bodies: A Study in Medieval Political Theology*. Princeton: Princeton University Press, 1957.

Kaplan, Alice. *French Lessons: A Memoir*. Chicago: University of Chicago Press, 1993.

Kelley, Kitty. *Jackie Oh!* Secaucus, N.J.: Lyle Stuart, 1978.

Kempf, Roger. *Dandies: Baudelaire et Cie*. Paris: Editions du Seuil, 1977.

Kermode, Frank. *The Genesis of Secrecy: On the Interpretation of Narrative*. Cambridge, Mass.: Harvard University Press, 1979.

Kermode, Frank. "Loie Fuller and the Dance Before Diaghilev." *Theatre Arts* (Sept. 1962): 6–23.

———. *Romantic Image*. London: Routledge and Kegan Paul, 1957.

———. *The Sense of an Ending: Studies in the Theory of Fiction*. New York: Oxford University Press, 1967.

Kleinert, Annemarie. "*La Dernière mode*: Une Tentative de Mallarmé dans la presse féminine." *Lendemains* 17–18 (June 1980): 167–78.

Kleist, Heinrich von. "On the Marionnette Theatre" (1810). In *Essays on Dolls*, translated by Idris Parry and Paul Keegan, 1–12. London: Penguin, 1994.

Koestenbaum, Wayne. *Jackie Under My Skin*. New York: Farrar, Straus & Giroux, 1995.

———. *The Queen's Throat: Opera, Homosexuality and the Mystery of Desire*. New York: Simon and Schuster, 1993.

Konrad, Linn B. "Villiers de l'Isle-Adam's Future Eve: A Textual Pheonix." *Romance Quarterly* 34, no. 2 (May 1987): 147–54.

Kracauer, Siegried. "The Mass Ornament." Translated by Barbara Correll and Jack Zipes. *New German Critique 5* (Spring 1975): 67–76.

Kravis, Judy. *The Prose of Mallarmé: The Evolution of a Literary Language*. Cambridge: Cambridge University Press, 1976.

Kuryluk, Ewa. *Salome and Judas in the Cave of Sex: The Grotesque: Origins, Iconography, Techniques*. Evanston, Ill.: Northwestern University Press, 1987.

Lafargue, Paul. *Le Droit à la paresse*. Paris: Editions H. Oriol, 1883.

Lathers, Marie. "Snapshots of a Future Eden." *Australian Journal of French Studies* 28, no. 1 (1991): 50–59.

Laver, James. *Taste and Fashion from the French Revolution Until Today*. London: George G. Harrap, 1937.

Le Bon, Gustave. *Psychologie des foules* (1895). Paris: Féix Alcan, 1908.

Lecercle, Jean-Pierre. *Mallarmé et la mode*. Paris: Librairie Séguier, 1989.

Legrand-Chabrier. "La Loie Fuller: D'Une Exposition à l'autre." *Art Vivant* (1925): 28.

Lehman, David. *Signs of the Times: Deconstruction and the Fall of Paul de Man*. New York: Poseidon, 1991.

Lemaire, Michel. *Le Dandysme de Baudelaire à Mallarmé*. Montréal: Les Presses Universitaires de l'Université de Montréal, 1978.

Leprun, Sylviane. *Le Théâtre des colonies: Scénographie, acteurs et discours de l'imaginaire dans les expositions, 1855–1937*. Paris: Editions L'Harmattan, 1986.

Lidsky, Paul. *Les Ecrivains contre la Commune*. Paris: François Maspéro, 1982.

Lista, Giovanni. *Loie Fuller: Danseuse de la belle époque*. Paris: Editions Somogy, 1995.

Le Livre d'or de l'exposition de 1900. Book 2. Paris: Edouard Cornely, 1900.

Loesberg, Jonathan. *Aestheticism and Deconstruction: Pater, Derrida, and de Man*. Princeton: Princeton University Press, 1991.

"Loie Fuller's Glory Laid to Light." *Chicago Tribune*, Jan. 8, 1928.

Lombard, Jean. *L'Agonie* (1888). Paris: Librairie Paul Ollendorff, 1901.

———. *Byzance* (1890). Paris: Librairie Paul Ollendorff, 1900.

Lorrain, Jean. *Une Femme par jour*. Reprint. Saint-Cyr-sur-Loire: Christian Pirot, 1983.

———. *Histoire de masques*. Introduction by Michel Desbruères. Saint Cyr-sur-Loire: Christian Pirot, 1902.

———. *Monsieur de Phocas*. Paris: Librairie Paul Ollendorff, 1901.

———. *Poussières de Paris*. Paris: Société d'Editions littéraires et artistiques, 1902.

Ludlam, Charles. *Ridiculous Theatre: Scourge of Human Folly*. New York: Theatre Communications Group, 1992.

Lukács, Georg. *History and Class Consciousness: Studies in Marxist Dialectics*. Translated by Rodney Livingstone. Cambridge, Mass.: MIT Press, 1985.

Magriel, Paul, ed. *Chronicles of the American Dance*. New York: Da Capo Press, 1978.

Mallarmé, Stéphane. *Collected Poems*. Edited and translated by Henry Weinfield. Berkeley: University of California Press, 1994.

———. *Correspondance*. Vol. 1, *1862–71*; Vol. 2, *1871–85*. Edited by Henri Mondor and Lloyd James Austin. Paris: Gallimard, 1959, 1965.

———. *Les Noces d'Hérodiade*. Paris: Gallimard, 1956.

———. *Oeuvres complètes*. Paris: Gallimard, 1945.

———. *Selected Prose, Poems, Essays, and Letters*. Translated by Bradford Cook. Baltimore: The Johns Hopkins University Press, 1956.

———. *Villiers de l'Isle-Adam*. Edited and with an introduction by Alan Raitt. Exeter: University of Exeter Press, 1991.

Mandell, Richard. D. *Paris 1900: The Great World's Fair*. Toronto: University of Toronto Press, 1967.

Marcus, Jane. "Salome: The Jewish Princess Was a New Woman." *Bulletin of the New York Public Library* 78 (1974): 95–113.

Marquèze-Povey, Louis. *Le Mouvement decadent en France*. Paris: Presses Universitaires de France, 1986.

Martin, Randy. "Dance Ethnography and the Limits of Representation." *Social Text* 33 (1992): 103–23.

Marx, Karl. *Capital*. Vol. 1. Translated by Ben Fowkes. New York: Random House, 1977.

Marx, Roger. "Loie Fuller." *Les Arts et la vie* (May 1905).

Maslin, Janet. "A Movie Within a Movie, with a Demure Madonna." *The New York Times*, Nov. 19, 1993, C14.

Mauclair, Camille. *Idées vivantes*. Paris: Librairie de l'Art Ancien et Moderne, 1904.

Mead, Rebecca. "The Philosopher of Fabulousness." *New York* (May 1, 1995): 52–55.

Meltzer, Françoise. "A Response to R. Girard's Reading of Salome." *New Literary History* 15, no. 2 (Winter 1984): 325–32.

———. *Salome and the Dance of Writing: Portraits of Mimesis in Literature*. Chicago: University of Chicago Press, 1987.

Merton, Robert K. Introduction to Gustave Le Bon, *La Psychologie des foules*. Paris: Félix Alcan, 1908.

Meyer, Moe. "Reclaiming the Discourse of Camp." In *The Politics and Poetics of Camp*, edited by Moe Meyer, 1–22. London and New York: Routledge, 1994.

Miller, Hillis. "Is Deconstruction an Aestheticism?" *Nineteenth Century Prose* 20, no. 2 (Fall 1993): 23–41.

Miller, Michael. *The Bon Marché: Bourgeois Culture and the Department Store, 1869–1920*. Princeton: Princeton University Press, 1981.

Miller, Richard, ed. *American Imperialism in 1898: The Quest for National Fulfillment*. New York: John Wiley and Sons, 1970.

Ministère du commerce et de l'industrie. *Compte des recettes et des dépenses: Exposition Universelle Internationale de 1900 à Paris*. Paris: Imprimerie Nationale, 1909.

Mitchell, Timothy. "Orientalism and the Exhibitionary Order." In *Colonialism and Culture*, edited by Nicholas Dirks, 289–319. Ann Arbor: University of Michigan Press, 1992.

Moers, Ellen. *The Dandy: Brummell to Beerbohm*. New York: Viking, 1960.

Moissonnier, Maurice. "Le Châtiment de la guerre à la commune." In *Histoire de la France contemporaine*, 3: 315–63. Paris: Editions Sociales, 1979.

Monahan, William. "Mort de Jackie." *New York Press* 7, no. 29 (July 20–26, 1994): 15–16.

Montorgeuil, Georges. *Paris dansant*. Paris: Théophile Bélin, 1898.

Moon, Tom. "Recordings: 'Oh, Whatever.'" *Rolling Stone* (Sept. 8, 1994): 75–76.

Morand, Paul. *1900 A.D.* Translated by Rollilly Fedden. New York: William Farquhar Payson, 1931.

Mornecque, Jacques-Henry. *Villiers de l'Isle-Adam Créateur et visionnaire*. Paris: Nizet, 1974.

Moses, Claire Goldberg. *French Feminism in the Nineteenth Century*. Albany: State University of New York Press, 1984.

Moynet, G. "Le Pavillon national des Etats Unis." *L'Encyclopédie du siècle*. Vol. 2. Paris: Montgredien, 1900.

Musée Rodin, Paris. Archive collection.

Néry, Alain. *Les Idées politiques et sociales de Villiers de l'Isle-Adam*. Paris: Diffusion Université Culture, 1984.

————., ed. *Textes politiques inédits de Villiers de l'Isle-Adam*. Paris: Diffusion Université Culture, 1981.

Noiray, Jacques. *Le Romancier et la machine: L'Image de la machine dans le roman français (1850–1900)*.Vol. 2, *Jules Verne-Villiers*. Paris: Librairie José Corti, 1982.

Nordau, Max. *Degeneration* (1892). Translator unknown. London: William Heinemann, 1913.

Nozière. "L'Ecole de Loie Fuller." *Matinale*, June 22, 1911.

Nunokawa, Jeffrey. "Homosexual Desire and Commodity Love in *The Picture of Dorian Gray*." Unpublished paper. Presented at the Oscar Wilde Conference, Princeton University, May 1991.

Nye, David. *Electrifying America: Social Meanings of a New Technology 1880–1940*. Cambridge, Mass.: MIT Press, 1990.

Penley, Constance. *The Future of an Illusion.* Minneapolis: University of Minnesota Press, 1989.

Phelan, Peggy. *Unmarked: The Politics of Performance.* London: Routledge, 1993.

Picard, Alfred. *Le Bilan d'un siècle.* Paris: Imprimerie Nationale, 1906.

———. *Rapport général administratif et technique.* Paris: Exposition Universelle, 1900.

Pine, Richard. *The Dandy and the Herald: Manners, Mind and Morals from Brummell to Durrell.* London: Macmillan, 1988.

Pinet-Cheula, Hélène. *L'Ornement de la durée: Loie Fuller, Isadora Duncan, Ruth St. Denis, Adorée Villany.* Paris: Musée Rodin, 1987.

Poggi, Christine. "Mallarmé, Picasso, and the Newspaper as Commodity." *Yale Journal of Criticism* 1, no. 1 (Fall 1987): 133–51.

Poggioli, Renato. *Teoria dell'arte d'avanguardia.* Bologna: Il Mulino, 1962.

Poulet, Georges. *La Distance intérieure.* Paris: Librairie Plon, 1952.

Praz, Mario. *The Romantic Agony.* Translated by Angus Davidson. Oxford: Oxford University Press, 1974.

Prendergast, Christopher. *The Order of Mimesis.* Cambridge: Cambridge University Press, 1986.

———. *Paris and the Nineteenth Century.* Cambridge: Blackwell, 1992.

Rabaut, Jean. *Féministes à la belle epoque.* Paris: Editions France-Empire, 1985.

Rachilde. *Monsieur Vénus.* Paris: L. Genonceaux, 1902.

Raitt, A. W. Introduction to *L'Eve future.* In Villiers, *Oeuvres complètes,* 1429–59.

———. *The Life of Villiers de l'Isle-Adam.* London: Clarendon, 1981.

———. *Villiers de l'Isle-Adam et le mouvement symboliste.* Paris: François Corti, 1965.

Rastignac. Article. *Courrier de Paris,* Jan. 14, 1893.

Rearick, Charles. *Pleasures of the Belle Epoque: Entertainment Festivity in Turn-of-the-Century France.* New Haven, Conn.: Yale University Press, 1985.

Renard, Jules. *Journal.* Paris: Gallimard, 1972.

Rhodes, S. A. Introduction to the American edition of Mallarmé, *La Dernière Mode.* New York: Institute of French Studies, 1933.

Richard, Jean-Pierre. *L'Univers imaginaire de Mallarmé.* Paris: Editions du Seuil, 1961

Rivière, Joan. "Womanliness as Masquerade." In *Formations of Fantasy,* edited by Victor Burgin, James Donald, and Cora Kaplan, 35–61. London: Methuen, 1986.

Roach, Joseph. *The Player's Passion: Studies in the Science of Acting.* Newark: University of Delaware Press, 1985.

Rodin, Auguste. "La Rénovation de la danse." *Le Matin,* May 30, 1912.

Ross, Andrew. *Strange Weather.* London: Verso, 1991.

———. "Uses of Camp." *Yale Journal of Criticism* 2, no. 1 (1988): 1–24. Reprinted in Bergman, *Camp Grounds,* 54–77.

Ross, Andrew, and Constance Penley, eds. *Technoculture.* Minneapolis: University of Minnesota, 1991.

Said, Edward. *Orientalism*. New York: Random House, 1978.

Sartre, Jean-Paul. *Baudelaire*. Paris: Gallimard, 1947.

———. *Mallarmé*. Paris: Gallimard: 1986.

Schor, Naomi. *Breaking the Chain: Women, Theory and French Realist Fiction*. New York: Columbia University Press, 1985.

Schuerwegen, Franc. "'Télétechnè fin de siècle': Villiers de l'Isle-Adam et Jules Verne." *Romantisme* 69, no. 3 (1990): 79–87.

Schweik, Robert C. "Oscar Wilde's *Salomé*, the Salome Theme in Late European Art, and a Problem of Method in Cultural History." In *Twilight of Dawn: Studies in English Literature in Transition*, edited by O. M. Brack Jr., 123–36. Tucson: University of Arizona Press, 1987.

Sedgwick, Eve Kosofsky. *Between Men: English Literature and Male Homosocial Desire*. New York: Columbia University Press, 1985.

———. *Epistemology of the Closet*. Berkeley: University of California Press, 1990.

———. *Tendencies*. Durham, N.C.: Duke University Press, 1993.

Seidel, Linda. "Salome and the Canon." *Womens Studies* 2 (1984): 29–66.

Seltzer, Mark. *Bodies and Machines*. New York: Routledge, 1992.

Severi, Rita. "Oscar Wilde, La Femme Fatale and the Salome Myth." In *Proceedings of the Tenth Congress of the International Comparative Literature Association, 1982*, edited by Anna Balakian, 458–63. New York: Garland, 1985.

Shaw, Mary Lewis. "The Discourse of Fashion." *Sub-stance* 68 (1992): 46–60.

———. *Performance in the Texts of Mallarmé*. University Park, Pa.: Penn State University Press, 1993.

Shewan, Rodney. "The Artist and the Dancer in Three Symbolist Salomes." *Bucknell Review* 30, no. 1 (1986): 102–30.

Showalter, Elaine. *Sexual Anarchy: Gender and Culture at the Fin-de-Siècle*. New York: Viking, 1990.

Silvagni. "L'Etonnante vie de la fée de la lumière." *Pour Tous*, Sept. 20, 1953.

Silverman, Debora. *Art Nouveau in Fin-de-Siècle France: Politics, Psychology and Style*. Berkeley: University of California Press. 1989.

———. "The New Woman: Feminism and the Decorative Arts in Fin de Siècle France." In *Eroticism and the Body Politic*, edited by Lynn Hunt, 144–63. Baltimore: The Johns Hopkins University Press, 1991.

Simonds, William Adams. *Edison: His Life, His Work, His Genius*. New York: Blue Ribbon Books, 1934.

Smallwood, E. Mary. *The Jews Under Roman Rule*. Leiden, Netherlands: E. J. Brill, 1976.

Smith, Anna Deavere. *Twilight Los Angeles, 1992: On the Road: A Search for American Character*. New York: Anchor Books, 1994.

Solomon-Godeau, Abigail. "The Legs of the Countess." *October* 39 (Winter 1986): 65–108.

Sommer, Sally. "Loie Fuller." *Drama Review* 19, no. 1 (Mar. 1975): 53–67.

Sontag, Susan. "Notes on Camp." In *Against Interpretation*, 275–92. New York: Noonday, 1966.

Spackman, Barbara. *Decadent Genealogies*. Ithaca, N.Y.: Cornell University

Spackman, Barbara. *Decadent Genealogies*. Ithaca, N.Y.: Cornell University Press, 1989.

Staiger, Janet. "Seeing Stars." In *Stardom: Industry of Desire*, edited by Christine Gledhill, 3–16. London and New York: Routledge, 1991.

Stanton, Domna. *The Aristocrat as Art*. New York: Columbia University Press, 1980.

Starobinski, Jean. *Portrait de l'artiste en saltimbanque*. Geneva: Skira, 1970.

Stephens, Mitchell. "Jacques Derrida." *The New York Times Magazine* (Jan. 23, 1994): 22–25.

Stoker, Bram. *Dracula*. In *The Annotated Dracula*, edited by Leonard Wolf, 1–334. New York: Clarkson Potter, 1975.

Swart, Koenraad W. *The Sense of Decadence in Nineteenth-Century France*. The Hague: Martinus Nijhoff, 1964.

Symons, Arthur. *The Symbolist Movement in Literature*. New York: Haskell House, 1971.

Terdiman, Richard. *Discourse/Counter-Discourse: The Theory and Practice of Symbolic Resistance in Nineteenth-Century France*. Ithaca, N.Y.: Cornell University Press, 1985.

———. *Present Past: Modernity and the Memory Crisis*. Ithaca, N.Y.: Cornell University Press, 1993.

Tocqueville, Alexis de. *Democracy in America*. Translated by Henry Reeve, revised by Francis Bowen and Phillips Bradley. New York: Random House, 1981.

Torgovnick, Marianna De Marco. *Crossing Ocean Parkway: Readings by an Italian-American Daughter*. Chicago: University of Chicago Press, 1994.

Valéry, Paul. *Variété III*. Paris: Gallimard, 1936.

Verne, Maurice. *Aux Usines de plaisir*. Paris: Editions des Portiques, 1929.

Viegener, Matias. "Kinky Escapades, Bedroom Techniques, Unbridled Passion, and Secret Sex Codes." In Bergman, *Camp Grounds*, 234–56.

Villiers de l'Isle-Adam, Jean-Marie-Mathias-Philippe-Auguste. *L'Eve future*. In *Oeuvres complètes*, edited by Alan Raitt and Pierre Georges Castex, with the collaboration of Jean-Marie Bellefroid, 765–1017. Paris: Gallimard, 1986.

———. *Eve of the Future Eden*. Translated by Marilyn Gaddis Rose. Lawrence, Kans.: Coronado Press, 1981.

Vuillermoz, Emile. "Le Ballet moderne." *La Revue musicale*, Dec. 1, 1921, 46–52.

Weber, Eugen. *France Fin de Siècle*. Cambridge, Mass.: Harvard University Press, 1986.

Weber, Max. *Economy and Society*. Vol. 3. Translated by Ephraim Fischoff. New York: Bedminster, 1968.

Wicke, Jennifer. *Advertising Fictions: Literature, Advertisement and Social Reading*. New York: Columbia University Press, 1988.

Wilde, Oscar. *The Artist as Critic*. Chicago: University of Chicago Press, 1968.

———. *De Profundis*. Vol. 8 of *The Works of Oscar Wilde*. New York: Lamb, 1980.

———. *The Importance of Being Earnest and Other Plays*. New York: Signet, 1985.

Wilde, Oscar. *The Letters of Oscar Wilde*. Edited by Rupert Hart-Davis. New

Wilde, Oscar. *The Letters of Oscar Wilde*. Edited by Rupert Hart-Davis. New York: Harcourt, Brace and World, 1962.

———. *The Picture of Dorian Gray* (1891). New York: Signet, 1962.

———. *Salomé*. Paris: Editions G. Cres, 1923.

———. *Salome*. (Author's own translation.) Boston: Branden, 1989.

Williams, Rosalind. *Dream Worlds: Mass Consumption in Late Nineteenth-Century France*. Berkeley: University of California Press, 1982.

Wollen, Peter. "Fashion/Orientalism/The Body." *New Formations* (Spring 1987): 5–32.

Worth, Katharine. *Oscar Wilde*. London: Macmmillan, 1983.

Wright, Barbara, and David H. T. Scott. *Baudelaire, La Fanfarlo and Le Spleen de Paris*. London: Grant & Cutler, 1984.

Zagona, Helen Grace. *The Legend of Salomé and the Principle of Art for Art's Sake*. Geneva: Droz, 1960.

Zeldin, Theodore. *France, 1848–1948: Taste and Corruption*. New York: Oxford University Press, 1980.

INDEX

ABOUT THE AUTHOR

Rhonda Garelick is Assistant Professor of French and Comparative
Literature at the University of Colorado, Boulder. She has written on
European literature, mass culture, female performance, and modern
dance. She is currently writing a book on the dancer Loie Fuller.